PROFESSING POETRY

JOHN WAIN

PROFESSING
POETRY

. . . A Poet, or one that doth profess Poetry. . . .
Deposition at the trial of George Chapman, 1617

Macmillan

© John Wain 1977

ISBN 0 333 22641 0

First published 1977 by
MACMILLAN LONDON LIMITED
*4 Little Essex Street London WC2R 3LF
and Basingstoke
Associated companies in Delhi, Dublin,
Hong Kong, Johannesburg, Lagos, Melbourne,
New York, Singapore and Tokyo*

Printed in Great Britain by
PITMAN PRESS LTD
Bath

To
Brasenose College

Contents

Of the lectures, 'Alternative Poetry' begins on p. 22, 'The Poetry
of W. H. Auden' on p. 72, 'Homage to Emily Dickinson'
on p. 104, 'On the Breaking of Forms' on p. 136, 'The Poetry
of Philip Larkin' on p. 160, 'Reflections on the First Night of
Comus' on p. 191, 'Poetry and Social Criticism' on p. 248, 'The
Poetry of William Empson' on p. 284, and 'Edward Thomas and
Helen Thomas' on p. 335.

Poems by Avril Bruten appear on p. 58, by Sally Purcell on
p. 62, by Andrew Harvey on p. 63, by Jill Haas on p. 67, by Alan
Hollinghurst on p. 126, by David Winzar on p. 218, by Andrew Mo-
tion on p. 220, by Isabella Fey and Anthony Cam on p. 243, and by
Peter Levi on p. 281.

Foreword

The design of this book is a simple one. Most of the Oxford Professors of Poetry have published their lectures. Some of these collections, notably those by Matthew Arnold, A. C. Bradley and W. H. Auden, are among the most interesting works of English criticism. But a volume of printed lectures is no different from any other book of critical essays. It cannot convey the unique nature of the Oxford Chair, nor the special atmosphere that surrounds it.

I think these things ought to be conveyed. So, in publishing the first nine of my fifteen lectures, I have set them in a continuum of narrative and reflection. This setting is not offered as a journal. Nor is it intended to be antiphonal with the lectures, to be 'personal' where they are 'impersonal', or anything of that nature. In some ways, the lectures are just as personal as the commentary. What the commentary offers is some account of what the Oxford Chair is, what it feels like to take it on, what kind of situations and what kind of people the Professor tends to find himself among. It is, to that extent, an account of my professional life during these years; it is also a small window on the life of a great university.

Those who find the commentary boring and/or trivial are invited to ignore it and simply treat the book as a collection of nine essays on poetry. I wish them, and all my readers, some pleasure and some illumination.

Believing that the Professor of Poetry ought to be a practising poet, I naturally think that one of my duties is to write poetry. The book therefore concludes with a selection of the poems I have written since 1973. A selection, because some have been omitted; not on grounds of quality, but for other reasons.

December 1976   JOHN WAIN

Acknowledgments

Faber & Faber Ltd for poems from *Collected Poems* by W. H. Auden and for poems and extracts from *The Orators* and *Journey to a War* from *The English Auden: Poems, Essays and Dramatic Writings*, edited by Edward Mendelson; Harper & Row, Publishers, Inc. for 'We Real Cool' from *The World of Gwendolyn Brooks* (1971), copyright © 1959 by Gwendolyn Brooks; the publishers and the Trustees of Amherst College for poems from *The Poems of Emily Dickinson* edited by Thomas H. Johnson (Cambridge, Mass.: The Belknap Press of Harvard University Press), copyright © 1951, 1955 by the President and Fellows of Harvard College; the publishers for extracts from *The Letters of Emily Dickinson* edited by Thomas H. Johnson (Cambridge, Mass.: The Belknap Press of Harvard University Press), copyright © 1958 by the President and Fellows of Harvard College, copyright © 1914, 1924, 1932 by Martha Dickinson Bianchi; Faber & Faber Ltd for an extract from 'Tradition and the Individual Talent' from *Selected Essays* by T. S. Eliot; William Empson and Chatto & Windus Ltd for poems from *Collected Poems* by William Empson and passages from *Seven Types of Ambiguity*, *Some Versions of Pastoral*, *Milton's God* and *Essays in Criticism*, vol. VI, pp. 323 and 481; D. J. Enright and Chatto & Windus Ltd for an extract from *The Terrible Shears: Scenes from a Twenties Childhood*; A. P. Watt & Son and Trinity College, Cambridge, for passages from *The Golden Bough* by J. G. Frazer; Macmillan London and Basingstoke for 'At a Hasty Wedding' from *The Complete Poems of Thomas Hardy* edited by James Gibson; Curtis Brown Ltd on behalf of the author for passages from *Lions and Shadows* by Christopher Isherwood; A. P. Watt & Son, the National Trust and Macmillan London and Basingstoke for lines from 'Danny Deever' from *The Definitive Edition of Rudyard Kipling's Verse*; Faber & Faber Ltd for poems and extracts from *The North Ship, The Whitsun Weddings, High Windows* and *Jill* by Philip Larkin (the quotation from 'Toads' by Philip Larkin is reprinted from *The Less Deceived* by permission of The Marvell Press); Cambridge University Press for a passage from *Studies in Words* by C. S. Lewis; the Trustees of the C. S. Lewis Estate for an extract from an article by C. S. Lewis from the *Oxford Magazine* (1938); Faber & Faber Ltd for 'Aubade' from *The Collected Poems of Louis MacNeice*; Oxford University Press, New York, for an extract from *The Poetry of W. B. Yeats* by Louis MacNeice; The Orwell Estate, Mrs Sonia Brownell Orwell and Secker & Warburg Ltd for an extract from *The Collected Essays, Journalism and Letters of George Orwell*; Faber & Faber Ltd for two extracts from Canto LXXXI from *The Cantos of Ezra Pound*; Myfanwy Thomas and Faber & Faber for 'No One So Much As You' from *Collected Poems* by Edward Thomas and extracts from *As It Was* and *World Without End* by Helen Thomas; Alfred A. Knopf Inc. and Laurence Pollinger Ltd for lines from 'Captain Carpenter' from *Selected Poems* by John Crowe Ransom, published by Eyre Methuen Ltd; R. S. Thomas and Macmillan London and Basingstoke for 'Via Negativa' from *H'm*; Constable & Co. Ltd for two poems from and an extract from the preface of *170 Chinese Poems* translated by Arthur Waley; A. P. Watt & Son, M. B. Yeats, Miss Anne Yeats and Macmillan London and Basingstoke for extracts from the prose works of W. B. Yeats and *The Collected Plays of W. B. Yeats* and lines from 'Ego Dominus Tuus' and 'Sailing to Byzantium' from *The Collected Poems of W. B. Yeats*.

Michael Garrick's setting of 'Children, Children' by John Wain, copyright © Michael Garrick 1975 (P.R.S. and M.C.P.S.), is reproduced by permission of the composer.

Portions of this book have appeared in print as follows: prose in *Encounter, The Malahat Review, Art International, The Lugano Review, Planet* and *The Carleton Miscellany*; verse in *Planet, New Poetry, Oxford Poetry* and *Thames Poetry*.

1
Four-to-One at Ladbroke's

It is an honour that I dream not of.

Romeo and Juliet

Poetry is the sound of human speech at those times when it comes closest to the speech of the angels and the speech of the animals.

I am a writer: that is, an artist who makes his mud-pies out of language rather than out of paint or clay or stone or the scraping of horsehair across catgut. As a writer I have less freedom than the other artists because they take their raw material directly from nature. Stone is rough or smooth, colour bright or dark, a note soft or loud, irrespective of what human beings say it is. Language, on the other hand, is what human beings say it is. Human societies make languages, and if the society becomes unmanageable the language is among the first casualties. Using a widely diffused language like English, one is continually brought up against the fate that has befallen it all over the English-speaking world: how bloated it is, how sagging, how out of touch with the springs of its vitality. Loaded with jargon and cliché, the language snarls like a camel, lurches like a sick mule.

My life's work is to tend the poor beast, to try to get it to take wholesome food and stop craving for offal and carrion; to lead it shambling and exhausted to a spring of pure water, a patch of sweet grass, and then on through the rocky passes.

I write poetry and I write prose. There are differences of mood and intensity, but in outline the two are the same. They both invoke the kind of *rapport* between me and the language that a camel-driver has with his camel. I must understand what

3

treatment brings out its best qualities, what kind of food makes for health, how much it can carry, and at what altitudes it can go on breathing. I must also do my best to beat off the predators who spoor it with murderous intention, and the parasites that grow obscenely fat on its flesh.

A person, or an animal, in full health and with a reasonable share of the joy of life will perform soberly and adequately in all the usual functions of survival, breeding, living and dying. But, over and above those functions, he will now and then give expression to the flow of life in his veins. He (or she!) will dance, now and then, rather than just walking, will sing rather than just talking or crying out.

Poetry is that dance, that song. It is the sign that a language, and the people who use it, have full health and a reasonable share of the joy of life.

In the library of Exeter College, Oxford, mounted in a hinged frame so that one can read both sides of it, is a letter from William Morris, dated 16 February 1877, courteously declining to stand for election to the Chair of Poetry. 'I am not the man to fill the post,' he says, and goes on:

> I suppose the lectures a Poetry Professor should give ought to be either the result of deep and wide scholarship in the matter, or else pieces of beautiful and ingenious rhetoric, such, for example, as our Slade Professor could give; and in both these things I should fail and do no credit either to the University or myself. It seems to me that the *practice* of any art rather narrows the artist in regard to the *theory* of it, and I think I come more than most men under the condemnation, so that though I have read a good deal and have a good memory, my knowledge is so limited and so ill-arranged that I can scarce call myself a man of letters: and moreover I have a peculiar inaptitude for expressing myself except in the one way that my gift lies. Also may I say without offence that I have a lurking doubt as to whether the Chair of Poetry is more than an ornamental one, and whether the Professor of a wholly incommunicable art is

not rather in a false position: nevertheless I would like to see a good man filling it, and, if the critics will forgive me, somebody who is not only a critic. I ask your pardon for writing so much about myself, but your kindness has brought it on your head.

My sentiments exactly. And the only reason why there is no similar letter from me in existence is because in my judgment the situation has changed in the last century, and the usefulness of the Chair is now conceived of in rather different terms.

One Saturday afternoon in the early summer of 1973 I was sitting in the garden of my house in Wolvercote, Oxford. It is a well-worn eighteenth-century house on the edge of a sea of green, and the garden is a long narrow strip of churned-up earth sheltered all along one side by a high and ancient-looking stone wall. It is churned up because my wife Eirian and I have three sons, and each of them has an average of three friends, so that there are never fewer than a dozen boys charging up and down the length of the garden. Even if I had made any serious attempt to keep it tidy, the strain of driving off an endless succession of boys would have broken me in mind and body; I prefer to tolerate a garden that is dusty in summer and muddy in winter, and in any case there are attractive and indestructible flowering shrubs.

In this pleasance I was sitting with half a dozen friends, as I might have done on any Saturday afternoon in the summer. Philip Larkin was there, and the composer Bernard Rands and his wife Susan, and my old friend Wallace Robson. Christopher Ricks and Anthony Thwaite had each dropped in at an earlier stage of the afternoon. It was a pleasant, sociable time. Peter Levi had been with us and would be again, but at the moment I am thinking of he was over on Port Meadow with our youngest son Toby, whose seventh birthday it was (that fixes the date as 26 May). The Whitsun fair was in full swing on the meadow, and Peter Levi had gone with Toby to enjoy some of the fun.

The moment I am thinking of was about four o'clock and,

though we were all behaving as if this were a summer afternoon
like any other, we were in fact conscious that our thoughts
wandered from time to time. They wandered two and a half
miles to the Sheldonian Theatre, where the M.A.s of Oxford
University had been voting that day, and on the previous
Thursday, to elect their thirty-seventh Professor of Poetry.

My name was among the half-dozen or so from whom the
graduates were to choose, and for some weeks I had been trying
my best to forget the fact. The Chair of Poetry, unlike any other
academic post I have ever heard of, is conferred not by an
academic board or committee but by democratic vote of the
senior graduates. Since Oxford only attracts the attention of the
outside world at moments of comicality, the election has been
widely portrayed as a personality parade interspersed with
slapstick, and I had been determined to keep clear of this side of
the matter, which was easy enough as long as I confined myself
to three activities: getting on with my work at home, drinking in
quiet pubs, and canoeing on the Oxford Canal. (The river, at this
juncture, was too public.) By this strategy, I had managed to re-
main oblivious, for long periods, of the build-up to the election,
and the high-pressure salesmanship of some of the candidates
had reached my ears only as a distant, and distasteful, echo.
Even so late as this afternoon, within hours – by now, within
minutes – of the announcement of the result, I was able to
preserve a calm that was not all a Thespian performance. This
calm was now disturbed by two events. One was the return of
Toby and Peter Levi from the fair on Port Meadow. Toby was
carrying a large coconut and both were in high feather. It
appeared that Toby had wanted to try the coconut-shy. This
was not of the traditional kind where the coconuts have to be
knocked out of iron rings by a wooden ball, which is usually
rigged so as to be impossible; in this case, a coconut could, in
theory, be won by throwing a dart at a microscopic point on a
distant playing-card. As Toby selected his darts, Father Levi
had taken the proprietress of the stall on one side and entered
into deep and subtle negotiation with her. Would it be possible
to stage-manage matters so that the lad appeared to have won a

coconut, believed himself to have won a coconut, and went home with a coconut, for which Father Levi would pay the full cash value? As they bargained and deliberated, Toby let fly his dart and with pin-point accuracy landed it on the ace of spades or whatever. The prize was his. There was no need of further haggling. In triumph, the pair returned to Wolvercote Green in time for the second calm-eroding event. The telephone shrilled; our eldest son, William, briefly spoke with someone, then came out into the garden and said to me, 'You've got it.'

I recall vividly the moment when it first entered my head that I might, by some combination of chances, occupy the Chair of Poetry. I was walking, one winter night, along New College Lane in company with Peter Levi. Just as we passed under the Ponte de Sospire and came out by the Bodleian, he asked me, apropos of nothing we had been saying, whether I would consider standing for election. He, it seemed, was being urged to stand, friends and supporters were willing to mount a campaign, and he had told them that he would not be willing to stand in opposition to me.

I was staggered by this, and have remained staggered ever since. That Peter Levi should be thought of as the ideal Professor of Poetry is entirely predictable. A superb poet, a scholar in many languages, admired by the young, respected by the old, he is in every way the perfect choice to represent the art of poetry within the University. Only one part of his discourse appeared to me logical, as we stood in the street on that dark night. He is five years younger than I am, and the term of office of the Professor is five years.

I went home and considered the matter. There were arguments on both sides. As a writer who had once been engaged in academic work and had given it up to devote my full time to writing, I knew that any involvement with teaching was too claiming, too fascinating and too exhausting to be combined with anything like an ambitious programme of imaginative work, and I had such a programme. On the other hand, I knew that the Professorship of Poetry carried light duties, commensurable with its small salary. Those who stood for election were in most cases the holders of full-time university posts already, so that they had to take for granted the part-time nature of the job. On the other hand again, it might mean the destruction of a happy, but quite possibly rather fragile, balance that I had achieved over the years. Any writer who settles in a university town will find sooner or later that he has a relationship with the university – the more quickly if he was educated there and already has contacts with it, the more slowly if he is a stranger, but it will happen. Many writers do a straight deal with the university and accept a teaching post, usually one that they hope will be part-time; this may work for them (Angus Wilson is a full professor and seems to enjoy it) but it would not work for me, for whom no teaching job can ever be part-time.

With Oxford – and I believe only with Oxford could I have managed it – I had achieved a relationship that was immensely fruitful (for me) and evidently more or less acceptable to them. No money changed hands; I was willing to co-operate with under-graduate literary and other societies who wanted an evening talk or a reading; I gave informal advice about, and sometimes contributed to, the various magazines that sprang up and died; young poets showed me their work. That was what I did for the University. What the University did for me was richer and more complex. It was mainly a matter of personal contacts. I had some old friends who had been in Oxford ever since my under-graduate days, and I steadily made new ones. Three colleges gave me common-room membership; at two of them, St John's and Brasenose, I was an ex-Fellow. Apart from that, there was the mere presence of the University, an international scholarly and intellectual community in an English Midland town, and the inestimable benefit to any literary man of having the Bodleian Library within bicycling distance. All these were solid benefits. Would they be tarnished, would complications set in, once I was no longer a zoo animal but a working member of the University? Back on the first hand again, most of the Professors in recent times had not lived in Oxford, and two of them, Auden and Graves, had not even lived in England; still, they had managed to jet in and stay a few weeks in every year, and perform the duties of the Chair to everyone's satisfaction, so perhaps I might reasonably hope to do so from a distance of two and a half miles without much alteration in my way of life.

What decided me, in the end, was the thought that, if I did not stand for election, I should never know whether the University, through the corporate will of its M.A.s, wanted me to do the job or not. For the rest of my life I should have wondered whether I had refused my services to Oxford; and, considering the amount Oxford has done for me, the thought would have been an uncomfortable one. I came to Oxford at the age of seventeen, from the most provincial of the provinces, and Oxford gave me a profession, an orientation, a circle of friends which I still have, and − less definably − the sense of belonging to a clerisy and sharing its responsibilities and ideals. If Oxford wanted me to serve as her Professor of Poetry, it would be worse than discourteous to refuse. And how could I find out, but by letting my name go forward? I would not, I promised myself, indulge in any campaigning; then, if the vote went to someone else, I should at least feel that the act of offering myself for election had settled a question and released me from a duty.

This lofty stance I had no difficulty in maintaining outwardly; but inwardly, throughout April and May of 1973, it became slightly less secure. Standing for election is a very personal business. Once you know that people are going to vote for you or against you, it becomes very difficult − in the end, I think, impossible − not to hope for their acceptance. I once talked with a man who had stood as a Labour candidate for Parliament in an entirely solid Conservative area; he had stood simply as a human sacrifice, because his party wanted to be represented at the hustings. Even in this situation, he told me, seeking only to attract a few votes and get publicity for his party's ideas, he had found it bitter when the results were read out. There was a primitive reaction − 'They have rejected *me*' − which nothing could overlay. I thought of this anecdote fairly often during the last week or two. Especially as my situation did not seem much

brighter than the candidate's had been. As the *Guardian* assured
its readers, 'no one seriously doubts that Stephen Spender will
romp home'. Mr Spender, with his authority as poet and critic,
his world literary reputation, his massive support from such
Oxford figures as W. H. Auden, Isaiah Berlin, Stuart Hampshire
and J. I. M. Stewart, certainly seemed a logical choice; I thought
so myself and, when asked who I thought should have the Chair
if I did not, invariably named him with complete sincerity. The
London poetry establishment, for its part, regarded it simply as
a job for Spender and dismissed the election as a tedious for-
mality; on the Friday evening before that Saturday, a bunch of
them discussed the event on the radio in exactly those terms.
Ladbrokes, the London chain of betting-shops, quoted Mr
Spender at 4–6. I was 4–1, and that seemed to be that, except
that Oxford has her own way of doing things and her ways are
sometimes inscrutable even to the appraising eye of the
bookmaker.

So matters stood as the sun shone down on our dilapidated
back garden, the casual talk drifted on, and the tall dark figure
and the little fair one homed with their coconut. But with the
telephone call and the 'You've got it' the scene quickly changed.
The circus which I had so carefully stayed away from now came
to me. Cars rocked to a standstill in our quiet road, and a rapid
stream of people began to come down the garden path past the
dustbins and the upside-down canoe on its trestles, most of them
representing some form of the dispersal of news. For the rest of
the afternoon and well into the evening, cameras were clicked
and flashed at me, tape-recorders whirred behind out-thrust
microphones, and pencils flew over shorthand notebooks. Not
that I had much to say. It would have been a waste of time to
work out in detail what I intended to do in a job until I knew
whether I had it. I said I was interested in the work of young
poets in their formative years, which is true and always has
been, and at some point I added that I might give a lecture or
two, during the five years, on the work of the Oxford young if it
seemed interesting enough to warrant so much attention.

I suppose the sudden change from a quiet Saturday afternoon

among friends to a monocycle race in a three-ring circus was no more than typical of what the publicity machine does to every situation into which it intrudes itself. Already, it seemed, a note of farce had crept in. My middle name happens to be 'Barrington', an elaboration perfectly useless; no one ever calls me by that name, and I have had to fill it in on thousands of forms, thus wasting hours of my life. When the appropriate university officer came to the door of the Sheldonian to announce the result of the election, he informed the bystanders that 'The successful candidate is Mr John Barrington Ward.' Fortunately someone pulled at his sleeve and got him to repeat the name correctly. Mr Barrington Ward, editor of the *Oxford Mail*, had not in fact stood for election as Professor of Poetry.

Food and drink were now called for. Happily, our wine merchant had made a delivery the day before, and there were enough bottles of inexpensive wine to go round and more than go round. Eirian disappeared into the kitchen and reappeared with taramasalata, cheese dip, and a large dish of veal and rice. Various people asked me for statements. I could not tell which of them were journalists, except for a large man with an elaborately whelked proboscis whom I had seen in Fleet Street pubs. Philip Larkin was heard to say, in the manner he reserves for making asides, 'Typical of the Press. . . . We've been here all along.' I got out my mouth-organ and played 'Turkey in the Straw' and 'Gwenith Gwyn'. A pretty girl in a wide-brimmed hat, whom I did not recall having seen before, came and sat firmly beside me, so that when the photographs appeared she was in all of them. I began to feel that the Great British Public was being given a somewhat misleading image of my everyday life. Someone asked William if he was glad his father was to be Professor. 'Yes,' he replied with twelve-year-old composure. 'As a matter of fact, I was the first to be informed.' I told the proboscis man the story about the parliamentary human sacrifice, adding that I had felt rather the same. The poet Dan McNabb, a burly red-headed figure in kilt and sporran who had been one of the candidates, played 'The Retreat' on a cassette tape-recorder. Our middle son, Ianto, broke into a *pas seul*. The shadows lengthened; the journalists departed, Jane Bown of the *Observer* taking a last picture through her car window as I saw her off.

Afterwards, there was the usual clearing-up and dish-washing, in which Eirian was helped by several sweet and generous women friends. We had just kicked off our shoes and sunk down to relax when a friend who had left the party a couple of hours earlier returned unexpectedly. He had quarrelled with a fellow-guest and gone to the Plough Inn to drink beer and polish up his *esprit de l'escalier*. The beer, coming on top of wine, had slightly clouded his responses, but he was still good company.

Later, I was touched to hear of two spontaneous tokens of rejoicing. The Brasenose College porters, on hearing of my election, had rung the chapel bell. And Philip Larkin and Peter Levi, having shared a taxi from Wolvercote into the centre of Oxford, had got out and suddenly broken into a jig together, on the pavement outside All Souls. Thinking of those two events – the bells calling out into the balmy evening air, and the two P.L.s dancing in front of the venerable walls – has been enough to take me out of many a fit of depression.

The aftermath, in terms of publicity, was predictable. A number of people wrote kind and generous letters. Stephen Spender, who during the run-up to the election had been away in America and had taken no more part in the campaigning than I had, sent a telegram of congratulations and good wishes immediately on hearing the result. The newspapers put up their usual performance. Most of them were bitchy; journalists, as a rule, don't like serious writers, whose existence is a reminder of standards they prefer to forget. The proboscis man, drawing on the story I had told him about the parliamentary candidate, said that my anxiety during the hours of waiting had been pitiable, or words to that effect, thus combining *suggestio falsi* with *suppressio veri*; the same man, in the confidence that Stephen Spender would be elected, had written in advance a graceful word-picture of that poet, which, rather than waste it, he led off with; fortunately it took about two-thirds of his space, so there was the less room for misrepresentation. *The Times Literary Supple-*

ment, in its anonymous 'Commentary' dated 27 May, scolded the
M.A.s for having made a silly mistake; I was, it seemed, a
charlatan who had fluked into the office by adopting a flattering
stance towards undergraduate poets. The next time I dined at
Brasenose, the man who sat next to me said that he found the at-
tack 'past bearing'. I, however, put a slightly different interpreta-
tion on the outcry. I saw it as heartening evidence that I had
flicked some bully on the raw, that I was in a position to be a
serious nuisance to the literary K.G.B. and to encourage the
samizdat.

Of course people who disapproved of my election had a right
to express their disapproval, and they did so in a variety of styles
which I found fascinating, all the way from the I.R.A. methods
of the *T.L.S.* to a refined and feline technique as evinced by the
University's Public Orator, Mr Colin Hardie, when a week or
two later he came to deliver the Creweian Oration.

This oration, delivered in the Sheldonian Theatre as part of
Encaenia, the University's chief day of ceremonial, is given year
and year about by the Public Orator and the Professor of Poetry.
Formally it is supposed to be an address of thanks to everyone
who has been a benefactor to the University, especially during
the preceding twelve months. But literary men are adepts at the
skilful and unobtrusive adapting of forms, keeping their outward
shape but filling them with a wide variety of matter, and it is an
old and good game to say one's piece about anything that
catches one's attention in the life of the University while for-
mally keeping within the bounds of 'remember our benefactors,
past and present'. Mr Hardie accordingly began his remarks on
the election to the Chair by recalling how it had been endowed
by Sir Henry Birkhead, of Monkwearmouth, County Durham,
D.C.L., Fellow of All Souls, in 1696 (thus mentioning a benefac-
tor of the University), made some interesting remarks on the
history of the Chair, and went on to deplore the fact that the
election had become a 'quinquennial jamboree'. In this, surely,
he voiced the opinion of all who dislike seeing the art of poetry
brought into ridicule or associated with ridiculous behaviour. Mr
Hardie allowed, however, that 'We make wise choices in the end,

though I do not always, or indeed ever, find myself in the winning majority'; and ended this section of his address by recommending that the term of the Chair should be cut from five years to one.

This was graceful, and pleased me. I enjoyed the deft way in which the Public Orator conveyed that he hadn't voted for me ('or indeed ever') and the way he managed to combine being entirely courteous to me with saying to the University, in effect, 'You wouldn't reform the Chair while you had the chance, and now look what you've done – landed yourselves with Wain for five years.'

And yet, what would a reform of the Chair of Poetry amount to, and what shape would it take? Of the various proposals that have been made, in public and private, the most moderate and sensible is to shorten the term of office: I think myself that three years would be enough for most incumbents; the five-year stretch is a survival from the time when the Chair was one more university office, a perquisite to be passed gently round among those dons who were interested. Obviously the institution has evolved a good deal, in nearly three centuries. The intention of its reverend founder, to pay a scholar to lecture on poetry three times a year to the whole University, reflects the needs of that epoch when there was very little University-wide activity; most of the lecturing and teaching was within the walls of individual colleges, so that it was a decisive step to endow three lectures a year which all members of the University were free to attend. But, in the vastly different Oxford that emerged from the wave of change in Victorian times, this function no longer counted for anything; the election of Matthew Arnold in 1857 raised the Chair to the status of a platform with some importance to the literary world in general; and, since then, it has evolved further, becoming Oxford's own individual version of the 'poet in residence'.

The boldest reforming notion, that put forward by Dame Helen Gardner, was very much in line with the idea of the 'poet in residence'. Dame Helen proposed that the funds available should be split up, part going to finance a series of lectures and the rest to pay a poet to come to Oxford and just be there. Certainly the matter should be put to the vote, and if this is what the M.A.s want they should have it, I suppose; but personally I am flooded with lethargy at the thought of more lectures by visiting celebrities – Oxford already pours cream down the sink in this respect; if there were half as many lectures by half as many famous people, they would be better attended – while the notion of paying a poet to come and be in residence, carrying on his calling in the full glare of institutional attention, never seems to me to work quite successfully; it is better to allow the poet, while writing poetry as his main activity, to keep up the legal fiction that he is doing something else. Poetry is a plant that grows better if we do not keep digging up the roots to demonstrate the manner of their growing.

All these considerations, coming in rapid succession during those summer days and suddenly my business, something I had to have an attitude about, naturally sent me into reflection and reminiscence. In my days as an undergraduate (1943–6) the Chair of Poetry, like much else, had been suspended till the end of the war. Its most recent occupant, Canon Adam Fox, ended his term in 1943 and the Chair remained vacant till 1946. Hardly anyone noticed. Canon Fox, about whom I have no wish to be harshly critical, was a cultivated and agreeable presence in Oxford, but no one could say now, or could have said at that time, that he was in any sense an important man of letters or that his opinions as critic, scholar or practitioner were likely to inspire anyone. The effect of his election, in 1938, was to close off one important avenue of ideas about poetry for five years.

   Why, in that case, was Adam Fox elected? The question may seem an unreal one; the M.A.s have the right to elect whom they like, and surely they are allowed an occasional mistake. If this were all, it would be simple. And, if this were all, I should certainly refrain from bringing up the matter at all; it is no pleasure to seem disrespectful to the memory of Canon Fox. But fairness to the M.A.s dictates that they must be defended from the charge of making this kind of mistake. The election of Adam Fox was, if I am to believe the anecdote I have heard many times from many different people, a put-up job. The Canon himself, needless to say, was entirely blameless and may even never have heard of the episode. What happened, or at least what I have been repeatedly assured happened, was this.

In that summer term of 1938, on the day of the election for the Chair of Poetry, there was a one-day conference of clergymen at Magdalen College: incumbents, I suppose, of College livings. After a morning spent in deliberation, they sat down to a lunch which no doubt reflected the traditionally high standard of Oxford hospitality; and as they neared the end of the meal (so the story goes) the College's tutorial Fellow in English, C. S. Lewis, stood up to address them. They had enjoyed the College's hospitality; now there was something they could do in return. A Magdalen man was standing for election as Professor of Poetry. It was a short walk to the Sheldonian Theatre, and most of them were M.A.s. Why not go along in a body and make sure that he was elected?

This they did; and thus was the Professor chosen who oc-cupied the Chair when I was a freshman. The story has always interested me, partly because it is just about the only dis-creditable thing I know about that good, brave and generous man who was my teacher. Many people, of course, will not find it discreditable; they will see it merely as an episode in the legitimate play and counter-play of university politics, getting 'our' man in and keeping the opposition out. But these are people to whom the art of poetry is of no importance, and Lewis was not one such. No, the explanation of this curious little episode (which does not find a place, by the way, in the semi-official biography of Lewis by the Reverend Walter Hooper and Mr Roger Lancelyn Green) is to be found in a facetious justificatory piece which Lewis wrote in the *Oxford Magazine*. This piece is headed 'From Johnson's *Life of Fox*' and is a brilliant example of that witty pastiche in which Lewis delighted to show his skill. It was Samuel Johnson's practice, in his *Lives of the Poets*, to break his discussion of each poet into two: first the life, then the work. Lewis begins with what would have been

Johnson's second half.

> The poetry of *Fox*, which is now to be considered, is more
> simple and unadorned than that of any other writer; nor
> need it excite the wonder of posterity if the regularity of
> nature and the sobriety of reason were not sufficient to save
> his compositions from disgust in an age when taste was
> formed on the incoherent excursions of *Eliot* and the
> petulant obscurity of *Pound*. But since the modes of error
> are agitated by continual change while truth remains
> always the same, his poetry now shines with undiminished
> lustre when the false wit of the *Fantasticks* is neglected by
> the polite, condemned by the judicious, and read by the
> learned with frigid indifference.

That, of course, gives Lewis's motive in a nutshell. It is in no
sense an unintentional give-away; he is frankly announcing his
motive for the world to see and take note. All his life, but with
especial truculence at about this time, Lewis was an opponent of
'modern' poetry; he feared Eliot as a doughty attacker of the
values he had grown up with, while Pound he detested as a
harmful charlatan. (I am not putting words into Lewis's mouth;
it is all in his printed work, and I myself many times heard him
express these opinions.) It must have seemed to him that the
election of Fox would keep the Oxford Chair, at least, free from
any taint of modernity. In this, he was perfectly right; but he
also knew that he was going conspicuously far in the opposite
direction, for the Johnson burlesque ends with a rather uneasy
passage of self-justification:

> So little were the merits of *Fox* perceived by his own age
> that his elevation to the Chair of Poetry in the University
> of Oxford is said to have excited wonder. By this event
> *Natvilcius* tells us that no rival was mortified and no fac-
> tion embittered, because all confessed that the supporters
> of Fox had neither over-awed resistance by the splendour
> of their names nor undermined it by policy; that they had
> won by mere numbers a contest in which numbers are the
> only lawful means of victory; and that they had enrolled
> these numbers by no subtler stratagem than that of dis-

seminating widely what they believed sincerely. It is
pleasing to learn that when the taste of the town was so
corrupt, the justice and candour of the University remained
thus unimpaired. Such are the obliquities of our vitiated
nature that in some ages those very qualities which *Nat-
vilcius* allows to the *Foxites* will be found more likely to
irritate than to allay the displeasure of an adversary; nor is
it recorded that *Goliath* found any consolation in reflecting
that he who slew him was a shepherd and a boy.

The reference to a fictitious chronicler called 'Natvilcius', there,
is one of Lewis's donnish jokes, which were usually quite good
of their kind. *Nat whilc* is Anglo-Saxon for 'I know not who';
Lewis often used this as a pen-name – for instance, his verse
contributions to *Punch* in the forties and fifties were signed
'N.W.', and this is also the origin of 'N. W. Clerk', by which
name he signed his very personal book *A Grief Observed* (a
clerkly person, identity unknown). 'Natvilcius' is Latinized to
make it look more like the kind of source that would be con-
sulted by Johnson.

When I call this episode discreditable to Lewis, I am thinking
of the slight but perceptible disingenuousness here. Obviously, if
'numbers are the only lawful means of victory', people are going
to use all kinds of tricks to get those numbers together; if the
story of the clergymen is true (and I am waiting for someone to
tell me that it isn't), Lewis had used a trick himself, and not
merely depended on 'disseminating widely what [he] believed
sincerely'. Enough of this matter. If Lewis was guilty of cutting
a corner here, he did so not out of frivolity (the usual cause of
such capering in Oxford) but from a burning conviction that the
invaders should not pass the gate. Or, to go back to my earlier
metaphor, it may have been his way of encouraging the *samiz-
dat*. He should not have done it; but it is a measure of his high
moral standard that what would seem in most dons a perfectly
ordinary piece of politicking, in him seems rather shocking.

In 1946 the Chair of Poetry was revived, C. M. Bowra was
elected and I went to his Inaugural. Bowra, a figure of authority,
has been described too often for me to describe him again. I sat

with rapt attention through his lecture on 'The Background of
Modern Poetry', not taking it all in but very much aware of its
general drift, which was that 'modern poetry', still stubbornly
resisted by the academic establishment, was an epoch of poetry
like any other epoch, that it had already produced a body of
serious work and that its basic tenets had been accepted by some
poets of genius and many others of important talent. Most dons
of Bowra's generation were still, in 1946, inclined to dismiss
'modern' poetry, and 'modern' art in general, as a hotchpotch of
charlatanism, largely attributable to the upheaval caused by the
First World War – which, be it remembered, was then closer in
time than the Korean War is to us. Bowra had published, during the
Second World War, one of the few important books of literary
criticism to appear in those chaotic years, *The Heritage of Sym-
bolism*, and in it had made clear that he accepted the achievement of
the Symbolists, bringing into alignment the work of poets like
Valery, Blok, Rilke, George and Yeats, and presenting us with a
unified, though rich and complex, chapter of literary history.

Watching the short, stocky figure standing solidly on the plat-
form, hearing the abrupt and rather barking delivery, I had
therefore the exciting sense of being present at a moment of
history; what Bowra's lecture signalled was that the traditional
strength of Oxford scholarship, based on a knowledge of 'the
best that had been thought and said in the world', was bending
itself to work for, rather than against, the modern idiom in
poetry, that idiom which had slowly and painfully established
itself in the preceding quarter-century, and which had suffered
about equally from the uncritical hostility of the rooted and estab-
lished literary intelligence and from the uncritical acceptance of the
rootless, the 'advanced' and those with an itch of modernity on
them. From now on, the 'modern' poet could no longer claim that
inside the academy he was misunderstood and vilified, so that it
was necessary to seek his alliances among people hostile to learning
and indifferent to tradition. (No, I am not forgetting Richards and
Leavis at Cambridge. But Richards had disappeared into Basic
English, and Leavis had made it very plain that the virtues he dis-
cerned in modern poetry were confined to a very few poets; and that

he had, moreover, no intention of commenting one way or the other about modern poetry as an *international* movement; his critical purism, laudable in so many ways, forbade him to comment on anything that was not in his own language, whereas Bowra plunged boldly into French, German, Italian, Russian, giving us the sense that what was happening there was also happening here.)

I admired Bowra; and, though I left Oxford a year after his election and did not manage to attend any more of his lectures, I read them in printed form and relished the intellectual adventurousness that led him into primitive as well as sophisticated areas. His implied message, always, was that we should enjoy what is there to enjoy, that we should take an intelligent interest in poetry as a human activity, growing up from many kinds of soil in many kinds of climate, but testifying always to a deep shared humanity.

Since Bowra combined learning with the practical experience of a man of letters, he represented a return to the tradition of Arnold and behind him to an eighteenth-century figure like Thomas Warton, who in later life was Poet Laureate. And during his tenure there were signs that opinion was moving over still further. The M.A.s, at some point, evidently made up their collective mind that they saw the Professorship as a job for a practitioner: they wanted a poet, preferably with scholarly leanings, rather than a scholar with an interest in poetry. From this decision they have never wavered. In 1951, they elected Cecil Day Lewis; in 1956, W. H. Auden; in 1961, Robert Graves; in 1967, Edmund Blunden; and then, when ill-health forced Blunden to retire a year later, Roy Fuller; then myself.

In spite of the obvious inhibition of having to include myself among the right decisions, I feel impelled to say that the M.A.s appear to me to have chosen sensibly in these last twenty-odd years. ('We make wise choices in the end.') There have been lunatic candidates, and there has been (to put it no more unkindly) lunatic behaviour on the part of some of the candidates; but always, when the chips were down, the choice has fallen on a man who has had something to say about the art of poetry and was able to underpin what he said with the evidence of a solid, sustained effort to contribute to that art.

These were my thoughts. Meanwhile, there was work to do. In November I had to get my Inaugural Lecture ready for delivery, but before starting work on it I had to finish my biography of Samuel Johnson, which was years overdue. After completing and delivering the Johnson book, I went up to Eirian's cottage in Wales to meditate on a suitable theme for the lecture; and I think the lecture I finally gave, 'Alternative Poetry', reflects all the various facets of my situation at that time. The lecture should, I thought, make clear where I stood on contemporary poetics generally; it should also have a certain historical sweep; and it should reflect the enrichment of my work and life that has come from the Celtic societies, and in particular Wales.

During those late-autumn days, I walked about the Caernarvonshire hillsides among the last of the season's heather flowers and rowan berries; I discussed the plight, and the opportunities, of the twentieth-century artist with my neighbour Victor Neep; and Emyr Humphreys enlightened me as to the perspectives of the English-language writer who has one foot in a Celtic language and a scholar's love of its literature. Stir this into a mixture, and add the fact that three years' immersion in Johnson had naturally made my thoughts focus on the eighteenth century, and you have the lecture I actually delivered on that dark afternoon in early December.

ALTERNATIVE POETRY

Of all the heroes of ancient Ireland, none has achieved a brighter or more lasting fame than Finn MacCumhail. For seven hundred years, the men and women whose language was Gaelic clustered eagerly to hear stories of the high deeds of Finn and his Fianna, or band of chosen warriors.

These stories, known to scholars as 'the Fenian Cycle', appear to have supplanted the earlier and more starkly heroic 'Ulster Cycle' in the imagination of the Irish people some time in the thirteenth century. They are presented as if both the narrator and his listeners believed in the historical existence of Finn and his companions; their setting is in the third century A.D., during the reigns of King Cormac MacArt and his son Caerbre. The Fianna are represented as a band of warriors who pay homage to the High King of Erin, but in other respects live independently, according to their own laws and traditions. They accept the hospitality of the people of Ireland and in return defend them against foreign invaders.

In the days of Cormac and Caerbre, Ireland had no foreign invaders, and the probability is that, if the Fenian Cycle has any nucleus of historical truth, the original of Finn MacCumhail may have been some local war-leader who offered resistance to the Scandinavian invaders of a later day, such as the diabolical Magnus Barelegs who brought fire and sword through the Hebrides in the late eleventh century and extended his marauding as far as the Isle of Man and Anglesey before being killed, I am glad to say, by Irish warriors in 1103. This would be borne out by the fact that the most deadly of the enemies against whom the Fianna defend Ireland are 'the men of Lochlin', the name given to

22

the north of Germany east of the Elbe and later to Denmark and Norway.

While such speculations are interesting, they concern us not at all when we approach the Fenian stories as literature. Their tone is consistently marvellous and other-worldly. Enchanters, giants, animals with human attributes, lakes and groves haunted by spirits of peculiar power occur everywhere. Most of the principal characters in the stories have some magical attribute or trace their descent at least partly from supernatural beings.

Thus Finn as a youth had put himself to school to an old Druid who lived beside the River Boyne. In a pool of that river, under a hazel tree that dropped on to the stream the nuts of knowledge, lived a salmon. Anyone who could catch this salmon and eat any part of its flesh would gain universal wisdom. The Druid had never succeeded in catching it, but after Finn became his apprentice he managed to do so, and gave it to Finn to cook, with instructions not to eat any of it himself. When Finn served the dish a change had come over his face, and the Druid asked him if he had eaten any of the salmon. 'No,' he replied, 'but when I was turning it over on the spit I burnt my finger, and put it into my mouth to cool it.' On hearing this the Druid set the salmon before Finn and told him to eat it and, having done so, to leave his service and go out into the world, for there was nothing left that the Druid could teach him. And for the rest of his life, if Finn wanted to foretell the future, or know what was happening at a distance, he had only to put his finger into his mouth and bite on it.

Finn's wife, Saba, he first encountered in the form of a deer fleeing from his hounds. Ordinary hounds would have killed her, but Finn's dogs, Bran and Skolawn, were the children of Tyren, sister of Murna who was Finn's mother. A woman of the Fairy Folk, having fallen in love with Murna's husband, had changed her into a hound, and in that form she had given birth to the hounds who were Finn's inseparable companions and had human knowledge. Instead of killing the fawn, they lay down beside her and began to lick her face and limbs, which alerted Finn to the fact that something magical was toward. He took the

fawn to his stronghold, whereupon she changed into the most
beautiful woman he had ever seen, and told him how she had
been put into the form of a deer by an enchanter whose love she
had refused. Finn married Saba, and they lived in great hap-
piness; but one day, while Finn was away doing battle with the
Norsemen in Dublin Bay, the enchanter reappeared, changed
Saba back into her former shape and drove her away, never to be
seen again. Finn, wild with grief, searched but never found her;
and one day, more than seven years later, he was hunting on the
slopes of Ben Bulben when his hounds discovered a naked boy.
Once more, the hounds of ordinary breed would have killed the
child, but Bran and Skolawn kept them at bay until Finn came
up. Struck by something in the boy's face and bearing, Finn took
him home and had him clothed and taught language; whereupon
he told how he had known no human mother but a gentle fawn,
who had lived in fear of a dark enchanter who had sometimes
visited them, and how one day the enchanter had come and
taken the fawn away, since when he had been alone. Finn named
his son Oisin ('Little Fawn'), and the child who had known no
human speech grew up to be not only a warrior but also a poet,
so that tales of Finn and the Fianna were commonly attributed
to Oisin, son of Finn; and Oisin became a poet in whom men
believed as they believed in Homer.

The Fenian Cycle acted as a powerful focus on Gaelic im-
agination and sentiment. Finn and his followers enjoy a free and
roving life in the open air, hunting and feasting, and the tales are
shot through with a nostalgia for the freedom and beauty of the
wild forest that places them beside the English stories of Robin
Hood. More importantly, they channelled to the people the
ideals of chivalry. The Fianna are protectors and rescuers, bound
by an elaborate code of service and a discipline like that of the
Samurai. Before a man can be numbered among them he must
prove himself a prodigious warrior; he must be buried up to the
waist in the earth, and defend himself with a shield and a hazel
stick against nine others who throw spears at him; if he is
wounded, he has failed in his test. He must be able to leap over a
stave level with his brow, and run at full speed under one level

with his knee, and pick out a thorn from his foot without slackening his pace; he must be learned in the Twelve Books of Poetry, and skilful himself in making verses. With all these accomplishments, he must be brave and generous. Of Finn himself it was said that he gave away gold like the leaves of the forest, and silver like the foam of the sea.

Finn and the Fianna are indeed the Gaelic counterpart of King Arthur and the Round Table. There is even, within the cycle, a parallel to the story of Lancelot and Guinevere. Finn, advancing in years but still a mighty warrior, is betrothed to Grania, daughter of Cormac the High King. To the palace at Tara come all the heroes of the Fianna to attend Finn's wedding feast. Grania, not welcoming the prospect of her marriage, surveys them and her choice lights on Dermid the brown-haired, a character who occupies in Celtic folklore something like the position of Adonis in Greek, irresistible to women, the hero of innumerable tales of love. Against his will she compels Dermid to flee with her, and the inevitable result is war between Dermid and Finn.

This war does not, however, lead to the breaking of the Fianna as the war between Arthur and Lancelot leads to the breaking of the Round Table. The Fianna are ultimately crushed by the power of the High King, to whom they have become a burden. Caerbre, who has succeeded to the throne, resolves to provoke a battle by making demands that the Fianna will never agree to fulfil. The battle duly takes place; Finn is not present – in some versions he afterwards arrives by sea to visit the battlefield, which may indicate that he has passed to the oversea kingdom of the dead. The Fianna are led by Oscar, son of Oisin, a man known for his hardness in war; but they are defeated, many of them are killed, and Caerbre and Oscar, in single combat, die by one another's hand. After the death of Oscar, Finn knows no more happiness; and for Oisin, too, his son's death is a theme of ceaseless lamentation. The story of this battle, which took place in the pass of Gavra, is more realistic and elegiac than the bulk of the Finn cycle; in its sadness and heroic awe, we hear a fitting swan-song for so noble a body of legend, and it is recorded that as late as the middle of the nineteenth century the shepherds and crofters who recounted the story of the battle at Gavra and the death of Oscar would do so with uncovered heads.

Many of the stories of the Fenian Cycle have no doubt been lost, but those that survive are abundant and various. Together, they form an imaginative statement of the highest possible quality: piercing in their beauty, profound in their wisdom and symbolism. Familiar as the material is, it is not yet familiar enough, and I cannot forbear giving two examples. The first is the story of how Dermid, the Adonis or Lancelot or Tristram of the cycle, became marked with the love-spot which no woman could see without becoming enamoured. Dermid was out hunting with Conan, Goll and Oscar, three fellow-warriors of the Fianna. At night, they came to a hut, in which were an old man, a wether sheep, a cat and a girl. They asked for shelter and were admitted. But, when they sat down to dinner, the sheep got up on the table. One after another the warriors struggled to cast it down, but none could do so; even the mighty Goll, who actually succeeded in flinging the sheep off the table, was overpowered by it. The old man then ordered the cat to lead the sheep away and lock it up, which it did forthwith. The warriors, bitterly ashamed, were for leaving the hut, but the old man explained that they had no need to feel disgraced. The sheep they had been fighting was the World, and the cat was the only power capable of bringing it to subjection, for the cat was Death. They retired to sleep in a large chamber, which the young maiden shared with them, her beauty making a light on the walls like that of a candle. One after another the heroes went to her bed (chastity, incidentally, is not an ideal in these stories), but she repulsed each in turn with the words 'I belonged to you once, and I never will again'. Last of all Dermid made his approach. 'Oh, Dermid,' said the girl, 'I belonged to you once, and I never can again, for I am Youth; but I will set a mark on you that no woman can see without loving you.' And she touched his forehead, which henceforth bore the love-spot that drew women to him while he lived.

Our second example is the story of the Chase of Slievegallion.

The story begins, as usual, with a hunting expedition. One day Finn's hounds started a fawn on the slopes of the hill of Allen, and followed it northwards until they reached the mountain of Slievegallion. Finn, becoming separated from the rest of the party, found himself beside the small lake at the top of the mountain, and beside it he saw a beautiful lady weeping bitterly. She told him that a gold ring she greatly loved had fallen from her finger into the water. Immediately Finn plunged into the lake, and after searching its every recess he found the ring and handed it up to the lady before leaving the water. She took it and disappeared, which (once again) alerted him to the presence of magic. On getting out of the lake, Finn was suddenly transformed into a very old man, feeble, dim-sighted, snowy-haired, so that even Bran and Skolawn did not know him, but ran round the lake searching for their master. The rest of the party now came up, and paused to ask the pitiable old fellow if he had seen Finn go by. Finn managed to convey to them that he was Finn, and that he suspected the enchantment had been put on him by one of the daughters of Cullen the Smith, one of those magical smiths who abound in folklore, who lived in the Fairy Mound of Slievegallion. Immediately the Fianna hurried to the Mound, carrying Finn on a litter, and when they got there they dug furiously for three days and nights, until they were deep inside. There, a maiden confronted them, offering a drinking-horn of red gold. Finn drank from it, and at once his youth and strength were restored. His hair was still white; another draught would have restored this too, but he chose to leave it as it was.

Surely this story is great literature. Its symbolism is as profound and as beautifully imagined as that of, say, *The Winter's Tale*. At the behest of a woman, and also of his own code of conduct, Finn plunges into the waters of knowledge and suffering. On emerging, he undergoes a period of weakness and despair; as a result of further quest and effort, his strength comes back (again through a woman), but he carries on him the mark of that painfully won experience which makes him fit to command and counsel his fellow-men.

The predominance of the Fenian Cycle in Irish literature

begins with the compilation, in about 1200, of the 'Colloquy of
the Ancients'. This is a collection of prose tales; the dominant
form of Irish medieval literature is the prose tale which breaks
into verse at heightened moments, usually in the form of a short
lyric poem uttered by one of the characters in the story. The
'Colloquy of the Ancients' is a large collection, amounting to
eight thousand lines even in the incomplete manuscript which
has survived. It takes the familiar medieval form of a collection
of stories contained in an envelope of narrative and situation.
Long after the Battle of Gavra and the dispersal of the Fianna,
two surviving members, Caolte and Oisin – both warriors, both
poets – meet and consider their situation. Each is attended by a
band of eight followers, all that are left of the Fianna. Melancho-
ly survivors, they talk over the glories of the past, then agree to
part. Oisin, of whom we hear little more, betakes himself to the
Fairy Mound to rejoin his mother, while Caolte journeys until he
reaches the dwelling of St Patrick and his monks. (St Patrick's
arrival and the conversion of Ireland are represented as
happening long after the exploits of the Fianna, though in terms
of historical fact they probably happened some six hundred years
before.) At first the monks are terrified by the appearance of
these enormous men with their wolf-hounds, but Patrick
sprinkles holy water over them, whereupon a thousand legions of
demons who have been hovering over them fly away and are lost
in the mountains and glens. Then they settle down to talk; St
Patrick asks what manner of ruler Finn was, and Caolte sings his
praises and launches into a story. At first the saint is reluctant to
listen to these idle tales when he should be praying and
meditating, but soon he is listening eagerly, and greets each new
tale with 'Success and benediction attend thee, Caolte!' They
journey through Ireland; Caolte sees in every hill, wood or
spring an association with Finn, and the collection has a
topographical framework. Relations between St Patrick and
Caolte are fair and courteous, and the saint thinks it probable
that the poet will be rewarded in heaven for his art.

   Thus the 'Colloquy of the Ancients'. The characteristic form
in which the Fenian Cycle has survived, however, is an enor-

mous mass of ballads, sometimes written down but mainly handed on by oral tradition. And the ballads give a very different picture of St Patrick, and of the relationship between Christianity and paganism. As they tell the story, it is Oisin who confronts St Patrick, and receives grudging hospitality; St Patrick has small patience with the old blind giant, scolding him for clinging to pagan beliefs and recounting pagan stories. He assures him that his beloved Fianna are all in hell for their pains, and often contrives heartless practical jokes intended to terrify Oisin into accepting baptism. At times the two break into a grotesquely humorous flyting. Oisin, irritated by Patrick's nagging and by his interminable prayers and psalms, threatens to twist his bald head off; Patrick has a good mind to beat Oisin with his holy bell.

These ballads, widely dispersed and long remembered, form the overwhelming bulk of the Fenian Cycle as we actually have it. They are a popular, oral form, and the isolated moments when they happen to be written down are the momentary lifting of a curtain, when we glimpse them in their progress through the centuries. In 1626 and 1627 an Irish soldier of fortune, Captain Sorley O'Donnell, employed a scribe at Ostend and another at Louvain to copy out a vast collection of ballads known as the *Duanaire Finn* ('The Poem-Book of Finn'). But long before the Fenian ballads thus wandered to the Continent they had spread all over the Gaelic-speaking world. For many centuries, little or no racial distinction was drawn between the inhabitants of Northern Ireland and those of the Highlands and Islands of Scotland. One name, Scotia, covered both; one language was spoken across the whole area. Over a century before O'Donnell's collection, one James MacGregor, a clergyman of the island of Lismore near Oban, wrote or caused to be written a collection of over eleven thousand verses of Gaelic poetry, subsequently known as *The Dean of Lismore's Book*. Twenty-eight of these poems are short, detached ballads belonging to the Fenian Cycle; above several of them MacGregor has written, 'Auctor hujus Ossin.'

When the methodical study of folklore began in the nineteenth

century the collectors were out again, and one of the most
energetic and scrupulous of them, J. F. Campbell of Islay, took
down from the lips of cottagers poems which differed scarcely at
all from those in *The Dean of Lismore's Book*. As late as 1860 a
Fenian ballad attributed to Oisin was taken down from recita-
tion on the Isle of Barra. Back and forth across the water the
ballads moved. Douglas Hyde, the friend of Yeats and historian
of Irish literature, heard one of the Dean of Lismore's ballads
from a peasant in County Roscommon in 1890. And so the age-
long story comes down almost to living memory.

Over much the greater part of this time, the Fenian stories, in
common with most Gaelic legends, remained firmly enclosed in
the comparatively narrow geographical area which is their
locale. For century after century, the European literary sensibili-
ty showed no awareness of their existence. The Europe of Dante
and Chaucer, of Boccaccio and Shakespeare and Cervantes, of
Villon and Racine and Dryden, knew nothing of Finn and Oisin.

But historical forces move in a mysterious way, their wonders
to perform. In the latter half of the eighteenth century, the
legends of the Fenian Cycle made a sudden appearance on the
wider stage of European literature: an appearance that was at
least partly an illusion; in which they were seen and not seen;
famous, yet still unknown; discussed and debated loud and long,
yet in an atmosphere more remarkable for heat than for light;
present to men's minds, yet present in a shape that was not their
own.

This is how it happened.

In the Highland village of Ruthven, on the banks of the River
Spey, there lived a poor farmer named Andrew MacPherson,
who was blessed with a bright, quick-witted son. This boy,
James, had shown so much aptitude at the village school that his
father decided, come what may, to take him from the fields and
put him to a learned profession. Since the only learned profes-
sion at that time open to a boy from so humble a background
was the ministry, a minister James MacPherson should be, and
with this aim he attended King's College, Aberdeen, and sub-
sequently the University of Edinburgh. In 1756, at the age of

about twenty, he had finished his studies at Edinburgh, or taken
them as far as he could afford, and, still too young to enter the
ministry, kept for a time the charity school in his native village.
Clever and ambitious, he yearned to attract notice. He wrote
poems and sent them to the *Scots Magazine*, at that time the
only literary periodical north of the Tweed. By some means or
other, he obtained a post as tutor in the family of Mr Graham of
Balgowan, and supervised the education of the young Graham
who afterwards became Lord Lynedoch, one of Wellington's
ablest generals. In the summer of 1759, MacPherson accom-
panied the Graham family to the fashionable spa of Moffat, and
there he made the acquaintance of John Home, author of the
play *Douglas* which had been a success both in Edinburgh and
London. Home took to MacPherson; they had many interesting
literary discussions; he declared the young tutor to be a good
Classical scholar; and, when their talk happened to turn on the
ancient Gaelic poetry of the Highlands, Home, a Lowland Scot,
found himself increasingly interested in what MacPerson had to
say on that subject too.

Perhaps it was Home who brought up the subject. He was,
without knowing anything about it, interested in the imaginative
world of the Celtic Scot. One of the earliest poems in English
literature to strike a chord responsive to that world is William
Collins's 'Ode on the Popular Superstitions of the Highlands of
Scotland, considered as the Subject of Poetry' – and Collins had
been moved to write this poem after a conversation with Home,
whom he had met at Winchester. Home was convinced that the
poetic imagination of the Highlander was splendid and beautiful.
But it was locked away in its (to him) impenetrable language.
When MacPherson, who had grown up in a Gaelic-speaking
village, mentioned that he knew the Gaelic poems and even had
some of them in his possession, Home pressed him to translate a
specimen. MacPherson demurred; the task was enormous, and
he lacked confidence. But Home persisted in his request to the
point where MacPherson felt it impossible to refuse. He under-
took to try; for the next few days he spent much time closeted in
his room; finally he came down and handed to Home a short

narrative and elegiac composition, in highly cadenced and ver-
sicular prose, entitled 'The Death of Oscar'.

As MacPherson came down those stairs, and handed over to
Home what he had written, European literature crossed one of
those frontiers that mark off one era of sensibility from another.
Home responded vibrantly to 'The Death of Oscar'; it had all
the qualities which he had long surmised the ancient Gaelic
poetry to possess, if he could only lay his hands on it in trans-
lation. He asked for more, and MacPherson obliged. On his return
to Edinburgh, Home took several of the pieces with him and
showed them to Hugh Blair, Professor of Rhetoric at the univer-
sity and a man whose learning, taste and sensibility were
respected in England as well as in Scotland. Blair, too, admired
the compositions. He made the acquaintance of MacPherson.
Determined to help the poems to reach the wider public they so
much merited, he contributed a preface to the small gathering of
quasi-Fenian poems that MacPherson published in 1760 under
the title *Fragments of Ancient Poetry, collected in the Highlands
of Scotland, and translated from the Gaelic or Erse language.*

MacPherson continued to publish his versions, and Blair con-
tinued to sponsor them. In the first flush of the enthusiasm
aroused by the *Fragments*, MacPherson made it known that he
had heard of the existence of a complete epic poem, *Fingal*,
which might still be claimed for the written culture if speedy ac-
tion could be taken. It was preserved in the memories of certain
residents of the Highlands; he mentioned in particular a country
doctor in Lochaber who knew it by heart from beginning to end;
and this was sufficiently remarkable, for it was nine thousand
lines long.

Scottish vigour and practicality came at once into play. A
dinner was held; subscriptions were quickly raised; and
MacPherson was sent on a tour of the Highlands to gather
material. He returned with good news. He had found the epic of
Fingal, preserved in its entirety. He published his translation of
it in 1762, and followed it with *Temora* in 1763. In the latter
year, Blair came out with his widely influential essay, *A Critical
Dissertation on the Poems of Ossian, Son of Fingal.* (Ossian was

what MacPherson called Oisin, and Fingal was what he called Finn.) Blair's essay presents the ancient bard as a poet the equal of Homer and in many respects the superior of Virgil.

> Both poets are eminently sublime; but a difference may be remarked in the species of their sublimity. Homer's sublimity is accompanied with more of a solemn and awful grandeur. Homer hurries you along; Ossian elevates, and fixes you in astonishment. Homer is most sublime in actions and battles; Ossian, in description and sentiment. In the pathetic, Homer, when he chooses to exert it, has great power; but Ossian exerts that power much oftener, and has the character of tenderness far more deeply imprinted on his works. No poet knew better how to seize and melt the heart. With regard to dignity of sentiment, the pre-eminence must clearly be given to Ossian. This is indeed a surprising circumstance, that in point of humanity, magnanimity, virtuous feelings of every kind, our rude Celtic bard should be distinguished to such a degree, that not only the heroes of Homer, but even those of the polite and refined Virgil, are left far behind by those of Ossian.

Blair also remarked the Classical regularity of Ossian's poetry, as exemplified by the six-book epic *Fingal*, when judged by the canons laid down in Aristotle's *Poetics*.

> Examined even according to Aristotle's rules, it will be found to have all the essential requisites of a true and regular epic; and to have several of them in so high a degree, as at first view to raise our astonishment on finding Ossian's composition so agreeable to rules of which he was entirely ignorant. But our astonishment will cease, when we consider from what source Aristotle drew those rules. Homer knew no more of the laws of criticism than Ossian. But guided by nature, he composed in verse a regular story, founded on heroic actions, which all posterity admired. Aristotle, with great sagacity and penetration, traced the causes of this general admiration. He observed what it was in Homer's composition, and in the conduct of his story, which gave it such power to please; from this observation

he deduced the rules which poets ought to follow, who
would write and please like Homer; and to a composition
formed according to such rules, he gave the name of an epic
poem. Hence his whole system arose. Aristotle studied
nature in Homer. Homer and Ossian both wrote from nature.
No wonder that among all the three, there should be such
agreement and conformity.

As reasoning, this is perfectly sound: if we accept Blair's ac-
count of how Aristotle arrived at his critical principles, it should
follow naturally that any unspoilt primitive poet would reach the
same point by the same route; indeed, the position is a familiar
one in neo-Classic criticism ('Nature and Homer were, he found,
the same'). It is merely an accident that the truth happens to be
even simpler – that the author of *Fingal* had learnt the precepts
of Aristotle from Blair's own lips in the classrooms of the
University of Edinburgh.

For MacPherson, strange to relate, had himself concocted
nine-tenths of the material which he offered as a modern English
version of ancient Gaelic. Even stranger to relate, he had in-
vented out of whole cloth the very first poetic narrative he
showed to Blair, 'The Death of Oscar'. As we know, the tales
and poems of the Fenian Cycle represent Oscar as having been
killed in the battle at Gavra in which the Fianna had gone down
to their heroic end. The stories also tell of another character
named Oscar, and he too was killed at Gavra, fighting on the
side of the High King. MacPherson, who presumably knew the
authentic story, chose to weave a tale of romantic love. He has
Oscar and Dermid in love with the same maiden; neither can
break free of her, but equally neither can bear the thought of
injuring his friend; they fight, each hoping to be killed, and
when in the end it is Oscar who kills Dermid he has no further use
for life and contrives a picturesque suicide at the hand of the
damsel herself. Of all this, Gaelic tradition knows nothing. Nor
does MacPherson's fragment make any recognizable gesture
towards such tradition. It is lachrymose and elegiac in the
fashion of mid-eighteenth-century pre-romanticism.

'Why openest thou afresh the spring of my grief, O son of
Alpin, inquiring how Oscar fell? My eyes are blind with
tears; but memory beams on my heart. How can I relate
the mournful death of the head of the people? Prince of the
warriors, Oscar, my son! shall I see thee no more?

'He fell as the moon in a storm, as the sun from the
midst of his course, when clouds rise from the waste of the
waves, when the blackness of the storm inwraps the rocks
of Ardanmidder. I, like an ancient oak on Morven, I
moulder alone in my place. The blast hath lopped my
branches away; and I tremble at the wind of the north.
Prince of the warriors, Oscar, my son! shall I see thee no
more!

'Dermid and Oscar were one; they reaped the battle
together. Their friendship was as strong as their steel; and
death walked between them to the field. They came on the
foe like two rocks falling from the brows of Ardven. Their
swords were stained with the blood of the valiant: warriors
fainted at their names. . . .

'By the brook of the hill their graves are laid; a birch's
unequal shade covers their tomb. Often on their green
earthen tombs the branchy sons of the mountain feed,
when midday is all in flames and silence is over all the
hills.'

In his subsequent compositions, MacPherson did not always
follow this policy of totally original invention. Often, he incor-
porated into the work fragments of material to which parallels
exist in the authentic tradition. But, while he was not totally averse
to using genuine Gaelic material, he remained obstinately averse to
the flavour, the style, the *haecceitas* of anything that he found either
on the lips of the people or in the manuscript collections. His taste
was entirely that of the 1760s – or, rather, to be more precise, it was
that of the 1770s and 1780s, manifesting itself a few years before it
was fully accepted and acknowledged.

To anticipate the next swerve of taste is exactly what every
popular writer longs to be able to do. MacPherson did it, and his
success was immediate and spectacular. No best-seller ever best-
sold like the works which he proffered as those of 'Ossian',

slightly modifying the bard's name to make it easy for the Anglo-
Saxon tongue. And not the Anglo-Saxon tongue only. Very soon
the name was being enthusiastically mispronounced in every
corner of Europe. In the next few years, translations appeared
into German, Italian, Spanish, French, Dutch, Danish, Swedish,
Polish, Russian and Greek. European men of letters as diverse as
Klopstock and Lamartine took up Blair's suggestion that a fruit-
ful comparison might be drawn between Ossian and Homer;
both preferred Ossian. The youthful Goethe, apparently
prompted by Herder, translated copious extracts from Ossian,
and introduced his poetry at a crucial point of *The Sorrows of
Werther*; it is the last book from which Werther reads aloud to
Charlotte, the night before he commits suicide. The immense
vogue of Goethe's book carried the vogue of Ossian along with
it. Napoleon Bonaparte was passionately fond of both. Napoleon
read the works of Ossian in the Italian translation of Cesarotti;
he is said to have modelled some of his despatches on their style,
which must have made them less effective as despatches; he
showed his admiration by founding an academy of Celtic studies
in Paris, and by rewarding Cesarotti. The Ossianic impulse
erupted into drama in Arnault's five-act tragedy *Oscar, fils
d'Ossian* in 1796, and even into music; when a composer named
Méhul wrote his opera *Uthal*, in the Ossianic style, he dispensed
with violins in the orchestra and used instead a chorus of tenor
voices, to heighten the effect of numinous melancholy.

The treatment of Ossian by the sprightly Mme de Staël in her
*De la Litterature, considerée dans ses rapports avec les in-
stitutions sociales* (1800) may fairly be taken as typical of the Con-
tinental approach. She is a strong believer in the influence of climate
and habitat on the literary imagination; to her, as to Herder, a
literature is primarily an expression of the deeper emotional and
spiritual nature of a people. Distinguishing two traditions in
Europe, *la litterature du midi* (the achievement of Greeks, Italians,
Spaniards, and the French of the epoch of Louis XIV) and *la
litterature du nord* (mainly English and German, with a side-glance
at Danish and Swedish), she finds the origin and fountain-head in
Homer and Ossian respectively. Mme de Staël wisely declines a

direct literary comparison between Ossian and Homer. She sees
them as representing different stages. Ossian is like one of those
primitive singers who made the rough popular ballads on which
Homer based his poems; his work is, so to speak, pre-epic, closer to
folk-material. For a somewhat similar reason, Ossian's poems,
though she had claimed them as the pure paradigm of 'northern
literature', do not in fact contain that wealth of philosophical ideas
and original speculation which, again according to her own ac-
count, distinguish *la littérature du nord* from *la littérature du
midi*. This, too, is owing to their early date; being of such antiquity,
they represent the human mind at a stage before the power of
speculation was developed; but they provide, in their intense and
brooding melancholy, the essential precondition and groundwork
of speculation.

Altogether, Mme de Staël shows more caution and good sense
than was common among the admirers of MacPherson's 'Ossian'
in the British Isles. She side-steps the question of the exact place
occupied by 'Ossian' in the family tree of northern literature, of
which poets were, and which were not, directly influenced by
him, and contents herself with the statement that, whatever
were the historical contours of the matter, Ossian is the perfect
diagram of *la littérature du nord* in its pristine state:

> Les chantes d'Ossian (Barde, qui vivait dans le quatrième
> siècle) étaient connus des Écossais et des hommes de lettres
> en Angleterre, avant que MacPherson les eût recueillis. En
> appelant Ossian l'origine de la littérature du nord, j'ai voulu
> seulement ... l'indiquer comme le plus ancien poète auquel
> l'on puisse rapporter le caractère particulier à la poésie du
> nord. Les fables islandaises, les poésies scandinaves du
> neuvième siècle, origine commune de la littérature anglaise
> et de la littérature allemande, ont la plus grande ressem-
> blance avec les traits distinctifs des poésies Erses et du poème
> de Fingal.

Mme de Staël, writing before the colossal effort of research
made by the nineteenth and twentieth centuries, is understan-
dably vague about the family tree of European literature in the

Dark Ages. But in her tastes and preferences she is perfectly clear-cut. She enjoys the poems of Ossian and finds them venerable, stimulating, authoritative. And so did Home and Blair; so did Goethe, Napoleon, Herder, Lessing, Schiller, Novalis and Chateaubriand. Only very slowly did the beliefs die out in Continental Europe that 'Ossian' was the Homer of the British Isles, and MacPherson his true and selfless intermediary.

Such, in bare outline, is the story of how MacPherson transformed Oisin into Ossian, and made of the Fenian stories a dish that pleased the palate of all Europe for a generation. It is a familiar story enough, and my excuse for recounting it once again must be a contemporary one. I believe there are lessons to be drawn from the story of MacPherson and his Ossian: that the literary upheaval of the 1760s has been very exactly paralleled by the literary upheaval of the 1960s; that the tolerance we extend, in retrospect, to those eminent critics who took 'Ossian' for the equal of Homer may have to be extended likewise to those critics of our day who are impressed by the outbreak of psychedelic and improvisatory verse, or versicular utterance, in the same years of our century.

Let me be specific. The years since 1960 have seen a mass turning-away from the notion of poetry as an art that used to have something in common with music, and towards a more or less improvisatory style which aims at one of two objectives: either to simulate the ravings of a drug-addict, or to inculcate very simple political and social messages. In either case it represents the deliquescence of a tradition. The former is a degeneration from the tradition of surrealism, and the latter from the tough and urgent 'committed' poetry of Mayakovsy, Brecht or the early Auden. What the two styles have in common is an impoverishment, a rejection of resources. Most of the in-struments and strategies that poets have used immemorially are cast aside. Form, which used to hold the precious liquor of a poem as a jug holds milk, is broken for no other purpose than to allow the milk to spill on to the ground. Verbal nuance and literary allusion are rejected as 'élitist', the implied directive being that what all cannot achieve no one must. The result is a poetry which can minister only to a warm feeling of togetherness, a collective *frisson*. Understandably, it flourishes better at 'poetry readings' (or, more flamboyantly, 'read-ins') than on the printed page, being written not for those who wish to read, and ponder, and reread, but for those who need each other's company in a crowded space and a poet up on the platform dealing with the latest important experience, glorifying the latest idol, in lines simple and porous enough to be rewritten, in a few minutes, to meet the demands of next week's political dénouement or social current.

The comparison holds because MacPherson, too, proceeded by the route of simplification and impoverishment. Of the richness he found in his sources, he retained very little. The whole of the narrative element went out of the window for a start. The Fenian stories as he found them were swift, colourful, full of invention and symbolism. Their tone was often melancholy and elegiac, but almost equally often gay and rejoicing, full of appreciation of nature and love of life. MacPherson flattened all this into a monotonous lachrymosity. In doing so he hammered at exactly the right point to produce a sharp reflex jerk from the literary nerve-centres of his generation. His work is in fact very similar to the prose churned out by advertising agencies. A few stock responses are walloped again and again. And the poetry of our present-day MacPhersons can be shown, by an elementary critical exercise, to exhibit the same resemblance. What we are discussing is the difference between depth and shallowness, between rich complexity and impoverished pattern-making. The real poet evokes the deep, universally shared archetype; the ad. man rings Pavlov's little bell.

It is not – perhaps I ought to underline here – a matter of conscious charlatanism. MacPherson was convinced that he was offering something valuable. He was, in his way, as firmly in the grip of a $\delta\alpha\iota\mu\omega\nu$ as the most authentic poet. This is proved, I think, by the fact that his first offering to Blair, 'The Death of Oscar', was a fabrication of his own. If MacPherson had been an astute opportunist, he would have used in that first exercise such authentic material as he had to hand, trusting that more would

come his way. The fact that he pushed aside such genuine
material as he possessed, and went ahead with the insipid con-
tents of his own mind, indicates that he, as much as any great
poet, wrote what he had to write.

Nor was it, in MacPherson's case – and here we note a parting
of the ways between MacPherson and the equivalent figures in
our own time – a question of issuing a direct challenge to the
prevailing literary modes and assumptions. MacPherson, faced
with the established literary culture of the eighteenth century,
wanted not to lick it but to join it. This is the significance of the
skirmish between him and Samuel Johnson. Johnson represented
Augustan literary culture, and he repulsed MacPherson's
attempt to be taken seriously within the citadel of that culture.
This was fair, because MacPherson had tried to get in at the
front door. Augustan culture set a very high value on the epic
poem, yet was itself unable, because of its prevailing rationalistic
and urbane atmosphere, to nurture an epic poet. The gap was
filled by translations of ancient epic poetry into the Augustan
mode. Hence the constant lip-service, and perhaps more than
lip-service, to two great translations, Pope's Homer and
Dryden's Virgil. To these two, MacPherson wished to add a
third – MacPherson's Ossian. No rebel he; in fact he can stand
as the type of the perfect *apparatchik*. His career was a model of
discreet and rapid climbing. He was patronized by Bute; went to
Florida as secretary to Governor Johnstone; on his return
became active in controversy on the government side; was
elected to Parliament for a Cornish borough; received a pension
from Lord North's government; became confidential agent to the
Nabob of Arcot, and by so doing amassed considerable wealth;
finally retired to his native heath, where he built a splendid man-
sion and was a beneficent landlord. He left instructions that he
was to be buried in Westminster Abbey, and the instructions
were carried out.

MacPherson's involvement in the pseudo-revival of ancient
Gaelic literature was an affair of his youth. His work was
finished by the time he was twenty-six, though at various times
in later life he was forced to spend some energy on defending his

position or evading detection. (The episode of his threatening
Johnson with physical harm, and receiving in reply the famous
letter of 20 January 1775, belongs to one of these later periods.)
But, like many men who later wander far from the paths of
literature, MacPherson was, for a few years in his youth,
genuinely in the grip of an imaginative impulse. The nature of
this impulse is easy to see. He was one of those who received
advance warning of the seismic upheaval of Romanticism. They
were a mixed band. We are sometimes apt to imagine, under the
influence of the all-pervading notion of 'progress', that the most
advanced artist, the one who most clearly anticipates the next
stage in the history of his art, is the best. But this will not stand
examination. In eighteenth-century poetry, for instance, it is
clear that Johnson and Goldsmith, who are conservative in style
and attitude, are better poets (in any sense that I can attach to
the word 'better') than Collins or the Gray of the Odes, though it
is these poets who point towards the new developments. Cer-
tainly they are far better than MacPherson. The privilege of
receiving a special message from the *Zeitgeist* is, like Grace as
imagined by the Jansenists, distributed with no regard for merit.
MacPherson, within his limitations (and they were formidable),
was stimulated into writing by the message of the *Zeitgeist*.

The *Zeitgeist* was also, of course, responsible for that
astonishing wave of antiquarian energy that fuelled the literary
research of the second half of the eighteenth century. Medieval
literature, both polite and popular, lay waiting to be discovered
after the studied neglect of the centuries of the Renaissance. The
collectors went out, after ballads, after minstrel poems, after
romances; and where the material they found did not match up
with their imaginative vision of what medieval literature should
be like they unhesitatingly altered it. Nowadays, with our
scrupulous and quasi-scientific standards in these matters, we
shake our heads over the buccaneering approach of the
eighteenth-century connoisseur. An editor like Percy, confronted
by several versions of a ballad, made his own recension by
picking out the verses he enjoyed most, and could seldom resist
the temptation to prettify the result still further in the direction

of eighteenth-century taste. The result was not scholarship, but it did something which a purer scholarship might not have been able to do: it attracted a mass public towards certain facets of medieval literature, and this public gave crucial support to Romantic poetry in its first phase.

The procedure of a man like Percy was governed mainly by a genuine curiosity about the material he was uncovering, and partly by a desire, unconfessed and perhaps not fully admitted to consciousness, to contribute to the imaginative literature of his own day. We can see the elements at work in many figures of that time. Occasionally, the impulse to fabricate overcame the impulse to preserve and edit so completely that the results have been called 'forgeries'; such are the works of MacPherson and Chatterton, and of that strange character Robert Surtees, who sent to Sir Walter Scott a series of ballads which he claimed to have had from the recitations of aged peasants, some of them his own servants, and as to whose provenance he gave minute particulars. Surtees himself, though Scott never suspected it, was the author of every syllable. Obviously what we have here is the impulse to write a certain kind of poetry, an impulse overwhelming in its intensity, yet not sufficiently self-confident to offer itself as that alone. To claim for one's own compositions that they are interesting, venerable survivals, invested with the mystery and beauty of a remote past, is to give them the protective colouring of something larger and more impersonal than one's own individual imagination.

For an interesting parallel, we might profitably glance in the direction of Iolo Morganwg, who performed for Welsh literature something like the same spectacular disservice as MacPherson did for Gaelic, but was in all other respects entirely different. MacPherson's escapade, as we have noted, was an affair of his youth; Iolo Morganwg spent the whole of his long life in the passionate study of Welsh literature and antiquities. Far better than anyone else in his day (the late eighteenth and early nineteenth century) he understood the nature of Welsh poetry from the fourteenth century onwards. But, exactly as in the case of MacPherson, he was afflicted from the beginning with a wish to intervene, to participate, to raise his own voice in the chorus of the great poets of the past. As a youth, Iolo Morganwg made the acquaintance of a clergyman, Thomas Richards of Coychurch, who had published a Welsh–English dictionary. This important work of scholarship contained many examples of the diction of the old bards, accompanied by illustrative quotations from their works. Iolo Morganwg made a careful study of these words. At the same time he coined hundreds of new ones, and for these too he provided illustrative quotations, made up by himself and attributed to bards whose names he found in the manuscripts he was already beginning to collect.

So it went on. Having noticed a resemblance between the work of the troubadours and that of Dafydd ap Gwilym, he formed the theory that the bards of Glamorgan in the twelfth century had been exposed to the influence of the troubadours during habitual visits to the Norman castles in the Vale. If he could have stopped there, he would have been a scholar. But he was also a poet, of the demented and underground type represented by MacPherson. He invented a poet, Rhys Goch ap Rhicert ab Einion ap Collwyn, and to this figure he attributed fifteen poems of his own composition.

Later in life, Iolo Morganwg became interested in the Druids, whom he regarded as the ancestors of the bards. He began to put together a vast comprehensive account of the Druidical thinking, and into this account he wove ideas he had come across in books on the Jewish Cabbala, Brahminism, Hinduism, theosophy and mysticism. Himself a man of the age of Rousseau, a believer in the political and social ideas which found their outlet in the French Revolution, he saw a connection between the Druids and the advanced thinkers of his own day. To a friend in London he wrote, 'I am giving you the patriarchal religion and theology, the divine revelation given to mankind, and these have been retained in Wales until our own day.' 'I am giving the venerable remains of the theology and economy of the primitive world.' And again: 'I am describing a state of society wherein the noblest and most benign of human affections had obtained the ascendancy.' And yet again: 'I have inherited the traditions of a world that had not

been corrupted by wealth and civilization.' Thus did Iolo
Morganwg fuse two white-hot elements – his vision of the
revolutionary or quasi-Pantisocratic future and his equally
ardent vision of the lost, but recoverable, Golden Age. The sheer
amount of information he marshalled in this process makes
MacPherson look like a child. So inextricable is the blend of
learning and fantasy that he muddied the waters of scholarship
for a hundred years. (Fragments of Iolo Morganwg, accepted in
good faith as the utterances of ancient bards, are to be met with
in Mr Graves's *The White Goddess*, and doubtless in many other
places.) What is more to our immediate purpose, the impulse to
learn, to discover and to disseminate was, in Iolo Morganwg,
identical with the impulse to create. The two formed a seamless
fabric.

So it was with MacPherson. He had already failed as a poet
within the accepted mid-eighteenth-century conventions. When
his imagination boiled up again, it did so within a form which
would never have been taken seriously unless he had presented it
under the umbrella offered by Home and Blair. His interest in
the Gaelic originals was minimal. In so far as he knew them at
all, he disliked them. Since MacPherson never visited Ireland
and had no contacts there, it is unlikely that he knew of the
prose tales which were preserved in Irish manuscripts. His own
research was mainly field-work, conducted in that one hurried
visit to the Highlands and Islands in 1759. What he found was a
mass of modern balladry, which he disliked both in matter and
manner. This wretched stuff could not possibly have been the
utterance of an ancient epic bard. It must be late, degenerate, an
importation from Ireland (for MacPherson, naturally, wished to
believe and therefore did believe that Oisin was a Scot like
himself). The melancholy tone of the Fenian Cycle, the grieving
over departed glories, he retained and grotesquely magnified.
But the other characteristic which virtually all the stories have in
common, their preoccupation with the marvellous, he rejected
with sarcasm. Indeed, the chief argument by which he sought to
demolish the authenticity of the Irish Fenian ballads, and thus
preserve the tradition intact as a Scottish possession, was that

the Irish poems were marked by absurdities which they must have collected during their passage through the Middle Ages, a period for which he felt as much scorn as any Renaissance humanist.

> I have just now, [he wrote] in my hands, all that remain of those compositions [sc. 'the Irish poems concerning Fion']; but, unluckily for the antiquities of Ireland, they appear to be the work of a very modern period. Every stanza, nay almost every line, affords striking proofs, that they cannot be three centuries old. Their allusions to the manners and customs of the fifteenth century, are so many, that it is a matter of wonder to me, how any one could dream of their antiquity. They are entirely writ in that romantic taste, which prevailed two ages ago. Giants, enchanted castles, dwarfs, palfreys, witches and magicians form the whole circle of the poet's invention. The celebrated Fion could scarcely move from one hillock to another, without encountering a giant, or being entangled in the circles of a magician. Witches on broomsticks, were continually hovering round him, like crows; and he had freed enchanted virgins in every valley in Ireland. In short, Fion, great as he was, passed a disagreeable life.

Just as MacPherson poured polite urban sarcasm on the subject-matter of the Fenian poems, so he held austerely aloof from the actual form in which he encountered them, which was that of the ballad. Even if he had had the skill to write convincing ballad-poetry while completely altering the stories of the originals, he would not have done so. The ballad was firmly identified with a tradition for which MacPherson had as little use as he had for the prevailing tradition of polite poetry. They were associated with folk-art, and MacPherson would have none of that. True, Ossian's poetry embodied the very spirit of a people, as Mme de Staël was to confirm when she saw in it the essential outlines of *la littérature du nord*; but this embodiment was a matter of a stately art, highly charged and elevated. Somewhat later than MacPherson, but very much under his influence, the German writers of the *Sturm und Drang* were to elaborate the theory of *Volkslied*; but *Volkslied*, if people's song at all, was no rude or homespun lyricism but works of an enormous grandeur among which they numbered the epics of Homer, the Bible, the Niebelungenlied and, inevitably, the works of Ossian.

In Iolo Morganwg, we find the same current of feeling on which MacPherson, some thirty years previously, had launched his Ossian. But, whereas Iolo Morganwg had kept his fabrications within the original language, MacPherson had launched his into the wide sea of European letters by the medium of English. And, to recapitulate, he had (1) exploited a widespread dissatisfaction with prevailing literary modes without issuing a formal challenge to those modes, seeking acceptance and inclusion rather than collision; (2) avoided tissue-rejection by passing off his original work as translation.

Both these procedures survived into our own century. When, round about 1914, a new generation of poets began to find the accepted modes of European poetry no longer possible to work in, they infiltrated their new procedures partly under the guise of translation, and partly under the umbrella of a criticism which set out to regroup the major works of the tradition without ceasing to pay attention to them.

The classic period of modern poetry, at any rate in the English language, began about 1914. (When it ended it is slightly less clear-cut, but that it *has* ended will need no demonstration.) Its central critical document is T. S. Eliot's essay 'Tradition and the Individual Talent', written in 1919. In that statement, made on the threshold of his life's work, Eliot faced the problem of an entrenched literary taste and a culture whose arteries were beginning to harden. In the orthodox literary opinion of that time, the classics were the classics, they were established beyond dispute, all that was needed was to take the most recent of them as one's starting-point and continue the line with a few minor and allowable variations – this was the 'continuous literary decorum' from whose adherents Bridges foresaw a resistance to Hopkins. Intent himself on innovation, Eliot urged that the relationship of the classics with the modern original mind was a fluid one. Not

only did the past, as everyone knew, influence the present; the
present could also influence the past, since the backward look
modifies the object. The order of precedence among the estab-
lished classics was not immutable; it could be altered by the
appearance of a new masterpiece, causing some to be shifted
slightly to one side, others to be brought nearer to the centre, as
the new work modified the sensibility with which we regarded
them. We continued to need them all, but the intensity of our
need and the direction of our gaze could vary; it was a living and
reciprocal process. Tradition, in Eliot's words,

> cannot be inherited, and if you want it you must obtain
> it by great labour. It involves, in the first place, the
> historical sense, which we may call nearly indispensable to
> anyone who would continue to be a poet beyond his
> twenty-fifth year; and the historical sense involves a
> perception, not only of the pastness of the past, but of its
> presence; the historical sense compels a man to write not
> merely with his own generation in his bones, but with a
> feeling that the whole of the literature of Europe from
> Homer and within it the whole of the literature of his own
> country has a simultaneous existence and composes a
> simultaneous order.

It is this simultaneous order which is constantly open to change
and adjustment, constantly responding to the developments of
the original and contributing mind, constantly open to what
Matthew Arnold called in another connection 'the soft play of
life'.

This attitude found, I think, its first systematic formulation in
Eliot's essay. But it was not totally new. It had long been
accepted as a working principle by the European literary mind.
When Blair, or Mme de Staël, went over the history of literature
with a mental crowbar in order to find a place for Ossian beside
Homer, and having established that relationship went on to
define and discuss it, they were being traditional in Eliot's sense;
they were arguing that they, and everyone else, would hence-
forth live in a slightly altered relationship with the Greek and Latin
epic.

MacPherson's other strategy, the avoidance of tissue-rejection by introducing the new material as translation, is equally in evidence in the early years of classical modern poetry. When Arthur Waley's *170 Chinese Poems* appeared in 1918, Waley certainly intended them to be taken seriously as literal translations, which they were. But the effect of these poems, coming as they did at the moment when the new modes of English and American poetry were just struggling into existence by means of Imagism and its kindred impulses, was profoundly encouraging. Waley did not present his translations as free verse; he had a definite system, which was, he explained, that

Each character in the Chinese is represented by a stress in the English; but between the stresses unstressed syllables are of course interposed. In a few instances where the English insisted on being shorter than the Chinese, I have preferred to vary the metre of my version, rather than pad out the line with unnecessary verbiage.

The result was a poetry that was bound to give crucial encouragement to the new approach to verse in English. The level diction, the detached, ironic tone which could yet adapt to the expression of profound emotion, fell refreshingly on ears hardened to such trumpeters as Kipling, Newbolt and Chesterton. A poem like this, for instance – 'Civilization', by Yüan Chieh.

To the south-east – three thousand leagues–
The Yüan and Hsiang form into a mighty lake.
Above the lake are deep mountain valleys,
And men dwelling whose hearts are without guile.
Gay like children, they swarm to the tops of the trees;
And run to the water to catch bream and trout.
Their pleasures are the same as those of beasts and birds;
They put no restraint either on body or mind.
Far have I wandered throughout the Nine Lands;
Wherever I went such manners had disappeared.
I find myself standing and wondering, perplexed,
Whether Saints and Sages have really done us good.

Another important statement in Waley's introduction was this: 'Above all, considering imagery to be the soul of poetry, I have avoided either adding images of my own or suppressing those of the original.'

The next few years saw a poetry which attempted to pare away all discursive elements and proceed almost entirely by images, grouped together as a painter might group them, and conveyed in unceremonious, immediate language. How could such Imagist poetry fail to take strength and comfort from Waley's collection, rich as it was in poems like this one? — 'Flowers and Moonlight on the Spring River', by the Emperor Yang-ti.

> The evening river is level and motionless —
> The spring colours just open to their full.
> Suddenly a wave carries the moon away
> And the tidal water comes with its freight of stars.

But there is no need of conjecture. Three years before Waley's book, an original poet with no more than the most impressionistic notion of Chinese had published a small but supremely important collection of poems which used the protective colouring of 'translation from Chinese' to introduce a diction and a rhythm that appeared strange at the time but soon became accepted and then conventional. This was Ezra Pound's *Cathay*, published in 1915. Pound was not a scholar like Waley; but he was a poet who had heard something. Perhaps it was his own voice that he heard; but the Chinese originals, however travestied, gave him the enduring cliff-face from which his voice could echo back to his own ears. And no young English or American poet, reading Pound's version of 'The River-Merchant's Wife: A Letter', would be able afterwards to get that rhythm quite out of his head.

I hope to have established, by now, that MacPherson's procedure in offering an 'alternative poetry' was one that survived, in all essentials, to the threshold of our own period of literary history. His methods, which we have surveyed, were two-fold. But neither is alive today. There has been a radical change in the situation of poetry.

When Blair or Mme de Staël rewrote the history of European literature, when the young MacPherson or the young Ezra Pound heard a new melody and a new rhythm inside his head, it was necessary immediately to confront the problem of domesticating the strange in the company of the familiar. They faced a public, a 'world of letters', which recognized certain assumptions and procedures and was unwilling to let go of them or to modify them very radically. Now there is no such public, no such world of letters. The habits and expectations which bound them together have melted away in the last twenty-five years — not a result of hostile action on the part of innovators who did not accept them, but simply as a result of the changes in the whole structure of our civilization.

These changes, as no one will need to be told, have been brought about by technology. Without argument, without appeal to any body of opinion, the vast reorganization in our circumstances has quietly, while we were looking the other way, dismantled anything resembling a 'tradition' either in the old-style conventional sense or in the refined sense postulated by Eliot. We see this in all the arts. In the world of Mozart, a composer during his formative years had very little opportunity to hear music other than that produced within his own society, springing directly from its physical and social conditions, played by orchestras made up of musicians who had learnt their techniques in a direct father-to-son manner, on instruments made by craftsmen whose skills were equally local and traditional. After recognition and fame, the composer might be enabled to travel, and perhaps hear music from outside his own area. But by that time his sensibility was formed. And *mutatis mutandis* this was the case in the visual arts. Compare our own time, when the budding composer has only to walk to the record-shop on the corner to be deluged with the sounds of every civilization, every epoch, every corner of the earth, with no one of them 'predominant'; when the developing painter or sculptor grows up in the feverishly mushrooming jungle created by the total availability of all styles.

It is M. Mauriac who has given us the basic metaphor for this aesthetic environment by coining the phrase 'le musée

imaginaire'. And it would be vain to imagine that where music
and painting and sculpture have gone literature could avoid
following. Of course language is a more dense medium than
sound or colour, and a poem or a novel cannot overleap national
frontiers without some effort and delay; but the notion of a cen-
tral core of tradition has crumbled just as effectively in literature
as in the other arts. The imaginary museum has no walls. Any
young poet growing into his art, from now on, will be saturated
with everything from Greek tragic choruses to *Beowulf*, from Tu
Fu to Baudelaire, from the oral tradition as we were considering
it at the beginning of this lecture to the popcrete/concrete photo-
poem as constructed by Shimizu Toshihiko – and all pell-mell.
In the face of this, it is not surprising that so many of them are
afraid to grow up at all, retreating into a know-nothing infan-
tilism by comparison with which MacPherson's ersatz would
actually seem rather interesting.

The right way to meet the situation created by the imaginary
museum is, of course, the same as the right way to meet any
situation: to exploit its advantages as well as putting up with its
defects. For the poet of today, virtually anything is possible. No
one starts from a more favoured position than anyone else, no
one is closer to or further away from the centre than anyone else;
no one (outside the busy but unimportant coteries who recruit
our literary secret police) is in fashion or out of fashion. A good
poet writing in English today might with perfect reasonableness
choose from among a wide range of approaches and methods. He
might be drawn towards surrealism, which has survived best in
the Latin countries; or to the all-digesting long poem that comes
down ultimately from Pound through channels as diverse as
Charles Olson and David Jones; or he might go to the other
extreme and meditate the possibilities of the short, intensely
radiating poem, *haiku* or *englyn*. Or he might turn to the
English alliterative line as developed with Classical tightness in
Anglo-Saxon poetry and loosened in the Middle Ages until it
becomes the supple and resilient medium of *Piers Plowman* and
Gawain and the Green Knight; or he might look outside Europe
towards the rich possibilities of a form like the *ghazal*, which oc-

cupies something like the same place in Islamic literature as the
sonnet in that of Europe, but with the great advantage of not
being tied to a fixed length. And so on. All these forms have been
used by great poets, but even that greatness did not necessarily
exhaust them. There is room in them for new soil and new roots.

One demand, in return, the imaginary museum will henceforth
make on every artist. He will have to take the reader, listener or
looker into his confidence. The poet will say to his reader, 'This
is how I propose to work – along these lines, starting from these
premises and working out my freedom within these conven-
tions.' It will have to be a relationship of trust, of friendship
even. The poet will not be ashamed to explain a little what he is
doing, to give his reader the ground-rules; in the imaginary
museum, no one knows where everything comes from and what
it is conveying. There will have to be an element of invitation,
with the poet saying to his reader, 'Will you come with me?
Shall we share this experience?'

Any such procedure, of course, would involve abandoning the
convention of *épater le bourgeois*, the imperative to spit in the
face of the public, to shock and wound. I believe this convention
is as out of date, in any case, as the top hat and the hansom cab.
There is no longer an entrenched conservative bourgeoisie of the
kind that existed in 1910, and we shall get on better when we
have ceased to make believe that there is.

The expression 'alternative poetry' has been coined just at the
time when the thing itself has disappeared for ever. There can
never again be an alternative poetry because there can never be,
in the arts, a simple either/or. And along with the obsolescence
of alternative poetry will go the obsolescence of its social
offshoot, poetry conceived as a test of fitness to survive. (If you
enjoy being bombarded with the right obscenities, applaud the
right political catch-phrases and generally show solidarity, you
are fit to live in the Cockaigne of radical chic in which all good
things will be made easy, and if you don't you will be cast out.)
If poetry is to survive as an art – and there are many people
among the readers of poetry and even among the writers of it
who would like this to come about – the choice is now clear. Is

the relationship of the poet and his audience to be that of St Patrick and Oisin, jangling and flyting and seeking always to up-stage and disconcert one another; or is it to be that of St Patrick and Caolte, with the hearer delighted by the wonderful things the poet has to tell, and his beautiful and memorable way of telling them: *success and benediction attend thee*?

*

I call that the lecture I delivered, though in fact I adopted the principle I have stuck to ever since, of standing up and uttering a spoken version of the lecture, from notes, and going home and writing it out afterwards. There is nothing to be gained from keeping up the pretence that speaking and writing are the same thing. To an audience, one *talks*; to a solitary reader, one *writes*. A lecture in its spoken form makes the same points as in its written version, but it makes them in a simpler and more rhetorical way, with much less in the nature of fine-meshed argument.

The experience of giving an Inaugural, in the Sheldonian Theatre, is not one I would have missed, nor is it one I would voluntarily repeat. I was nervous, and my nervousness was not helped by the physical concomitants of the occasion. An hour beforehand I stole into the building to test the microphone; they had proudly installed the very latest kind, which needed no wires and was multi-directional; but when I wanted to hear myself on it the apparatus was not working. Only when I was confronted with the real thing, when the Vice-Chancellor and I, preceded by the mace-carrying Bedell, had made our entry and the audience was waiting, did I actually hear what my voice sounded like over this marvel of technology. It was harsh, and loud, and distorted. I said, 'Mr Vice-Chancellor, ladies and gentlemen,' and my voice seemed to bounce back at me in a grotesquely parodied form. I was nonplussed, and did not become plussed for the rest of the occasion. And, then, the audience seemed to be grouped in an off-putting fashion; they faced me in a solid square, marshalled into the middle of the floor with acres of unfriendly space all round them, and towards this square I had to pitch my voice with the aid, or non-aid, of the electronic miracle; the nearest of my hearers was some twenty feet away. However, it passed off without any disasters, and at the end I was reasonably satisfied as we all went across the road to the King's Arms for beer and sausages and a let-down of tension.

The Times Literary Supplement sent someone down to cover the lecture, and made it the occasion of another hysterical attack on me. At the time I was slightly annoyed, but looking back I feel rather flattered.

2
Living Vessels

There cannot have been a time when Oxford was without poets: not only the young aspirants who pass through the university more or less rapidly, with more or less effect on its life and their own, but the poets who make Oxford their home, for long or short periods. In our century, Yeats lived for a time in Broad Street ('No emperor does himself so well as an Oxford don,' he remarked after a dinner given for him by Maurice Bowra), Masefield made his home in the country nearby, Bridges lived on Boar's Hill, Robert Graves kept the village shop at Islip. When I came back to live in Oxford in 1963, two established poets were working at the University as dons, John Fuller and Peter Levi; and one, Elizabeth Jennings, was living there simply from choice.

About Elizabeth I can say nothing that I did not say in my poem to her, 'Green Fingers', one of the *Letters to Five Artists* I published in 1969. Patient under the dreadful affliction of repeated breakdown, her mental balance disturbed by recurrent depression and, in recent years, her physical health undermined, largely (one suspects) by the drugs with which that depression has been treated, she has unwaveringly gone on writing poetry, dedicated always to expressing her experience of life, actual as well as imaginative, in words, rhythms, images. This dedication has given her, as dedication always does, an inward strength; even at moments when she declares herself unable to cope with life and sinks into the protection of her friends, in some deep central core of her being she seems stronger than they. In 1963 she was a fresh-coloured, pretty, rather solidly built girl; now her flesh has left her bones and physically she seems what she is,

57

the frail victim of great suffering,

> A fiery soul that, working out its way,
> Fretted the pygmy body to decay,
> And o'er informed the tenement of clay.

But the strength of a directed imagination still shines out of her eyes, and her later poems rise on stronger wings than her earlier.

A woman poet of equal fineness, who for some inexplicable reason has not met with the recognition that has crowned Elizabeth's efforts, is Avril Bruten, a don at St Hugh's, slight of figure, crop-haired, chain-smoking, humorous, one of the wittiest and most vital people in Oxford, but shy and avoiding company. Her poems are the paring-away of experience until its spare, essential outlines stand out at last: they are lyrical, analytic, meditative, at the same time; if this were an age that cared for the finer and subtler notes of poetry, she would be famous.

POEMS BY AVRIL BRUTEN

Valentine's Park

> The name was always inappropriate:
> Attacks on caged birds, women, old men, trees,
> Just as the slow black bell swung
> Closing-time, were always making news.
> Swung by itself, we thought as frightened children,
> Like a decisive god. Moved in a painted tower
> Its unanswerable tongue.
>
> There were ways out: forced railings, rusting gates, —
> Ways that the children and the soldiers made
> Into the trenched allotments, breaking
> From the blaze of V.E. Day street-parties
> Into their separate nights. Yet any god exacts,
> The children found, remorse for broken rules.
> The black bell worked against us.

Once, in the ornamental lake, I dropped
Our front-door key; and nights and nights I lay
Hearing the marshalled burglars of East London
Slip back the lock and softly tread the stairs.
Night after night, the parties in the streets,
And the effigies of Hitler burnt to cheers.
But the black bell mocked all this.

Now I would think of some inane Greek chorus
Bleating a mindless comment on great deaths.
There would be something now to say of cedars
Supported by their own axed limbs for safety.
But to the children they were only castles;
The hollow yellow ilex just a dungeon,
Though the slow black bell was God.

The Wanderer

Now I am how I am

As weather
worries
sap in the bark;
as heat
harries
the nap of dark
leaves,
belief in
any kind
shifts in my mind,
as a devised
anchor
moves in the prised
sea-sand.

Then autumn
inches flame
throughout
the land;
and,
since I gaze
too long,
the same
red rays
of the continuing
sun
show black
in the slack
eye.

Description of a Medieval Drawing

Adam the blank,
surprised at the prised
ripped flank;
and the oxidised moon,
which once had been white.

The first pair.

It could all be true;
but I know that the crow,
and the bland lion too, —
and the God and the unicorn know,
that it could not be right.

They were there.

There is breaching of sides;
there is bearing the thrust;
there is taking of sides;
there is giving in trust.

> Strange, Adam was first
> to feel the skin burst;
>
> and repair.

Still among the women, and let no one wonder that women poets play such a part in this story, since poetry has from the beginning been a field as open to the witch as to the warlock, we seem suddenly to lurch back six hundred years. Sally Purcell is in love with the Middle Ages. As sometimes happens with people who give their imaginative fealty to an epoch, she has taken on something of its look. (I remember, suddenly, how David Nichol Smith had the face of an eighteenth-century man of letters.) Sally, with her pale gentle face and long straight fair hair, often has the withdrawn tranquillity of a fourteenth-century madonna.

It must be this tranquillity that supports her through her precarious way of life. She is a representative of that type that must have been always present in Oxford, though never in large numbers: the scholar who has nothing to do with the official machinery of scholarship. Her learning in medieval French, Latin and Provençal is as deep as that of any don in her subject, and her instinctive adherence to austere standards of scholarship might serve as an example to any of them, but she will not seek an academic post or even accept academic piece-work (the supervising of research, for example) when it is offered to her. Her way is closer to Villon's, though she is a gentle, feminine Villon, without the violence and rascality. She supports herself by working as a barmaid, and at closing time in the afternoon goes across the road from the King's Arms to the Bodleian, dividing her working hours between the tavern and the study. In this she is profoundly wise. The tug and thrust of teaching, the plaster-of-Paris rigidity of an academic routine, would make her far less likely to work effectively as a poet, and her poetry is the centre of her life.

Andrew Harvey, though so devoted to Sally and so heedful of her example, has a different approach. He needs the constantly shifting pattern of ideas and information. His mind is always in racing motion: his eyes, direct and clear behind rimless lenses, are always looking ahead to the next interchange, the next connection he can make between two areas of his knowledge. When I first knew him he was an undergraduate: I used to think that, if he had read a book every day since he was born, there would still not have been time for him to have read all the books he knew. He must have been born a polyhistor. Now he is a Fellow of All Souls, started no doubt on a life-long journey that will take him to the lonely intellectual heights. May the world never beat him down to an acceptance of compromise, or any dialogue with the second-rate.

He writes poetry all the time: with the same incredible speed with which he reads and assimilates information. Inevitably, under these circumstances, some of his earlier poems lack body: they remind one of a powerful car with its wheels spinning on soft ground. But increasingly he is finding a grip on hard earth. For that matter, everything he is producing now will one day be seen as his 'early work' — juvenilia, almost. By the age of twenty-one, he had written reams of perfectly respectable verse. All poets write juvenilia, even if they only compose them in their heads and never get as far as writing them down. Andrew Harvey is the opposite, in this, of my younger self: at the age of twenty-six I published a little volume of nineteen poems, all I had written that I felt able to show to the world. Nineteen poems! Andrew must write as many as that in a month, and his poems are certainly as good as mine were then.

Let these poets speak for themselves.

POEMS BY SALLY PURCELL

facilis descensus

Under your darkness without hope of dawn
tangled the living lie, Master:

enchanted by the huge simplicity
of abdication, they renounced the sun.

No-one need learn / the black paternoster,
all know it; he asks / mere acknowledgement.

He moulds them with oppression they first chose,
as nightmare rides each will
        once offered joyously —

all is not harvest & the witch is never dead.

Gloss on Vita Brendani

Seeking a desert in the ocean,
destined place of each one's resurrection,
holy men kingly in their scarred leathery skin,
richly feasted on wild root & leaf,
drop the oars overboard when land lies behind them
too far to be seen,
and all God's will ahead —
every passion in a single obedience
offered to the secret journey,
pattern of that last one
whose beginning only is known.

POEMS BY ANDREW HARVEY

What makes me tell myself that I am lost
When I know most nights I can cool most lacks
In work or walks downriver in pure wind
And birds in the wind?

What makes me tell myself I have no hope
When I know one cherry tree in full bloom
Or food with friends and music on a hill
Stun me with such hope

I can scarcely speak? The moon with white hands
Anointing all our futures ... why do I still
Still, with such mean precision, have to prove
I am not worth your love

When you forgave me myself long ago?
From what do these too-prompt despairs guard me?
Joy, is it? Joy that might break all safeties
With rods of white light?

formas atque animos sub iuga aenea

'I'll write only if you leave me alone'
Spring in the window-box. Brahms on the
    gramophone.
It isn't enough, my love, it isn't enough.

'I'll SEE you. Can't promise any more than that'
A fat woman's spying from the opposite flat.
Never wanted this, my love, never wanted this.

'You said I stopped you writing. Now you can.'
It's not a fat woman but a fat man.
It isn't enough, my love, it isn't enough.

'You don't even take my hate seriously'
Why's the fat man laughing? Is it you or me?
Never wanted this, my love, never wanted this.

'Sometimes I think you want me to go mad'
Is it the playing or recording that's bad?
It isn't enough, my love, it isn't enough.

'What do we do now? Will we ever KNOW?'
Why is the scherzo so serious, so slow?
Never wanted this, my love, never wanted this.

The title of that second poem indicates a free and tenuous, but
nourishing, relationship with one of Horace's Odes (Book I, ode
33). In that poem, Horace is commenting in his vein of lyrical
wryness on the twisted sense of humour of the goddess of love.
Venus enjoys seeing people smitten with a fatal attraction for
others who are completely different from them and hopelessly in-

compatible; she brings dissimilar minds and bodies under her brazen yoke ('formas atque animos sub iuga aenea'). It seems to me that the reader who doesn't get the reference (as I didn't, till he pointed it out to me) is missing nothing. Putting that line up on the masthead is Andrew Harvey's signal to himself, rather than to the reader, that this is the kind of effect he is aiming for. Though, having said that, I must add at once that a reader who happens to share his passion for Horace will find many of the poems even more interesting.

The question comes back to me often: is there such a thing as a poetic temperament? I have known so many poets – young, old, men, women, from many nationalities and races – is there anything they have in common? Can I, after all these years, tell a poet when I meet one?

Musing over this question at different times and in different moods, I never find myself returning a definite No to it. There are times when it seems to me simply unanswerable; but at other times I feel that there is a basic substratum of character, that all the poets I have known, wildly different in almost every way, are linked by one common thread. Perhaps, in this book, I shall move towards defining that thread, or perhaps it will turn out to be indefinable.

Meanwhile, the poets who are my neighbours here in Oxford, whom I meet regularly in the street, provide a diverse enough galère. Jill Haas, for instance, a friend of both Sally and Andrew but different on the surface from either of them. She is a New Yorker, very much a product of a cultivated metropolitan background, who decided quite suddenly that New York was not a place where she could write poetry; and, thinking over where to go, she seems to have picked on Oxford just because it sounded right to her; never having been there, knowing no one, she packed a suitcase and arrived. That was three years ago, and now her Oxford life has taken root and put out blossoms. Behind that soft, courteous manner with its flashes of quick vivacity, she is intensely serious and dedicated. On first arriving, she set herself a formidable programme of study to fit herself for her vocation. It was at this stage that I was able to give her the only piece of practical help in my power, by introducing her to the Bodleian and sponsoring her application to be admitted as a reader. At once she started reading purposefully, filling gap after gap, knowing that poetry can't be written by amateurs who don't know what has been done already and in what ways. One of the books on her reading-list was Arthur Golding's translation of Ovid's *Metamorphoses*, which Ezra Pound always urged on young poets as a quarry and an example. Jill's search for this book occasioned a merry little pantomime which she looks back on, amusedly, as one of the stages in her adaptation to Oxford. Consulting the Bodleian catalogue, she went to the pre-1920 volumes — naturally enough, for a sixteenth-century book. All she wanted was a readable text, but the catalogue sent her to the edition of 1575. She ordered this up, and was told that in accordance with the Bodleian's practice she must read it in Duke Humphrey's Library, where incunabula are studied. Obediently she went to that sumptuous place with its decorated ceiling and rich smell of calf bindings, was reverently handed the immense folio, and began to read it. But the Elizabethan print was confusing to her eyes, and she went to the desk and asked if they could lend her a magnifying glass. With this, she laboured on until it finally occurred to her that if she looked in a different volume of the catalogue she could find a spick-and-span modern paperback produced in the 1960s. It was not in fact necessary for a young New York lady to read Golding's text in the elegant but rococo typography of the sixteenth century, with the aid of a magnifying glass.

The first poems by Jill Haas that I read were beautifully cadenced but entirely opaque. For some years in New York she had been following a course in the writing of poetry given by Jose Garcia Villa, a poet I respect and whose work I used to read with interest twenty-five years ago, though I have lost touch with what he has been doing in recent years. Villa, as I remembered, was a hermetic, ceremonial poet, and from Jill's account it seemed that he had, naturally enough, sought to foster these qualities in the fledglings who came to him for advice. (Partly owing to the stubborn American conviction that anything that can be done can be taught, American poetry tends to arrange itself in a pattern of master and disciples, which has always seemed to me one of the things that we in England ought not to copy from them.) Jill worked very hard over those early poems and, though she never showed it, was, I think, rather disconcerted by the obvious incomprehension of everyone to whom she showed them. After about twelve months she began to loosen the texture of her poems and inject more in the way of ordinary discursive statement. Jose Garcia Villa might not have approved, but the poems certainly began to communicate much more effectively, without losing their essential spare elegance.

POEMS BY JILL HAAS

Lament

The world consented to a
    mankind lamb. The lamb,
unconsenting, bore the
    world in its slaughter.

My brothers, my teachers:
    I come to the ordure,
a fortunate Jew (one to
    the million, the modern

proportion.) Unschooled in
    the gas-stands; un-
fettered, untorn — as
    strange to your tears

as the tears of your
    butcher. Pardon me,
pardon — for my dead
    nonchalance.

Hear O Israel: this lament;
　　my contrition.

(from a sequence of poetry and music, 'The Winds')

'Lilith', they whisper
　　(the men with full beards)
'Lilith',
　　and go softly to their beds.

No need to call —
　　I am here ... in this
desert where satyrs roam
　　among the wolves. ....

'Lilith'
　　I shall come — as always
on the womanless nights, or
　　nights when you are deep in

your aching dreams. I shall
　　come, wearing the face
of Sheba ... am I Sheba or
　　a cunning demon?

'Lilith'
　　Do not whimper my name
in the darkness. Honour it,
　　instead, with ringing terror:

Lilith, your mistress
　　is the Night-Monster
A succuba, in whose fearful
　　wings, sleeps your shame ...

and a western wind.

The spade-work goes on. The best pattern for my thrice-yearly lectures, I have decided, is: in the autumn, a lecture on some general topic to do with poetry; in the spring, on a living poet; in the summer, anything that seems to suggest itself.

I hope to find living poets in England who seem to me of sufficient stature to be held up as examples. If I took in American poetry the quest would be easier, but I do not feel I could speak of American poetry with any authority, though I have always been interested in it; besides, I wish to avoid ministering to the widespread notion that English and American poetry are more or less the same thing.

For my first living poet, the choice made itself. W. H. Auden was alive, and living in Oxford, and his world reputation had recently made another leap forward. There is, indeed, an interesting contrast between the Auden of the 1970s, who came to live in a grace-and-favour cottage at Christ Church, and the Auden of the 1950s, when he was Professor of Poetry. He was, of course, an excellent Professor: his lectures were very interesting and he was amiable and approachable in his dealings with people. And then 1956, the year of his election, had been very much a pivotal year in Auden's life. Not quite twenty years previously he had left England and taken American citizenship. It had seemed to most people then that we had lost him; the expression 'Brain Drain' had not yet, I think, been invented, but we were already starting to experience the phenomenon. Yet somehow Auden, during those years of teaching in various East Coast colleges and living mainly in New York, had become an ex-Englishman without becoming an American. His personality was, in fact, beginning to turn inwards; he was getting towards middle life, when a man draws more and more on whatever resources he happens to have inside him. His circle of friends was international, and in the end, I believe, he settled down into a pattern in which one could discern some elements shared with the cultivated middle class of the entire Western world from Seattle to Berlin, and some elements of the English intelligentsia brought up in the aftermath of the First World War; and perhaps, at the bottom, a little hard pebble of the northern

English professional class, which came out in his carefulness
with money, his devotion to regular habits, his church-going,
and his annoyance when meals were unpunctual.

One obvious difference stemmed from the changed attitude of
the academic world towards him. In 1956 there was not, as yet,
much academic study of Auden. The major seat was still firmly
occupied by T. S. Eliot, and the academic industrialists were un-
certain whether it would be a good thing to invest time and
effort in Auden. This was fortunate, because it meant that he
was free to get on with life and work without the deadly circle of
note-takers, so much resembling the ring of fire within which the
scorpion stings himself to death. Auden was, in 1956–61, doing
two things at once during his visits to Oxford: he was attending
to the duties of the Chair, and he was re-introducing himself to
English life, picking up threads he had dropped two decades
earlier, delighting in the conversation of old friends like Nevill
Coghill, and more recent friends like C. S. Lewis and David
Cecil, and in the fresh and spontaneous companionship of the
young. It was a good time for him, and he radiated and
expanded.

In 1972, when he came back to end his life among the
dreaming spires, the Oxford experience was much more limited,
and rather flat and sour. The academic hounds were in full pur-
suit; if he followed his earlier custom of making himself available
at a café table, he would find himself confronted not by young
poets eager to show him their work, but by graduate students
relentlessly feeding him questions arising from theses they were
writing on him. Add to this that he was tired and unwell, and
that the Oxford crime-wave made itself felt in a thoroughgoing
burglary early on in his *villegiatura*. . . . But younger people could
still interest and stimulate him; Andrew Harvey has golden
memories of their conversations, and Elizabeth Jennings found
him kind and responsive.

I had met him two or three times over the years, but during
the first months of his Oxford stay I had not happened to run
into him, and after the election campaign got under way I felt in-
hibited about doing so, because he very naturally supported

Stephen Spender, his old friend and earliest publisher. (It was the youthful Spender's hand-press that gave to the world Auden's *Poems* of 1929.) Since I was standing in opposition to Spender, I was by definition crossing Auden's wishes, and this gave me sorrow; I knew I should have very little to say to him if we met, so made no move towards him. But now the election was over and the past could be buried, and I looked forward to trying my best to make an effective assessment of his work; and, whether he took any interest in my view or not, perhaps enjoying a few meetings with a poet who had given me pleasure steadily since my adolescence.

So I began to read for my lecture on 'The Poetry of W. H. Auden'. But I had not been reading for long when a telephone call from the *Observer* informed me that he had died suddenly in Austria. Would I write the expected salute? I did so, with a heavy heart, and telephoned it to them within a few hours. But the lecture – that, obviously, must be given. Auden's heart might have stopped beating, but I had decided on him as my first 'living poet' and in that spot, firmly, he would remain.

So, discarding with a sigh of relief the heavy trappings of an Inaugural, I lectured one cold winter day in the domestic tranquility of Brasenose hall, on:

THE POETRY OF W. H. AUDEN

'The whole world is stalled today. Capitalism runs down, ceases to function; Communism makes little progress. The nations and the classes wait. We go neither forward nor back, we hardly know which way we are facing.' The words are Edmund Wilson's, the year 1935. Wilson is reporting on his visit to the Soviet Union; he had gone there with all the high hopes of a 1930s progressive, and during his stay he had, for all his shrewdness, not quite realized the nature of what he was looking at. Coming from an America in the grip of the Depression, where the capitalist way of running a society seemed finally to have proved itself a failure, he wanted, as millions like him wanted, to find that Communism had the answer; but in Moscow he found himself appalled by the joyless atmosphere, the cowed silence of the people in the streets, the way no one talked or laughed as they moved slowly along, the sense that among these people the art of happiness had been lost or perhaps had never been known.

Throughout his sojourn in Russia, Wilson's constant point of reference and comparison was America. These two giants were both, in those years, torpid, locked in their internal problems. In terms of world politics, both were offstage. Nevertheless, Wilson's sad verdict could apply to those countries that were in the limelight as well as those that were out of it. Everywhere was the sense that 'we go neither forward nor back', that 'we hardly know which way we are facing'. And in England a young poet who had recently begun to publish was already accepted as a spokesman for this stalled society, a painter of this landscape of dead slag-heaps, a diagnostician of 'This England where nobody is well'.

> Get there if you can and see the land you once were proud
>   to own,
> Though the roads have almost vanished and the expresses
>   never run.

That is the voice of the early Auden. But then so is

> This like a dream
> Keeps other time
> And daytime is
> The loss of this;
> For time is inches
> And the heart's changes.

And so, for that matter, is

> Though heart fears all heart cries for, rebuffs with mortal
>   beat
> Skyfall, the legs sucked under, adder's bite.
> That prize held out of reach
> Guides the unwilling tread,
> The asking breath
> Till on attended bed
> Or in untracked dishonour comes to each
> His natural death.

From the beginning, Auden had expressed himself not in one style but in a sheaf of styles. He moved from the crudely exhortatory to the sly and confiding, from the clarion-call of a leader to the antics of a privileged clown, from the barest simplicity to the densest obscurity. Yet, even in these days of his youth, he had already on him the mark by which one recognizes the major poet: all his styles were one style, his voice was always his own voice. The young Auden described and reacted to the world of the 1930s so incisively and memorably that the epoch seems, in retrospect, to be coloured by his way of perceiving it. To speak of the thirties is to speak like Auden. So that, even in the fragment of Edmund Wilson's prose with which we started, the

words 'The nations and the classes wait' sound faintly like a
quotation from early Auden, from one of those gnomic poems in
short lines.

Auden was an Englishman of the professional middle class,
born shortly before the First World War and growing up in its
aftermath. Since 1945, England, like all other middle-sized coun-
tries, has had no hope of influencing world events save by exert-
ing some kind of influence on America or Russia. But in those
days the decisive actors on the world stage were England and
the Continental European powers. A decision taken in London,
Paris, Berlin or Rome had immediate repercussions throughout
the world. To belong to any kind of ruling class, to enjoy any
position of privilege or immunity, in any of these countries was
to feel the weight of a great and immediate responsibility on
one's shoulders – one's own shoulders, not someone else's.

The class to which Auden belonged was comfortable and
privileged in a way that has now vanished from the world. Their
incomes, modest as they sound today, were effective enough in a
country where a working man, if he were lucky enough to have a
job at all, seldom earned more than two or three pounds a week.
This comfort was, to the young, extremely uncomfortable. It
made them feel that something important was expected of them
in return, if they were to be anything better than detestable
parasites. Hence the rush into left-wing politics. An out-of-date
and unjust political system had led to the Great War in which
many of their fathers had been killed; now, twenty years later,
the same system prevailed, and under it the nations were once
again arming for battle.

By a historical accident, Auden began writing at the exact
moment when the conditions of life changed so abruptly that a
new poetry was obviously called for – one with a changed subject-
matter and a changed set of perspectives. 'What a wonderful
opportunity' will be the reaction of those inexperienced in the ways
of literature. More seasoned minds will be more aware of the
dangers and pitfalls. The new progressive poetry of reform and
zeal had a prepared public, waiting to be given back its own con-
victions. And to ride on such a public is to ride on a tiger. If you

get off, you are eaten – as, in the 1960s, some of the most
talented writers of the black community in America were eaten.

Auden's situation in the early thirties was, in fact, one of acute
danger. He shared, with not many reservations, the outlook and
opinions of the public who demanded an anti-Fascist, Socialist,
progressive art that would help the world towards its new birth.
This audience, with the best intentions, ruined poet after poet.
Some recovered, others did not. But anyone with the curiosity to
turn over the pages of the progressive literary magazines of that
decade, or of such anthologies as *New Signatures*, can see the
depths of complacent silliness which seemed, in the climate of
that time, perfectly respectable. (I hasten to add that this prin-
ciple obtains in every period in which a strong tide of opinion
creates a pervasive fashion. The vogue of the Beats, or the
Liverpool poets, has had just as disastrous an effect on the
weaker brethren.)

Auden was the acknowledged leader of this movement; he was
loyally served by his followers, and never for a moment looked
like anything else but its leader. Yet he was successful in
avoiding all its worst faults. Not for him the cheap catch-phrases
and the impoverished language and rhythm that go with at-
titudes taken over ready-made and never imagined from the in-
side. He managed to take the whole rather second-rate bag of
tricks and somehow breathe life into it. It is worth considering
how he managed to do so.

His chief strategy, from the beginning, was the bland refusal
to be tied down. Already, in these earliest works, we find an
essential feature that never altered right to the end. It would
certainly not be true to say that Auden never made a literal
statement. Protean and restless as his mind was, he claimed for
himself the right to make any conceivable kind of statement and
to make it at any time. But this was part of his policy of un-
expectedness. He never clears his throat, fixes you with a grave
look, and says, 'I want you to pay particular attention to this
next bit, because it is deadly serious.' He slips in his most
serious and literal statements, those which communicate his
truth most nakedly, between passages that are highly figurative,

riddling, joking, argufying. As a result, there has never been complete agreement among his readers as to what the literal content of his work exactly consists of.

The key books of the earliest period are *Poems* (1930) and *The Orators* (1933). Both convey, unmistakably, a sense of impatience, an idealistic and impetuous movement towards change. And there the 'unmistakable' element in either book comes abruptly to a halt. We are in a world of shifting mirrors. Everything is what 'Paid on Both Sides' is called in its sub-title, 'a charade'. Even where the poems are not densely obscure (and they tend to be so in proportion as they are gnomic), they slide in and out of seriousness in such a way as to make them ungraspable. To turn to *The Orators* is particularly disconcerting for the reader who wants an extractable, portable message. This brilliant book operates continuously on a level of hilarious parody and burlesque, in-group jokes, private reminiscences, with sudden outbreaks of direct sermonising. Its theme is renewal, rebirth, getting rid of 'the old gang' who have involved us in tired, unworkable conventions and obsolete ways of seeing the world. The old gang are to be removed and 'we', the new men, the young, the original, the clever, the switched-on, are going to take over and save the situation. This is, of course, exactly what the Nazis were were saying in Germany and what Communists were saying all over the world. But, whereas these groups of conspirators intended nothing for their dinosaur predecessors except simple slaughter, *The Orators* hovers about this direct and unattractive solution like a moth round a candle-flame. There are times when the old fogies do appear to be threatened with mere extinction:

> 'You've got some pretty stiff changes to make. We simply can't afford any passengers or skrimshankers. I should like to see you make a beginning before I go, now, here. Draw up a list of rotters and slackers, of prescribed persons under headings like this. Committees for municipal or racial improvement – the headmaster. Disbelievers in the occult – the school chaplain. The bogusly cheerful – the games master. The really disgusted – the teacher of modern

languages. All these have got to die without issue. Unless
my memory fails me there's a stoke hole under the floor of
this hall, the Black Hole we called it in my day. New boys
were always put in it. Ah, I see I am right. Well look to it.
Quick, guard that door. Stop that man. Good. Now boys
hustle them, ready, steady — go.'

Hustling the stubborn and unnecessary people down into the
Black Hole is precisely what the totalitarian governments of
Europe were already, quietly and efficiently, getting on with.
But, if one tried to accuse the youthful Auden of advocating the
same tactics, one ran up against the whole preposterous prep-
school ethos, the riddles and jokes, the scraps of reminiscence.
The essential commentary on the early Auden is that provided
by Christopher Isherwood's autobiographical novel, *Lions and
Shadows*. This book begins by describing how Isherwood, in the
course of a conventional English public-school education, forms
an alliance with a fellow-pupil named Chalmers, a highly gifted
and rebellious youth. The two go up to Cambridge together,
where they spend months plotting various forms of resistance
against the people who embodied the Cambridge ethos (called
variously 'the other side' and 'the Poshocracy') and constructing
a fantasy about a place called Mortmere. The opposition finally
flares into actual combat (the butter-fight in Chalmers's rooms),
after which Chalmers drifts into a subordinate place in the story,
and his place as the dominant influence is taken by an Oxford
poet called 'Weston' (Wystan Auden). Weston dominates
Isherwood's imagination as thoroughly as Chalmers (Edward
Upward) has done earlier. The portrait of Weston is the single
most important aid to the study of Auden's early work; if it had
not been written, that work would be far less intelligible.
    When the two first meet again, having not seen each other
since prep school, they begin by reviving memories.

    ... we began to chatter and gossip: the preparatory school
    atmosphere reasserted itself. We revived the old jokes; we
    imitated Pillar cutting bread at supper: ('Here you are!

Here you are! Help coming, Waters! Pang-slayers coming!
Only one more moment before that terrible hunger is
satisfied! Fight it down, Waters! Fight it down!') We
remembered how Spem used to pinch our arms for not
knowing the irregular verbs and punish us with com-
pulsory fircone gathering. We tried to reconstruct the big
scene from Reggy's drama, *The Waves*, in which the villain
is confronted by the ghost of the murdered boy, seated in
the opposite chair: ('The waves ... the waves ... can't you
hear them calling? Get down, *carrse* you, get down! Ha, ha
– I'm not afraid! Who says I'm afraid? Don't stare at me,
carrse you, with those great eyes of yours. . . . I never
feared you living; and I'm demned if I fear you now you're
– *dead*! Ha, ha! Ha, ha! Ha ha ha ha ha ha ha!') Weston
was brilliant at doing one of Pa's sermons: how he wiped
his glasses, how he coughed, how he clicked his fingers
when somebody in chapel fell asleep: ('Sn Edmund's Day
... Sn Edmund's Day ... Whur ders it *mean*? Nert – whur
did it mean to *them, then, theah*? Bert – whur ders it mean
to *ers, heah, nerw*?') We laughed so much that I had to
lend Weston a handerchief to dry his eyes.

The Orators faithfully makes use of these fragments. Its
opening section, 'Address for a Prize-Day', begins:

Commemoration. Commemoration. What does it mean.
What does it mean? Not what does it mean to them, there
then. What does it mean to us, here now? It's a facer, isn't
it boys? But we've all got to answer it.

And, in one of the 'Six Odes' which make up the third section,
we hear again the voice of 'Pillar cutting bread at supper'.

Auden at this stage was very firm about the need for
'austerity'; everything had to be scientific and clinical. And his
Icelandic ancestry was also finding expression.

'Austerity' was also mixed up with Weston's feelings about
the heroic Norse literature – his own personal variety of
'War' – fixation. Naturally enough, he had been brought up
on the Icelandic sagas; for they were the background of his

family history. On his recommendation, I now began, for
the first time, to read *Grettir* and *Burnt Njal*, which he had
with him in his suitcase. These warriors, with their feuds,
their practical jokes, their dark threats conveyed in puns
and riddles and deliberate understatements ('I think this
day will end unluckily for some, but chiefly for those who
least expect harm'): they seemed so familiar – where had I
met them before? Yes, I recognized them now: they were
the boys at our preparatory school. Weston was pleased with
the idea: we discussed it a good deal, wondering which of
our schoolfellows best corresponded to the saga characters.
In time, the school-saga world became for us a kind of
Mortmere – a Mortmere founded upon our preparatory-
school lives, just as the original Mortmere had been
founded upon my life with Chalmers at Cambridge. About
a year later, I actually tried the experiment of writing a
school story in what was a kind of hybrid language com-
posed of saga phraseology and schoolboy slang. And soon
after this, Weston produced a short verse play in which the
two worlds are so confused that it is almost impossible to
say whether the characters are epic heroes or members of a
school O.T.C.

The joking and riddling are all there in *Poems* and *The
Orators*; and, naturally, the familiar *dramatis personae* of the
author's friends make their cosy and joking appearances:

And in cold Europe, in the middle of Autumn destruction,
Christopher stood, his face grown lined with wincing
In front of ignorance – 'Tell the English', he shivered,
'Man is a spirit.'

In the face of all this, how could anyone accuse *The Orators* of
presenting in attractive terms a murderous conspiracy to
overthrow and destroy? It was all too funny and too cosy. Even
the old gang, the people who had got us into this mess, were not
necessarily marked out for destruction. They were to be
replaced, yes, and in some passages it appears that they are to be
hunted down and destroyed, but then comes the healing scatter
of psycho-analytical terms; perhaps after all they can be saved, if

they will submit to being made over anew; and in the last of the 'Six Odes' it is they who appear to be speaking:

Not, Father, further do prolong
Our necessary defeat;
Spare us the numbing zero-hour,
The desert-long retreat.

Against your direct light displayed,
Regardant, absolute,
In person stubborn and oblique
Our maddened set we foot.

These nissen huts if hiding could
Your eye inseeing from
Firm fenders were, but look! to us
Your loosened angers come.

The impossibly clumsy inversions, the 4–3 metre, indicate that this is a hymn, and not just any hymn but a vintage 'Hymns Ancient and Modern' piece, the sort of thing the old gang drone out Sunday after Sunday before going home to roast beef. Again the mistiness, the shimmering, the impression that parody has taken over from the thing parodied. If they are in church, are they appealing to their God? Does the 'Father' really exist, and will he indeed temper with mercy their 'necessary defeat'?

Questions of this kind are unanswerable. Auden is simply not going to make these things plain. And for a good and sufficient reason. What both *Poems* and *The Orators* are intended and shaped to convey is a *mood*. Change must come, the obsolete and infirm must go, England and Europe must renew themselves. This is conveyed by every means – the rhythms, the images, the tone of voice, the whole way the poems move and speak and comport themselves. To any young reader of the time, it would be natural to get out of his chair and follow where Auden led. And this is precisely why it would have been fatal to lead in too precise a direction, as far as political programming was concerned. With that formidable hypnotic power, that gift of obtaining the assent of a generation, Auden could so easily have degenerated into a demagogue or, even worse, a Gauleiter/Commissar.

Many people, of course, would have liked him to do exactly that. The world had already entered the age in which we are still living – the age of publicity and propaganda, when every journalist who interviews a writer wants the writer to make a Statement. The direct expression of opinion, in capsule form, is what the journalist and his big daddy the politician always want from the artist; they cannot understand that there could be any motive for utterance other than the direct communication of a snap judgment or a directive. As W. B. Yeats remarked, sadly, at the beginning of this epoch of saturation journalism:

> If one writes well and has the patience, someone will come from among the runners, and read what one has written quickly, and go away quickly, and afterwards write out as much as he can remember in the language of the highway.

It was this 'language of the highway' that Auden, as a poet with a very special impingement on the political and social scene, had to avoid. Otherwise he would have ended up among all the other purveyors of empty slogans and street-corner arguments, those poets whose work after ten years is as amusingly dated as an old news-reel. He had to avoid this, yet avoid it without turning away altogether in the direction of the 'timeless' statement, which was not suited to his genius. The work in his first three or four volumes adds up to an impressive testimony to his skill in achieving this.

Not that the result was satisfying to everyone. The people who have not liked Auden's poetry, and such people do exist and do include some who are fully competent to understand poetry, have always at bottom disliked it for this reason: that they cannot be sure how far Auden means what he says. Sometimes he seems to be making a statement just to see how it sounds, at other times he is joking or trailing his coat. The whole effect is tiresome and repulsive to a certain kind of reader – to F. R. Leavis, for instance, who from first to last has dismissed Auden as a clever undergraduate who wouldn't grow up. Even critics

much less severe on Auden than Dr Leavis, critics very ready to
regard him as an important poet, have been troubled by the
same misgiving; as when Mr W. W. Robson, in the course of an
alert and sensitive discussion of Auden's Inaugural lecture as
Oxford Professor of Poetry, notes that it is very difficult to sort
out those passages which Auden intends with full seriousness
from those he intends comically or quizzically, since 'Mr Auden
excels in that celebrated Oxford talent for making *any* opposi-
tion sound like the protests of a solemn fool who doesn't know
when his leg is being pulled' (*Critical Essays* (1966) p. 78).

Auden himself has a comment on this situation as it applies to
The Orators. When he authorized a reprint in 1966, he provided
a foreword which began by indicating a complete dissociation
from his earlier self.

> My name on the title-page seems a pseudonym for
> someone else, someone talented but near the border of
> sanity, who might well, in a year or two, become a Nazi.

After discussing briefly the probable literary influence behind
the work, Auden goes on:

> The central theme of *The Orators* seems to be Hero-
> worship, and we all know what that can lead to politically.
> My guess today is that my unconscious motive in writing it
> was therapeutic, to exercise certain tendencies in myself by
> allowing them to run riot in phantasy. If to-day I find
> 'Auden with play-ground whistle', as Wyndham Lewis
> called him, a bit shy-making, I realise that it is precisely
> the schoolboy atmosphere and diction which act as a moral
> criticism of the rather ugly emotions and ideas they are
> employed to express. By making the latter juvenile, they
> make it impossible to take them seriously.

This is not the kind of explanation that is likely to work with
Dr Leavis or those who think like him. 'Why,' such a person
might ask, 'why take the trouble to bring out a whole book of
material that has been carefully booby-trapped to prevent its
being taken seriously?' The objection has force: if we are not to

take the work seriously, why should we be asked to take it at all? To treat it simply as a diversion, a joke, good for a few minutes' amusement, is forbidden by the energy, the elaboration, the out-cropping moral earnestness, of the work itself. No, it is the later and rather embarrassed Auden who is (to take over the proffered expression) 'shy-making' here. These early books do convey something important: a mood, an imperative, an appetite for renewal.

The kind of trouble that Auden would have got into, if he had not adopted this double-exposure method, is well illustrated by what happened in the case of 'Spain'. This, published in pamphlet form in May 1937, is a totally and unequivocally 'committed' poem. It is written in support of one side in a war, and one can't get more 'committed' than that. At the same time, it avoids the usual ferocious imbecilities of battle-poetry. The need for com-bat and sacrifice is simply taken for granted as an urgent neces-sity, Fascism is clearly focused on as an evil thing, yet there is no atrocity-talk and no name-calling: it is simply 'to-day the struggle'. The organization of the poem, it will be recalled, is a tripod: yesterday, tomorrow, today. Yesterday the unfurling of the great umbrella of European civilization; tomorrow the ulti-mate conquest of material difficulties; but today the umbrella is torn and rent and the difficulties are no nearer solution, and the present generation has been fated to arrive on earth at the moment of 'struggle'.

> Tomorrow for the young, the poets exploding like bombs,
> The walks by the lake, the weeks of perfect communion;
> > To-morrow the bicycle races
> Through the suburbs on summer evenings. But to-day the
> > struggle.
>
> To-day the deliberate increase in the chances of death,
> The conscious acceptance of guilt in the necessary murder:
> > To-day the expending of powers
> On the flat ephemeral pamphlet and the boring meeting.

The phrase about expending powers on 'the flat ephemeral

pamphlet and the boring meeting' wasn't at all to the taste of the orthodox Socialist. Come, come! Meetings at which loyal party members listen to the exposition of doctrine, and accept criticism of their actions and attitudes, can't, by definition, be 'boring' — and as for 'the flat ephemeral pamphlet', that's no way to talk about party literature! And at the same time, from another exposed side, the poet was attacked for too complacently accepting the doctrine that 'the end justifies the means'. George Orwell, in the title essay of his energetic polemical book *Inside the Whale* (1940), quoted the two stanzas I have just given, and went on:

> The second stanza is intended as a sort of thumb-nail sketch of a day in the life of a 'good party man'. In the morning a couple of political murders, a ten-minutes' interlude to stifle 'bourgeois' remorse, and then a hurried luncheon and a busy afternoon and evening chalking walls and distributing leaflets. All very edifying. But notice the phrase 'necessary murder'. It would only be written by a person to whom murder is at most a *word*. Personally I would not speak so lightly of murder. It so happens that I have seen the bodies of numbers of murdered men — I don't mean killed in battle, I mean murdered. Therefore I have some conception of what murder means — the terror, the hatred, the howling relatives, the post-mortems, the blood, the smells. To me, murder is something to be avoided. So it is to any ordinary person. The Hitlers and Stalins find murder necessary, but they don't advertise their callousness, and they don't speak of it as murder; it is 'liquidation', 'elimination', or some other soothing phrase. Mr Auden's brand of amoralism is only possible if you are the kind of person who is always somewhere else when the trigger is pulled. So much of left-wing thought is a kind of playing with fire by people who don't even know that fire is hot.

In the case of 'Spain', Auden had the good sense to concede, tacitly, Orwell's case: when he reprinted the poem in *Another Time* (1940), the 'necessary murder' had become, more unobtrusively, 'the fact of murder'; and the title was changed to 'Spain 1937', the addition of a date categorizing and distancing the poem as 'occasional'. Soon, as we all know, it was dropped entirely from the canon.

But the episode, however Auden in later years contrived to snow it under, is an instructive one. When an unprotected literal statement was liable to this kind of attack from all sides, one could hardly blame the young Auden if he deliberately scrambled his message, presenting it in a bewildering kaleidoscope of fun-and-games, burlesque, hyperbole and anacoluthon. Yet to put it that way might be a hampering over-simplification. Exactly how 'deliberate' it was, he couldn't remember and no one now can say. Probably it was a matter of temperament. Auden's mind was constantly on the move, constantly testing, comparing, seeing how an idea looked from this side or that, from above or below. Most of us, when we get hold of an idea and are satisfied that we understand it, leave it at that. Auden, once he had taken on an idea, at once started to put it through the hoop. He related it to all his other ideas, tried how it would work in this context and then in that, made the blacks into whites and vice versa to see how it looked as a photographic negative, and generally kept it on the move. In his early period he did this with the ideas of Socialism and psycho-analysis, which were his fundamental faiths at that time, and in the later period he did it with the ideas of Christianity. It was, quite simply, his way of dealing with ideas. However fundamentally he agreed with and accepted them, he was never content to leave them lying in his mind like a book on a library shelf. The pages had to keep turning, and the words in the book had to be translated into as many mental languages as possible.

There were, of course, other reasons for the immediate success of the early Auden, apart from his power of rallying his generation under the banner of impatience for change and renewal. There was his Englishness, for one thing. The generation of poets and readers of poetry who were young in the 1930s had, up till then, been presented with an either—or choice that was slightly uncomfortable. 'Modern' poetry, which as modern

young people they naturally wished to read, was international
in idiom; it was by Edgar Allan Poe out of Baudelaire and
then reintroduced into English by the work of two expatriate
Americans. Poetry with a specifically English flavour, on the
other hand – which used language with an English intonation
and rhythm, and made familiar use of English points of reference
– tended to be written by poets of a more traditional bent, poets
whom the young associated, rightly or not, with the generation
of their parents. Suddenly, here was a poet who was totally
English and totally middle-class, whose poems were stuffed with
place-names and private associations, whose images and
cadences, and above all the spoken rhythm of whose verse, were
in tune with what they had been accustomed to, in the 'real'
world outside poetry, all their lives. Even Auden's fondness for
alliterative verse, 'kennings' and the rest of it, picked up from his
undergraduate years reading the English School at Oxford,
aligned him with his class and generation; a knowledge of
Anglo-Saxon was the shared badge of everyone who had been
through (or under, or over, or round) a university course in
'English', but here suddenly was a poet who could fit his own
words to what had seemed an obsolete tune, could turn the dead
lumber of 'an education' into living material. Auden spoke for a
tightly organized, homogeneous group, sharing their cadences,
their vocabulary, their landmarks. His experience (prep school,
public school, university, then back to be a master at the same
kind of school as that at which he had been a pupil) was as everyday
as theirs; he had not found it necessary, in order to be a poet, to join
the French Foreign Legion, or starve in a garret in Bohemia; he just
got on with an ordinary job and an ordinary life, and made poetry
out of it – poetry, what was more, that embodied all the hopes and
fears and fevers of the young in that decade. No wonder they
idolized him. He was so much nearer to them than Eliot, that Har-
vard mandarin, and so much more contemporary than Graves
(away in Majorca since 1929, in any case) or Blunden.

   At this point, it is appropriate to stop commenting and
generalizing in the abstract, and put a real poem on the page.
Here is one from *Look, Stranger!*, Auden's volume of 1936, a

book that takes us into the heartland of the 'English Auden'.

Now from my window-sill I watch the night
The church clock's yellow face, the green pier light
Burn for a new imprudent year;
The silence buzzes in my ear;
The jets in both the dormitories are out.

Under the darkness nothing seems to stir;
The lilac bush like a conspirator
Shams dead upon the lawn and there
Above the flagstaff the Great Bear
Hangs as a portent over Helensburgh.

But deaf to prophecy or China's drum
The blood moves strangely in its moving home,
Diverges, loops to travel further
Than the long still shadow of the father,
Though to the valley of regret it come.

Now in this season when the ice is loosened,
In scrubbed laboratories research is hastened
And cameras at the growing wood
Are pointed; for the long-lost good,
Desire like a police-dog is unfastened.

O Lords of limit, training dark and light
And setting a tabu 'twixt left and right:
The influential quiet twins
From whom all property begins,
Look leniently upon us all to-night.

Oldest of masters, whom the schoolboy fears
Failing to find his pen, to keep back tears,
Collecting stamps and butterflies
Hoping in some way to appease
The malice of the erratic examiners.

No one has seen you. None can say of late,
'Here – you can see the marks – they lay in wait.'
But in my thought to-night you seem
Forms which I saw once in a dream,
The stocky keepers of a wild estate.

With guns beneath your arms, in sun and wet
At doorways posted or on ridges set,
By copse or bridge we know you there
Whose sleepless presences endear
Our peace to us with a perpetual threat.

We know you moody, silent, sensitive,
Quick to be offended, slow to forgive,
But to your discipline the heart
Submits when we have fallen apart
Into the isolated personal life.

Look not too closely, be not over-quick;
We have no invitation, but we are sick
Using the mole's device, the carriage
Of peacock or rat's desperate courage,
For we shall only pass you by a trick.

At the end of my corridor are boys who dream
Of a new bicycle or winning team;
On their behalf guard all the more
This late-maturing Northern shore,
Who to their serious season must shortly come.

Give them spontaneous skill at holding rein,
At twisting dial, or at making fun,
That these may never need our craft,
Who, awkward, pasty, feeling the draught,
Have health and skill and beauty on the brain.

The clocks strike ten: the tea is on the stove;
And up the stair come voices that I love.
Love, satisfaction, force, delight,
To these players of Badminton to-night,
To Favel, Holland, sprightly Alexis give.

Deeper towards the summer the year moves on.
And what if the starving visionary have seen
The carnival within our gates,
Your bodies kicked about the streets,
We need your power still: use it, that none

O from this table break uncontrollably away
Lunging, insensible to injury,
Dangerous in the room or out wild-
-ly spinning like a top in the field,
Mopping and mowing through the sleepless day.

What one notices first about such a quintessentially
Audenesque poem is the blend of the familiar and the mysterious
– of the unabashedly familiar and the intensely mysterious.
Auden accepts the ordinariness of his occupation and setting: he
is a schoolmaster, looking meditatively out of the window after
the day's work; the younger boys are asleep in the dormitories,
and the older ones, Sixth-Formers, prefects, are doing their prep
in their studies. At ten o'clock, they come upstairs for a light
supper before going to bed. All this is the matter-of-fact
framework of the poem; everything is accepted, including the
actual names of the boys, Favel, Holland, Alexis. Within that
framework we encounter the mysterious. Who exactly are the
'lords of limit'? Since they train dark and light and set 'a tabu'
(not, we notice, a rational distinction, but a totemistic
prohibition) between 'left and right', they may stand, perhaps,
for our human sense of the possible, our respect for proportion,
our willingness to impose restraints on our conduct in order to
have a life at all; they may be a twinned manifestation of the Ego
as opposed to the Id. On the other hand, they are not sweetness
and light; they are jealous, vengeful, like the Old Testament
God, and 'we shall only pass [them] by a trick' – why is this?
The poet addresses them in a tone of urgent supplication: 'We
have no invitation, but we are sick'; and they are, like so many
healing presences, manifested in dreams.
    The dream-state is there again, strongly, in the last stanza
with its vision of madness and disintegration, and especially in

the brilliant concluding line. The 'day' usually is sleepless; what we normally fear is the sleepless night; but 'Mopping and mowing through the sleepless day' is a perfect verbal equivalent of a scene from a nightmare.

Such poetry is the achievement of Auden's first decade. At the end of the thirties, he moved to the United States and took American citizenship. This, the great hinge event of his life, also marks the beginning of an entirely different phase of his work. The shift, broadly speaking, is from Active to Contemplative. And also from corporate to lonely. The new Auden has ceased to advocate practical intervention in the world's affairs; henceforth his main message will be that what we do matters less than what we are. He has also ceased to 'speak for' any particular group of human beings. The identification with a country, a class, a generation, has gone. From now on he speaks for himself. When asked why he had made the move to America, he answered, 'To be alone.' This, unlike some of his statements, is worth taking at face-value. Going to America was, for him, a means of removing himself from any close-knit relationship with one particular society; it was, as nearly as possible, to go nowhere. In ceasing to be an Englishman, Auden did not become an American. He merely ceased to have any marked national affinities at all. Unlike his fellow-expatriate Isherwood, who went all the way to Hollywood and almost destroyed himself as a writer in the process, Auden stopped at New York – and 'America', as we know, 'begins at the Hudson River'. In Manhattan, Auden's life-style was international; his friends were people like Jacques Barzun, Lionel Trilling, Dag Hammarskjöld. In his verse, there are no traces of American rhythms or cadences; any more than in his speech he adopted what is called 'an American accent'. (It is true that he conscientiously used the short *a* in words like 'glass', but then a majority of the inhabitants of the British Isles use the short *a*.)

The change coincided, of course, with a shift in Auden's philosophical position, from a basically activist bundle of attitudes in which the central item was Socialism to a basically quietist bundle in which the central item was Christianity. It is

possible to make too much of this transformation. In some ways
the resemblances are as important as the differences. Both a
reforming creed like Socialism and a penitential creed like
Christianity hold that the suffering of life is not inherent in the
nature of things but results from man's wrong-headedness and
wickedness. In the middle of the Active period, Auden wrote one
of his most celebrated poems, 'As I Walked Out One Evening',
and we find there an attitude far from impossible to reconcile
with Christianity.

> 'O look, look in the mirror,
> O look in your distress;
> Life remains a blessing
> Although you cannot bless.
>
> 'O stand, stand at the window
> As the tears scald and start;
> You shall love your crooked neighbour
> With your crooked heart.'

Christianity, too, asserts that 'Life remains a blessing/
Although you cannot bless'; the beauty and fertility of the earth,
the immense possibilities of joy and creativity, placed at our dis-
posal by the Creator, are available if we will only untie our hands
and reach out to take them. But our hands are so often tied by
'sin' (Christianity) or 'error/mismanagement/conspiracy of the
possessing class' (Socialism). Both are equally far from a cosmic
pessimism that would declare the sources of all life poisoned in
the spirit of Housman's

> Ay, look: all heaven and earth ail from the prime
>   foundation.

The exact moment when Auden crossed the plank bridge from
his version of Socialism to his version of Christianity is not, so
far as I know, on record. But hindsight can discern it clearly ap-
proaching in the poems of the later thirties. These poems
frequently contain patches of weak, generalized writing in which
Auden appears to be trying to say something very important

without being able to make up his mind what terms to use for it
or indeed what exactly it consists of. Thus, in 'Spain':

> As the poet whispers, startled among the pines
> Or, where the loose waterfall sings, compact or upright
>   On the crag by the leaning tower:
> 'O my vision. O send me the luck of the sailor.'
>
> And the investigator peers through his instruments
> At the inhuman provinces, the virile bacillus
>   Or enormous Jupiter finished:
> 'But the lives of my friends. I inquire, I inquire.'
>
> And the poor in their fireless lodgings dropping the sheets
> Of the evening paper: 'Our day is our loss. O show us
>   History the operator, the
> Organiser. Time and refreshing river.'
>
> And the nations combine each cry, invoking the life
> That shapes the individual belly and orders
>   The private nocturnal terror:
> 'Did you not found once the city state of the sponge,
>
> 'Raise the vast military empires of the shark
> And the tiger, establish the robin's plucky canton?
>   Intervene. O descend as a dove or
> A furious papa or a mild engineer: but descend.'

All these groups or categories of people are asking for an avatar,
the descent of a god; but Auden, although his thoughts are
already beginning to turn in that direction, cannot bring himself
to use the word 'God', with or without a capital letter; it is the
(lower-case) 'life' they address and which returns them a disap-
pointing answer, putting the responsibility squarely back on
their shoulders.

> And the life, if it answer at all, replies from the heart
> And the eyes and the lungs, from the shops and squares of
>   the city:
>   'O no, I am not the Mover,

Not to-day, not to you. To you I'm the
Yes-man, the bar-companion, the easily-duped:
I am whatever you do; I am your vow to be
    Good, your humorous story;
I am your business voice; I am your marriage.

What's your proposal? To build the Just City? I will
I agree. Or is it the suicide pact, the romantic
    Death? Very well, I accept, for
I am your choice, your decision: yes, I am Spain.'

'The life' here is clearly something like History in the Marxist
vision — the collective will of humanity; but whereas the Marxist
sees history as an irresistible power, the sum of millions of un-
conscious acts of decision, the 'life' of which Auden speaks here
is represented as the conscious will of humanity at a moment of
crisis. It is a thin concept, and in its concluding lines the poem
not surprisingly returns to 'History', which will not 'pardon' the
defeated.

    This reaching-out for an abstraction beyond the coming and
going of practical life, some larger pattern to which the in-
dividual will can relate itself, is also seen in the closing lines of
Auden's remarkable work of 1938, 'In Time of War'. This, sub-
titled 'A Sonnet Sequence with a Verse Commentary', forms the
concluding section of *Journey to a War*, the book about China
under Japanese attack which Auden wrote with Isherwood. 'In
Time of War' is a magnificent achievement, in some ways the
high-water mark of Auden's work up to that time; the sonnet
sequence is highly figurative and introspective, and the verse
commentary that follows it is much more open and topical in
character, a kind of Audenesque equivalent of Louis MacNeice's
Autumn Journal. It concludes with a prayer uttered by 'the
voice of Man':

    'It's better to be sad than mad, or liked than dreaded;
    It's better to sit down to nice meals than to nasty;
    It's better to sleep two than single; it's better to be happy.

Ruffle the perfect manners of the frozen heart,
And once again compel it to be awkward and alive,
To all it suffered once a weeping witness.

Clear from the head the masses of impressive rubbish;
Rally the lost and trembling forces of the will,
Gather them up and let them loose upon the earth,

Till they construct at last a human justice,
The contribution of our star, within the shadow
Of which uplifting, loving, and constraining power
All other reasons may rejoice and operate.'

This is not particularly good writing, especially to conclude a
work of such sustained brilliance; my reason for quoting it
rather than one of the poem's completely successful passages is
to indicate once more the embarrassing and untidy presence of
this hovering abstraction, the Something-Out-There that Auden
wants so much to invoke and to talk about, but cannot find
words for.

Very soon afterwards, he took the decision to call this abstrac-
tion 'God' and to let it absorb some of his restlessness and
Angst. The result is the shift from Active to Contemplative and
all the other changes that go with it. But the poems are still ob-
viously coming from the same man. Auden's personality did not
change radically, though his gaze was in a different direction. If
the Active, pre-Christian Auden could see so clearly that life is a
blessing, the step to the specifically theocentric resignation of the
Contemplative Auden is a short one; as in prose he said, 'My
duty to God is to be happy,' so in verse he addressed his physical
senses:

Be happy, precious five,
So long as I'm alive
Nor try to ask me what
You should be happy for;
Think, if it helps, of love
Or alcohol or gold,
But do as you are told.

I could (which you cannot)
Find reasons fast enough
To face the sky and roar
In anger and despair
At what is going on,
Demanding that it name
Whoever is to blame:
The sky would only wait
Till all my breath was gone
And then reiterate
As if I wasn't there
That singular command
I do not understand,
Bless what there is for being,
Which has to be obeyed, for
What else am I made for,
Agreeing or disagreeing?

Once one accepts the change of tone, accepts that the poetry
now comes out of a different centre – no longer the close-knit
community threatened by outside enemies and internal decay, but
rather the *polis*, the City Without Walls of a civilization whose
main hoped-for virtues are to be tolerant, to be interested, to be
diverse and survive – one sees many continuing strands between
the Active and the Contemplative Auden. The fertility of invention
is undiminished; confronted with any subject, the powerful mind
gets busy, throwing up suggestions, comparisons, illuminating
fragments of information, burrowing down to the foundations,
coming at the matter from this or that unexpected angle. My
favourite of Auden's many exercises of this power is the series of
poems on various geographical entities – Wind, Woods, Moun-
tains, Lakes, Islands, Plains, Streams – to which he gave the title
'Bucolics'. This sequence manages to convey so much – about the
earth, about human society, about the poet himself and his at-
titudes – that one can read it again every few months and have the
sensation each time of reading a new work.

The variety of tone is also still there, though it is no longer felt
within the individual poem; part of the later Auden's doctrine of

'good manners' towards the reader seems to have dictated a
gentler artistic decorum. But the switch of tone from, say,
'Bucolics' to the title-poem of the same collection, 'The Shield of
Achilles', is as great as anything in the earlier work. The 'Shield'
is a totally unvarnished, direct, non-ironic statement; as much as
'Spain', it shows us Auden speaking without any reservations or
distancings; it uses the brief and poignant fable as a means of
voicing the poet's deepest convictions about the human
condition.

Tracing the continuity of Auden's work, the survival of the
earlier poetry into the changed world of the later, is fascinating,
and an important part of the interest with which one approaches
him. The more's the pity that the poet himself tried so hard to
deprive us of that fascination and interest by his persistent
efforts, through 'revision', to iron out his earlier poetry and make
it resemble his later. Even if one is reading in a large and well-
equipped library, it is no easy matter to read the work of the
Active Auden without the intrusive mediation of the Con-
templative; for the ordinary, unofficial reader, wishing only to
enjoy the poetry by his fireside – that is, the only reader who
matters – it must be next door to impossible. I hope Auden's
publishers have in hand a genuine 'collected' edition, giving us
the text of each poem as it appeared at the time. This is
necessary for two reasons. First, the Active poems are in nearly
every case much better in their original form. Poets, like
everyone else, change as they move on through life, and while it
may be permissible to revise and alter a poem within a year or
two of its composition – at certain times when one is not
developing very fast, possibly as much as three or four years –
after a lapse of years it becomes as unpardonable as tampering
with a poem by someone else – *is*, in fact, tampering with a
poem by someone else. Second, Auden's tinkering and clipping
were quite useless; they served no purpose. If he felt em-
barrassed by certain things he said, he had in his power the only
remedy that any of us have: he could have stated firmly what his
opinions were *now*, and in what respect they had changed, and
leave his early utterances to their fate. By going back to the work

of the thirties with a basket of fig-leaves, he only succeeded in drawing attention to what he considered his lapses. In any event, the self-censorship was quite useless.

There is a striking example of this uselessness in the poem 'September 1, 1939'. This is one of the most celebrated poems in *Another Time*, the last utterance of the Active, pre-American Auden. It begins with the poet sitting in a New York bar, thinking back across the Atlantic to a Europe about to be swallowed up in war, and thence to the state of the world and the condition of man. It is a famous poem and it deserves to be famous.

> Into this neutral air
> Where blind skyscrapers use
> Their full height to proclaim
> The strength of Collective Man,
> Each language pours its vain
> Competitive excuse:
> But who can live for long
> In an euphoric dream;
> Out of the mirror they stare,
> Imperialism's face
> And the international wrong.
> Faces along the bar
> Cling to their average day:
> The lights must never go out,
> The music must always play, .
> All the conventions conspire
> To make this fort assume
> The furniture of home;
> Lest we should see where we are,
> Lost in a haunted wood,
> Children afraid of the night
> Who have never been happy or good.

A little later, we come to the stanza:

> All I have is a voice
> To undo the folded lie,

The romantic lie in the brain
Of the sensual man-in-the-street
And the lie of Authority
Whose buildings grope the sky:
There is no such thing as the State
And no one exists alone;
Hunger allows no choice
To the citizen or the police;
We must love one another or die.

The last line there is one of Auden's most celebrated
utterances. For years, it was one of his most-quoted lines. It is,
like everything he wrote, many-faceted. One reacts to it in a
number of different ways simultaneously. Perhaps the first reac-
tion is, what a shockingly bad reason for loving one another! Or
perhaps it is simple agreement; men survive by co-operation,
and there has never been any hope for a human society that is
not founded on goodwill towards each other and not mere
goodwill but something deeper and stronger, love. Then there is
the immediate application in any time of world-wrecking con-
flict: 'If we don't learn to love one another we shall very soon kill
one another.' And there is the application to the individual
psyche: people who have no love in them are in any case dead
already, and if the whole society becomes loveless the race will
go down.

However we take it, that line is a memorable one. Quite
possibly it is the line that most literate people, asked without
warning to quote something by Auden, would come up with.
But, we should note, it has stamped itself on our memories in the
face of determined opposition from its parent. Auden decided
very soon that he did not like that line. Perhaps he no longer
believed that we must love one another or die; perhaps he just
thought that he ought to have expressed the notion in some
other way. At all events, he began to try to censor it out. *Another
Time* came out in 1940. Four years later Auden published, with
Random House in New York, the first of his 'Collected' volumes.
Already, in that collection, the poem appears without that line.
And in every subsequent reprint. The selection he made for

Penguin Books in 1958 doesn't contain the poem in any form. (But, then, the omissions from *that* volume are egregious and deserve an essay to themselves. 'Spain' isn't there, for instance; while from 'In Time of War' only a few sonnets survive, largely meaningless out of their context.)

So, 'We must love one another or die' became and remained one of Auden's most famous lines despite his efforts to prevent it, and despite the fact that it was only before the public officially, so to speak, for five years. The situation is not without its amusing sides. Words, once written and published, are like ferrets that have been carelessly let out of their cage. Auden spent a lot of time and energy running after his ferrets and trying to get them back into the cage, but they are still at large, still hiding in the long grass and waiting to bite somebody.

Auden suspected, rightly, that the critics who so carefully checked up on his revisions were nosing out ideological changes. In point of fact, what the revision usually succeeds in doing is to drain the original of colour and flavour by removing local associations, wrenching out the roots of time and place. In the poem we considered earlier, for instance, 'Now from my window-sill I watch the night', the revised version simply snips out all the prosaic detail, the actuality, the names, the whole physical setting; the school disappears, so that 'The jets in both the dormitories are out' becomes 'The lights of nearby families are cut'; but the last stanza is retained, and since it so clearly refers to a school dining-hall the images of breaking away from the table and running out to spin like a top in the field are left in a void. Worse, the mysterious heart of the poem (the lords of limit and the poet's appeal to them) is left beating without a rib-cage round it.

One day soon, no doubt, the present useless 'Collected' volumes of Auden, both the shorter and the longer poems, will be replaced by the genuine article and his 'revisions' relegated to footnotes as interesting curiosities. In 1976, this gap began to be filled by Mr Edward Mendelson's valuable edition of Auden's *Collected Poems*. Mr Mendelson also promises a companion volume, *The English Auden*. And then, I believe, we shall be in a better position to appreciate the flowering and survival of this extraordinary poetic mind: a mind *rusé*, self-protective, worldly and yet visionary. As we noted earlier, no poet has understood better the dangers that beset the artist in an age like this, dominated by journalists and seekers after encapsulated opinion.

Auden could permit himself, now and again, a totally direct statement, but over the broad span of his work he found himself having to insist, late as well as early, in the Contemplative phase as in the Active, that a poem is *not* this morning's newspaper, *not* a speech by a politician, not a 'flat ephemeral pamphlet'. In this connection it is worth lingering over a statement that, while it is hardly one of Auden's best poems, is indeed hardly more than a piece of clever light verse, conveys his mature opinion on the question of literalness and non-literalness, private language and public utterance. I refer to the poem in *The Shield of Achilles* addressed to Edgar Wind, the distinguished art-historian, and entitled 'The Truest Poetry Is the Most Feigning'.

This poem, in witty conversational couplets, offers advice to poets. If you are writing a love poem, pile it on – art is made of ingenious hyperbole, not grey precise truth:

And do not listen to those critics ever
Whose crude provincial gullets crave in books
Plain cooking made still plainer by plain cooks,
As though the Muse preferred her half-wit sons;
Good poets have a weakness for bad puns.

This seems like a defence of Auden's semi-seriousness, his inverted commas, against strict-minded judges like Leavis. The poem then goes on to recommend duplicity. If rifle-fire breaks out in the street outside while he is writing his love poem, the poet must immediately take out the name of his beloved and substitute that of Big Brother, retaining the fervour of devotion.

Some epithets, of course, like *lily-breasted*
Need modifying to, say, *lion-chested*,
A title *Goddess of wry-necks and wrens*
To *Great Reticulator of the fens*,

> But in an hour your poem qualifies
> For a State pension or His annual prize,
> And you will die in bed (which He will not:
> That silly sausage will be hanged or shot).
> Though honest Iagos, true to form, will write
> *Shame!* in your margins, *Toady! Hypocrite!*
> True hearts, clear heads will hear the note of glory
> And put inverted commas round the story,
> Thinking — *Old Sly-boots! We shall never know*
> *Her name or nature. Well, it's better so.*

The poem concludes with a short passage explaining the deeper reasons for this advice. Man is suspended between the straightforward simplicity of the animals and the total perspicuity of the Divine, and is so liable to self-deceit and mistake that it is a waste of time for him to try to express himself with complete naturalness:

> What but tall tales, the luck of verbal playing
> Can trick his lying nature into saying
> That love, or truth in any serious sense,
> Like orthodoxy, is a reticence.

This is a highly characteristic statement of the Contemplative Auden. The view of man ('Imago Dei who forgot his station') is traditionally Christian, but the interpretation in terms of the writer's professional and moral obligations is highly personal. There can be no doubt that the poem is serious in its central statement: art can survive under repression (and most governments, at most times, are repressive), but only if it takes on protective colouring. Write out of your real feelings, but disguise the object of them — like a man writing a love poem to a mistress and slotting in the name and hair-colour of his wife for the sake of domestic peace. It sounds a sensible strategy when we put it in those small-scale terms, or even when we think back to Ancient Rome with its short-tempered emperors and its machinery of banishment and confiscation. But what happens to such white lies in the case of a Pasternak or a Solzhenitsyn?

Would it have been better if *they* had feigned a loyalty to the
regime which they were far from feeling, for the sake of a quiet
life and dying in bed? Would the Auden of *Spain* have looked
with approval on a Fascist poet who had sung the correct tune,
with whatever inward reservations, for the sake of a 'State pen-
sion or His annual prize'?

Auden might, of course, reasonably reply that he was in-
dicating a general strategy for the artist; that there are certain
levels of savage totalitarian repression at which the strategy
would become useless; that, nevertheless, it holds good in most
cases at most times. Certainly it fits in with the later Auden's
consistent attitude: the world is in a more or less hopeless mess;
Man, the inveterate mistake-maker, isn't likely to put his house
really in order, but meanwhile if there are crannies here and
there in which he can live a decent, sane, tolerant and civilized
life, let him live it, for after all

  Life remains a blessing
  Although you cannot bless.

                                *

A few weeks after giving that lecture, I was in America, Auden's
adopted country for so many years of his life. My friend Mary-
Alice Matthews drove me for two days across the endless plains
of Minnesota and Nebraska. Although the car was running at
sixty miles an hour, we might as well not have been moving at
all; at the end of a day's driving, nothing had changed; the
landscape was the same colour, no sea or mountains had come
into view, the little grid-planned towns were interchangeable.
What it must have seemed like to the first settlers, who crawled
slowly over the earth in wagons drawn by mules or oxen! The
ones who came from a small, densely populated country like
England must have been bewildered and diminished; perhaps it
is not surprising that in this part of America the Scandinavians
fared best. But that unfenced expanse, that sense of the same
thing going on and on for miles, must have driven many an im-
migrant into black moods, into a *cafard* that finally became

suicidal – as we know for a fact that it often did.

Slumped in my seat, watching the ribbon of road and the un-changing horizon, I mused once again on the folly of trying to import American attitudes into Europe. And in particular on the folly of pretending that English writers ought to write like Americans. The two literatures grow out of two entirely different physical, mental and historical settings. And yet it goes on, year after year, the claim that the English tradition in poetry has been finally supplanted by the American tradition. Some time during my five years I must, I suppose, make some effort to oppose this stifling little orthodoxy, to chip away at its foun-dations and expose their weakness. For the moment, all irritability lulled by the vast expanses of earth and air, and by the gentle kindness of my companion, I forget the foolishness and conceit of literary law-givers and think receptively, sym-pathetically, of the situation of the American poet, trying to make the English language speak of things so far from its original scope, trying to adjust to those deserts and mountains and prairies, those tornadoes and dust-storms and earthquakes. Since I must begin to think of a subject for my summer lecture, I decide to speak of Emily Dickinson. A very different setting, hers, from this immense featureless plain: I visited her house in Amherst one autumn afternoon, and found the atmosphere more Jane Austenish than anything that survives in England; yet it was Jane Austen with a metaphysical undertow. When my friends had gone into the house and I was standing alone in the garden in the deep, still twilight, I felt Miss Emily's presence very strongly, and it was the presence of a lonely, questioning spirit. However domestic, American life till the end of the nineteenth century was lived in the presence of the wilderness, and this made their literature not social like English or French, but lonely and metaphysical.

So I reread Emily Dickinson's poems, in Minnesota, in New York, in the aeroplane going home, and at home looking across Port Meadow and the pastoral Thames, and then I stood up in Brasenose hall to pay her my tribute.

HOMAGE TO EMILY DICKINSON

> Perhaps you smile at me. I could not stop for that – My
> Business is Circumference – An ignorance, not of Customs,
> but if caught with the Dawn – or the Sunset see me –
> Myself the only Kangaroo among the Beauty, Sir, if you
> please, it afflicts me. . . .
>
> E.D., letter to Higginson, July 1862

In April 1862, the *Atlantic Monthly* carried a leading article,
'Letter to a Young Contributor', which offered advice to the
aspiring writer. Its author was Thomas Wentworth Higginson,
a respectable and responsible man of letters whose literary taste
was exactly that of most educated men of his time: the very
person, in fact, to write such an article. The ability to recognize
genius is necessarily given to only a few, but sound practical advice
can be given by any kindly and tolerant man who accepts the world
on the world's terms.

As he expected, Higginson received a number of letters
prompted by his article, some of them enclosing specimens of
their writers' work – none of which, he informed the editor of
the *Atlantic*, seemed to him worth publishing. And Higginson
did not except from this judgment one letter, enclosing four
poems, which aroused his interest. This letter was not signed,
but in the envelope was a small card, itself firmly contained in its
own envelope, bearing the name 'Emily Dickinson'. The letter
ran:

> Mr Higginson,
> Are you too deeply occupied to say if my Verse is alive?
> The Mind is so near itself – it cannot see, distinctly –

and I have none to ask —
    Should you think it breathed — and had you the leisure to
tell me, I should feel quick gratitude —
    If I make the mistake — that you dared to tell me —
would give me sincerer honor — toward you —
    I enclose my name — asking you, if you please — Sir — to
tell me what is true?
    That you will not betray me — it is needless to ask —
since Honor is it's own pawn —

With this message Emily Dickinson enclosed four poems, all
of which are to be found in her collected works:* 'Safe in their
Alabaster chambers', 'I'll tell you how the sun rose', 'The nearest
dream recedes — unrealized', and 'We play at paste'. The first of
these poems is a passionate meditation on the sleeping dead who
await the Resurrection; the second, within the framework of a
beautiful, if more or less conventional, piece of natural descrip-
tion, treats of life and death, of the nature of awakening and the
nature of falling asleep; the third concerns the unsatisfied
longings innate in the human spirit; the fourth is an intensely
focused metaphor of development, or metamorphosis indeed,
from the evanescent to the eternal. These four glasses of Miss
Emily's immortal wine, poured together into one bottle, proved
too strong for Higginson. He wrote back, evidently — for his side
of the correspondence has not survived — with the judgment,
between the lines or on them, that this poet would not appeal to
a pre-existing class of readers and could not expect publication.
    One has a good deal of sympathy for Higginson. He thought
that Emily Dickinson's poems were not good enough to be
printed in the *Atlantic Monthly*, for reasons very similar to
those that led the Catholic editor of *The Month* to send Gerard
Manley Hopkins back 'The Wreck of the *Deutschland*' in 1875.
According to his understanding of what made a good poem, hers
weren't 'good'. There was no technical smoothness; the rhymes,

The Complete Poems of Emily Dickinson, ed Thomas H. Johnson (Boston: Lit-
tle, Brown & Co., n.d.). This masterly edition is itself a reduction of Mr Johnson's
three-volume critical edition with the same title (Belknap Press, Harvard
University, 1955).

though governed by an ear of exquisite delicacy, are rather far apart ('pearl' and 'fool' would not please him, nor 'noon' and 'stone'); there is no seducing prettiness, no image to be copied into an album. In saying this one is not despising Higginson, a decent and capable man. In putting her question to him, Emily Dickinson wanted to hear the voice of consensus, of 'the world of letters'. She heard it. And though she continued to correspond with Higginson, allotted him indeed a considerable role in her life, the urgency, after that first letter, has gone. Henceforth, though their relationship is pleasant, no greater question hinges on his judgment.

Though his verdict was essentially negative, Higginson was interested and attracted by the personality he sensed behind the poems. His letter questioned her. Who and what was Emily Dickinson? Her background, her acquaintance, her reading? She answered — as it seemed — readily enough:

Mr Higginson,
    Your kindness claimed earlier gratitude — but I was ill — and write today, from my pillow.
    Thank you for the surgery — it was not so painful as I supposed. I bring you others — as you ask — though they might not differ —
    While my thought is undressed — I can make the distinction, but when I put them in the Gown — they look alike, and numb.
    You asked how old I was? I made no verse — but one or two — until this winter — Sir —
    I had a terror — since September — I could tell to none — and so I sing, as the Boy does by the Burying Ground — because I am afraid — You inquire my Books — For Poets — I have Keats — and Mr and Mrs Browning. For Prose — Mr Ruskin — Sir Thomas Browne — and the Revelations. I went to school — but in your manner of the phrase — had no education. When a little Girl, I had a friend, who taught me Immortality — but venturing too near, himself — he never returned — Soon after, my Tutor, died — and for several years, My Lexicon — was my only companion — Then I found one more — but he was not contented I be his scholar

– so he left the Land.

You ask of my Companions Hills – Sir – and the Sun-
down – and a Dog – large as myself, that my Father
bought me – They are better than Beings – because they
know – but do not tell – and the noise in the Pool, at Noon
– excels my Piano. I have a Brother and Sister – My
Mother does not care for thought – and Father, too busy
with his Briefs – to notice what we do – He buys me many
Books – but begs me not to read them – because he fears
they joggle the Mind. They are religious – except me – and
address an Eclipse, every morning – whom they call their
'Father'. But I fear my story fatigues you – I would like to
learn – Could you tell me how to grow – or is it uncovered
– like Melody – or Witchcraft?

You speak of Mr Whitman – I never read his Book but
was told that he was disgraceful –

I read Miss Prescott's 'Circumstance', but it followed
me, in the Dark – so I avoided her –

Two Editors of Journals came to my Father's House,
this winter – and asked me for my Mind – and when I
asked them 'Why', they said I was penurious – and they,
would use it for the World –

I could not weigh myself – Myself –

My size felt small – to me – I read your Chapters in the
Atlantic – and experienced honor for you – I was sure you
would not reject a confiding question –

Is this – Sir – what you asked me to tell you?

Your friend,
E – Dickinson

This second letter, which seems so artlessly confiding, in fact
illustrates Miss Emily's inviolable privateness. She is perfectly
ready to make a friend of Higginson, and to confide in him up to
a point; he became an important life-line to her, providing her
with an audience, even if an audience of one. But this did not
give him the right, nothing gave anyone the right, to walk into the
inner chamber of her life and personality. The letter charts
the boundaries of her experience, in perfectly sufficient outline;
we, who have the benefit of scholarly biographies, can give

names to the emblematic actors in the story. The friend who ventured too near immortality and never returned was a young law student who worked for a time in her father's office, leaving to set up his own practice and shortly afterwards dying of tuberculosis; Emily Dickinson had shared books and thoughts with him. The infinitely more important figure who 'was not contented I·be his scholar − so he left the Land' was evidently the Reverend Charles Wadsworth, the man to whom she appears to have given her heart and given it once and for all. I say 'appears' because no one has found a signed statement that Emily Dickinson loved Wadsworth. But the evidence can fairly be called conclusive. Dickinson *père* was a Congressman for a time, and Miss Emily as a girl of twenty-five visited him in Washington. On her way home, she stayed in Philadelphia as the guest of a childhood friend, and there she met Wadsworth, a man in his late forties, a powerful and successful personality, a paterfamilias, a minister of religion. It was unthinkable that he should give up all this and run away with her to a vagabond bliss, nor did Emily Dickinson ever think it. Instead, she returned home to Amherst and settled into what was to be the pattern of her life, a pattern of love and renunciation. She seems to have accepted that it was her destiny to be a bride, but a bride who would never know fulfilment in human terms. Only after death could she look for reunion with the loved one. Shortly thereafter she took to wearing white from head to foot; and there appeared in her verse, never to leave it, the theme of the absent beloved and the reunion beyond death.

Most, though not quite all, of these poems could go as they stand into any anthology of religious verse. In tone and content, they are indistinguishable from the way a fervent and mystically inclined Christian poet might speak of the long patience of life and the looked-for bliss of union with the Saviour. My reason for not so taking them must be partly that, on her own statement, Emily Dickinson was a metaphysical doubter rather than an accepter, and partly that certain poems exist which I find impossible to interpret except in terms of human, rather than divine, love. One such poem, written about 1862, seems to me not one of her finest if judged purely as a poem, but infinitely

touching in what it reveals of the silent suffering of the woman
behind the poems.

I cannot live with You —
It would be Life —
And Life is over there —
Behind the Shelf

The Sexton keeps the Key to —
Putting up
Our Life — His Porcelain —
Like a Cup —

Discarded of the Housewife —
Quaint — or Broke —
A newer Sevres pleases —
Old Ones crack —

I could not die — with You —
For One must wait
To shut the Other's Gaze down —
You — could not

And I — Could I stand by
And see You — freeze —
Without my Right of Frost —
Death's privilege?

Nor could I rise — with You —
Because Your Face
Would put out Jesus' —
That New Grace

Glow plain — and foreign
On my homesick Eye —
Except that You than He
Shone closer by —

They'd judge Us — How —
For You — served Heaven — You know,
Or sought to —
I could not —

Because You saturated Sight —
And I had no more Eyes
For sordid excellence
As Paradise

And were You lost, I would be —
Though My Name
Rang loudest
On the Heavenly fame —

And were You — saved —
And I — condemned to be
Where You were not —
That self — were Hell to Me —

So We must meet apart —
You there — I — here —
With just the Door ajar
That Oceans are — and Prayer —
And that White Sustenance —
Despair —

With such a poem freshly in mind, it is difficult (for me, impossible) to take as a purely religious lyric such a poignant and fully achieved statement as this one:

He found my Being — set it up —
Adjusted it to place —
Then carved his name — upon it —
And bade it to the East

Be faithful — in his absence —
And he would come again —
With Equipage of Amber —
That time — to take it Home —

Not that the Christian overtone is anything but perfectly deliberate; either planned, or fully permitted, by the poet. There need be no deep conflict, since part of the human imagining of heaven has always been that it is a place where the sundered will

find each other at last. The passionate longing in such a lyric as
'Wild Nights' is, to my mind, certainly a human longing, yet it is
always open to any reader to take it as a mystical adoration like
that of St Teresa, or those poems Hopkins sent up as cries 'to
dearest him that lives, alas, away'.

These poems on the theme of the absent beloved may serve to
lead us into Emily Dickinson's work, and put us in a position to
begin to take a grip on the whole range of her mind. 'Range',
however, is not quite the word; she is deep rather than wide; if
she writes one poem on a subject, she will probably write several
score that come at that same subject in one way and another.
Her concern is with ultimates, bedrock realities. Apart from a
few innocuous poems of natural description in the early years,
and one charming little poem about the newly opened railway ('I
like to see it lap the miles', c.1862), she has scarcely a poem
which does not go deeply to the root of existence.

In this, of course, she is in line with the general tendency of
nineteenth-century American literature. From the time of its first
characteristic masterpieces, the middle nineteenth century,
American literature is already very different from that of any
European country. When the European settlers reached that
large and unfriendly land-mass, they found themselves having to
change profoundly. Europe has been there for so long, has
weathered such fantastic changes and still contrived to exist in a
more or less recognizable shape, that even communities to whom
terrible things have happened can still find in their thinking a
strand of reassurance in sheer continuity; habit and tradition can
appear as guarantees of survival. But when they reached North
America they found a situation in which it was perfectly possible
that the old solutions would simply not work; no habit, no tradi-
tion, would guard them against the possibility of disintegration.
The nascent American mind was thus thrown on to ultimate
questions, a habit of thinking *ab ovo*; today, when the American
political and social tradition, from being one of the newest in the
world, has become one of the oldest, that habit still clings about
the American mind – but how much more closely did it cling in
those early years, how commandingly evident it is in Whitman,

in Melville, in Poe, in Hawthorne, in Emily Dickinson!

The colossus of nineteenth-century American poetry is Walt Whitman, not because he necessarily wrote the finest poems, but because his mind covered, and covered with dramatic energy and effectiveness, the whole span of the American experience; he is fascinated by the individual and equally fascinated by the national scene; his mind turns inward and outward with equal power.

> One's self I sing, a simple separate person,
> Yet utter the word Democratic, the word En-Masse

— not very good lines, those two, yet they have somehow contrived to stick in my mind since I first read them thirty years ago. Miss Emily is content with half of that programme. She nowhere utters the word en masse. The Civil War of the 1860s, to Whitman the hinge experience of his life, seems to have made very little impression on her. When Higginson went and served at the head of a regiment of black soldiers, and was wounded and invalided out with the rank of Colonel, she wrote him a letter of concern and sympathy — but very much as if she were commiserating with him for having been kicked by a runaway horse; the larger issues seem to have occupied her mind scarcely at all. We do not fault her for this; her single shaft goes deep into the rock; she drills where Whitman cannot follow her, though he sees and understands the complexity and value of the simple separate person.

In her luminous and self-forgetting absorption in the self, Emily Dickinson is in the great tradition of romantic poetry, and the romantic poet always proceeds by intense self-scrutiny. We can know other people only by conjecture; we can generalize about humanity only by extrapolation; but if we study our own identity we can come to know it deeply, and perhaps the truths we discover will be useful to other people. In any case, we have no choice, since there is an order of truths that can only be perceived by the lens of the self.

Miss Emily's subject is her own identity, her self, her inner-

most essence, her spirit, her soul — whatever label we wish to
attach to the crumb of identity that is 'I' and no other. She
searches and questions, passionately and unceasingly, to know
what this self is and what it is capable of and patient of. Natural-
ly she watches most carefully when the self is visited by some
extreme experience, something that takes it to the furthest boun-
dary of joy or of suffering — it hardly matters which, since the
self reveals and defines itself against either. One of her most
famous poems is that in which she states, quite simply, why pain
is valuable: once it gets to a certain intensity, it strips away
pretence and falsity; how we react then is how we *really* react,
not how we think we should:

> I like a look of Agony,
> Because I know it's true —
> Men do not sham Convulsion,
> Nor simulate, a Throe —

> The Eyes glaze once — and that is Death —
> Impossible to feign
> The Beads upon the Forehead
> By homely Anguish strung.

This intensity of seeing, this burning-glass concentration on
her own identity, gives to Emily Dickinson's poetry its lofty and
strenuous purity. Simple and unpretentious in form (there are
no metrical pirouettes and no indulgence in virtuosities of
language for their own sake), it strikes through to the roots of
being: not only is it irradiated always with the naked light of
consciousness, at its most characteristic it takes that same con-
sciousness for its subject.

> This Consciousness that is aware
> Of Neighbors and the Sun
> Will be the one aware of Death
> And that itself alone

Is traversing the interval
Experience between
And most profound experiment
Appointed unto Men —

How adequate unto itself
Its properties shall be
Itself unto itself and none
Shall make discovery.

Adventure most unto itself
The Soul condemned to be —
Attended by a single Hound
Its own identity.

The final image, there, is wonderfully pregnant. The soul is on
a hunting trip, and 'identity' is the faithful hound that will do the
running about, picking up scent and fetching the game. But of
course there is an insistent suggestion that the 'single hound' of
identity is the hound that *follows* the soul and cannot be shaken
off. The soul is both hunter and hunted.

When we contemplate Emily Dickinson, we cannot fail to be
struck by the contrast between her calm, eventless outward
existence, and the titanic struggles going on within. She makes
this one of the themes, naturally ('I tie my hat, I crease my
shawl', etc.); equally, she relates all natural phenomena to the
perceiving and experiencing self:

There's a certain Slant of light,
Winter Afternoons —
That oppresses, like the Heft
Of Cathedral Tunes —

Heavenly Hurt, it gives us —
We can find no scar,
But internal difference,
Where the Meanings, are —

None may teach it — Any —
'Tis the Seal Despair —
An imperial affliction
Sent us of the Air —

When it comes, the Landscape listens —
Shadows — hold their breath —
When it goes, 'tis like the Distance
On the look of Death —

That innermost core of being, 'where the meanings are', is the
locus of Emily Dickinson's poetry, the arena of its heroic
struggles. Poetry, for her, was something that involved the whole
being — there was nothing 'literary' in her approach. Higginson
made some notes of a conversation with her in 1870, and records
her as saying: 'If I read a book and it makes my whole body so
cold no fire can ever warm me I know *that* is poetry. If I feel
physically as if the top of my head were taken off, I know *that* is
poetry. These are the only ways I know of. Is there any other
way?'* In both reading and writing, she was equally uncom-
promising. Her aim is always to explore those supreme
experiences that test the self and force it towards definition; but
definition is also brought about by experiences that are un-
graspable, evanescent, so that to record them is like giving a very
precise description of something you can only see out of the
furthest corner of your eye.

Presentiment — is that long Shadow — on the Lawn —
Indicative that Suns go down —

The Notice to the startled Grass
The Darkness — is about to pass —

I have been quoting rather liberally in this section, mainly
because the matters under discussion are such as can be talked
about effectively in Miss Emily's voice and not at all effectively
in mine; so let me quote one more entire poem, this time one of

*Jay Leyda, *The Years and Hours of Emily Dickinson*, 2 vols (1960), vol. II,
p. 151.

her most famous – it sums up the central situation explored by
her work.

> Because I could not stop for Death –
> He kindly stopped for me –
> The Carriage held but just Ourselves –
> And Immortality.
>
> We slowly drove – He knew no haste
> And I had put away
> My labor and my leisure too,
> For His Civility –
>
> We passed the School, where Children strove
> At Recess – in the Ring –
> We passed the Fields of Gazing Grain –
> We passed the Setting Sun –
>
> Or rather – He passed Us –
> The Dews drew quivering and chill –
> For only Gossamer, my Gown,
> My Tippet – only Tulle –
>
> We paused before a House that seemed
> A Swelling of the Ground –
> The Roof was scarcely visible –
> The Cornice – in the Ground –
>
> Since then – 'tis Centuries – and yet
> Feels shorter than the Day
> I first surmised the Horses' Heads
> Were Toward Eternity –

This poem is the diagram of all Emily Dickinson's poems.
The carriage that moves in a leisurely, inexorable way through
the scenes of temporal life, passing the school which is
childhood, the ripe grain which is middle life, and the setting sun
which is age, is occupied by the self, and Death, and Immortali-
ty. The third must be present if the other two are, just as it must
be 'Eternity' towards which the horses' heads are pointed. These

are the conditions, the defining terms, of existence. (There seems also to be a suggestion, in the poem, that the self is dressed in bridal costume, gossamer and tulle; the soul is the chosen mate of death, or perhaps of immortality.) In the enclosed space of this carriage, which is time, the self journeys towards the grave in the company of Death and Immortality; and everything that happens on the way is important or trivial in *that* context. Miss Emily's scale of measurement is an uncompromising one. Wars and international upheavals meant scarcely anything to her; on the other hand, one of her most vivid poems concerns the simplest and most ordinary form of insect life ('I heard a fly buzz when I died'). This fly with its 'blue, uncertain, stumbling buzz' came between the dying eyes and the light from the window, in the moment of extinction of consciousness; and so the tiny, busy speck of life, intent on its own purposes, becomes a point of focused significance. This is life that will continue when the human life on the bed is stilled; and, since at any given instant some life is being snuffed out, some continuing and some coming to birth, the significance is everywhere. Contemplating a fly, we see that everything is important.

Life seen at the moment of death, or from the other side of death, or those who have preceded us into death seen from our side of the divide: these are constant themes with Emily Dickinson. One thinks of such poems as 'Of nearness to her sundered things' and ''Twas just this time, last year, I died'. She broods on death continually, not out of morbidity but because death is the point at which time-bound human existence abuts on the timeless. I would expect even the most decided atheist to respond to this strain in her work, since even from his point of view it could not be maintained that when the body dies life is simply switched off like an electric light bulb. The mere fact that I am writing this essay on Emily Dickinson, and you are reading it, indicates that *her* life has not come to an end; she is influencing our consciousness; and though this is most conspicuously true of artists, who leave their work behind them in an intact state, nevertheless it is true in some fashion of every human being. Even in a blankly anti-metaphysical view of experience, death

has the importance that Miss Emily accords to it, forming as it
does the intersection between one dimension and another. But
death is not only important to the person who dies; a death in-
fluences the survivors; and this is the theme of her great elegy,
'The last night that she lived'. The whole poem revolves round
the change of consciousness in those who watch by the dying
woman's bedside; when the death has happened, and there is
nothing more to do for her,

> We placed the Hair –
> And drew the Head erect –
> And then an awful leisure was
> Belief to regulate –

The closing word is beautifully chosen; it suggests a clock, and
our beliefs are like clocks because they are what we live by, and
the authority we quote to each other ('I'll see you at five o'clock',
and there is no arguing as to what is meant by five o'clock). But
the transforming experience of our kinswoman's death, transfor-
ming not only her but us, makes us take our beliefs down from
the shelf and 'regulate' them.

After such knowledge, what forgiveness? This spinster lady
looked into depths we can only just bear to know about, pushed
against frontiers we shrink away from; she was not a perfect
poet, being often too cryptic and sometimes given to repeating
herself, but the spare and haunting melody, the seemingly casual
rhymes and cadences that show her perfect pitch, served her as
nothing else would have done, because they served her to convey
the truth she had discovered for herself. When we read her
poems, we are in the presence of something as pure and as cold
as water that comes up from hundreds of feet deep in the rock,
or 'breath of vernal air from snowy Alp', and on such things
nobody puts a price-tag. In so far as we are able to understand
the extent of what she has done for us, we pay her homage.

•

High summer. Ten months have gone by since my election, and
the Oxford year has reached that pinnacle of hospitality,
peacock-pride and ceremony that the University allows itself
once a year. People float on the river in punts, drink wine on
shaven lawns, put aside books and papers (except for the poor
devils who are taking examinations) in favour of a round of
party-going, and for three or four weeks one might almost be
walking around in the Oxford of Zuleika Dobson.

All this is entirely good and necessary. Of the thousands of
young people who are at the University at any given time, the
great majority will be swallowed up very soon into the vast grey
world of the professions or business, or the strident arena of
politics. If their lives are ever to know a brief season of flowering
elegance, it will be now or never. Most of them work very hard
during their three or four years here, and if for a week or two
they can slacken off and enjoy the river and the gardens and one
another, put on outdoor plays and indoor dances that go on till
breakfast-time, this is a sweetener that may help to keep them
human through the long, grinding years of duty. As for the older
people, the dons who are responsible for the running of the place,
about a third of them will have to begin, within a few days, on
the slavery of reading mounds of examination papers, with
endless meetings and consultations; and beyond it the summer
vacation, an essential period of recharging, before having to be
back in September to get ready for the next wave of freshmen,
the next round of lectures and seminars. For the whole academic
population, these are the brief weeks of bright plumage, when
the bird sings in his cage.

I am to give the Creweian Oration. Nathaniel, Lord Crewe,
was an eighteenth-century bishop who evidently felt an affection
for Oxford, where he had been a don and head of a college in the
1670s and 1680s. When he died in 1721 he left a sum of money
to the University to provide for a yearly oration to com-
memorate its benefactors. As an inducement to the senior dons
to attend this oration, he put down an additional £10 a year (the
present-day equivalent would I suppose be about £500) to
provide some refreshment beforehand and thus make a social

occasion of it. What form this refreshment took when the series, after more than ten years' delay, got going is not recorded, but the tradition now seems to have stabilized at strawberries and champagne. So we assemble at ten in the morning, in the Hall of Jesus College, everybody in full fig, resplendent in black and gold and scarlet, wolfing down strawberries and champagne. Originally a separate occasion, the Creweian Oration has, during the twentieth century, gradually become absorbed in Encaenia, Oxford's high-flown equivalent of a school speech day, when under the watchfully benevolent gaze of the Chancellor and the Vice-Chancellor honorary degrees are given, various prize-winners stand up to be seen, and speeches are made.

So, with a glass of champagne in one hand and a bowl of strawberries in the other, stiffly aware of the encumbrance of my gown and hood and (for this ceremonial occasion) bands, yes, those flat strips of linen one sees pictures of eighteenth-century clergymen wearing – I had to go out and buy a pair and then ask somebody how to put them on – I stand and look round at the notabilities who crowd the hall. This is the first time in my life that I have ever seen such a concentration of academic notabilities; not being by nature an attender of ceremonies, I have never witnessed Encaenia, and now suddenly I am to per-form in it, I am to address these people and try to hold their attention. For days, I have been poring over the huge mass of documents provided for me by the University's Information Officer: all the grants for scientific research, the bequests of books and manuscripts. Money from industrial firms. Money from private donors. Money (in one instance) from the United States Air Force. A new gallery for the Ashmolean Museum; a new room for the Taylorian Institute. A housing scheme for married graduates; someone who remained nameless gave £100,000 for this purpose a couple of years ago, chipped in another £80,000 a few months later, and now hands over another £83,000. Who is this who gives fortune after fortune to the University? Was he, or she, once a lonely young graduate, living in the kind of dingy and freezing lodging-house I remember, and now finding satisfaction in helping young Oxford people, at that difficult in-between stage of academic life, to be housed like human beings?

Most of the material I have to recite is entirely dead; to stand up and spout it out is a mere formality, a necessary observance. At only two points does my material offer a chance to hold my hearers' attention. One is a human interest story. A year or so ago, there died in Chicago an old, solitary, shabbily dressed man named Walter Harding. He was a musician, though never a successful one; in the days of the silent cinema he accompanied the flickering images on the piano; later, he switched to theatre organ. At best, he extracted a living from the keyboard. But he had a hobby, the collecting of musical scores. With very small funds, but with a musician's discriminating eye and increasingly with a collector's passion, he filled his little house with books and scores, mostly of the seventeenth and eighteenth centuries, until his collection was worth a million dollars.

Today, that collection is on its way to the Bodleian Library. For Walter Harding was an Englishman, though it was eighty-six years since he had seen his native land. As a small child in a Victorian family, he had been taken to America, and he never returned. But, anchored to the thought of England and of Oxford by some still green tendril, he declared in his will that his collection should go to that old, far-off, magical place he had never seen.

The other live ingredient I have at my disposal is political. During this academic year of 1973–4, Oxford has been disturbed by repeated outbreaks of hooliganism. The urge to disrupt something, understandable enough in a fat society after thirty-five years without a shooting war, focuses naturally on the University. After all, it is (oh dear, yes) a symbol of 'privilege', with its ancient buildings and traditions; and, then, it is not patrolled by security guards, like the banks, or tucked away behind barriers like a Defence establishment; it is so open, so unguarded, so delightfully vulnerable. Oxford has no 'campus police'; nor is it, like the Sorbonne, unsleepingly watched by the baton-swinging *garde mobile*. A courteous, mild-eyed surprise seems to be the initial Oxford reaction to the appearance of Dervishes vowed to its destruction. On the other hand, a little way

down, there is steel. Of all the English universities that have been
plagued by politically inspired mob demonstrations, Oxford
alone has stood firm and sent the worst offenders down. So there
is a campaign, a well-marshalled and concerted campaign, to do
Oxford as much harm as possible. Two organizations are prin-
cipally behind it; both are nation-wide; neither has more than a
few members in Oxford, but both are prepared at a moment's
notice to load demonstrators into buses and pour them in, all the
way from Coventry and Essex to Broad Street and Radcliffe
Square.

As text-book revolutionaries, these whizz-kids know that the
classic technique is to exploit a grievance. In most societies there
are plenty of genuine grievances and it is just a question of
picking the one that will command the biggest crowd; but at
Oxford grievances have to be invented. An Oxford under-
graduate gets the best teaching in the world, on a system
which combines freedom with discipline in exactly the right
proportions – the compulsory weekly essay, but no compulsory
lectures – to unfetter the brilliant student without allowing the
dullard to fall out of sight. He is under the care of a paternalistic
college where his identity is a real one and his problems are
taken seriously. He has an unlimited choice of leisure activities,
a service to advise him on the choice of a career, and, as the
background to his daily life, the shabby comfort of the Junior
Common Room and the beer-cellar, with his own inviolable
study to escape to if he wishes neither of these. All that is asked
of him in return is that he should try to acquire some informa-
tion and develop some ideas. And this he does in the knowledge
that no grim-faced officialdom waits to check on whether this in-
formation is within permitted areas, or these ideas sufficiently
orthodox. No repressive slave-system is waiting to use his ser-
vices as a cog; instead, he is made free of a tradition of intellec-
tual independence, which he is asked to respect in others while
he cultivates it in himself.

Under these circumstances, resentment against 'the system'
can only be imitative. The Oxford undergraduate must be made
to feel inferior if he does not behave as savagely as his contem-

poraries all over the (Western) world. If the ragged students of the Sorbonne, living like rats in the holes of their great city, pale with bad food, crowding in their hundreds to hear lectures on overspill microphones, never seeing their professors face to face, have a sense of grievance, why, so must the undergraduates of Oxford. Nobody at the age of twenty likes to be short of a *casus belli*.

So the trumped-up grievance is duly produced, and it turns out to be the absence of a Central Students' Union. This makes a good rallying-cry and can even be made to seem reasonable to people who know nothing about Oxford (the average journalist, for instance). Those who know Oxford know, of course, that the functions of a Students' Union are filled by the colleges, with their common rooms and bars and dining-halls, with the Oxford Union Society as a political debating club. But, for outside consumption, the cry goes up: 'Oxford has no Central Students' Union. It is the only University without one. Why can't we have what everyone else has?'

If there were such a Union, of course – if the University were to bow to this demand and spend a vast sum of money on a building designed to house it – then the path of the disrupter and agitator would become very smooth. If the entire student population of Oxford were taken out of its Junior Common Rooms and Middle Common Rooms and massed in a central organization, it would be far easier to mobilize them into a political battering-ram at the service of radical change. In a very few years the University would be unrecognizable. This, of course, is the objective. 'We disapprove of the college system,' one of these Visigoths remarked to me in conversation. 'Why come up to Oxford,' I asked him, 'if you don't like the college system?' Looking at me pityingly, he replied, 'Because Oxford has the prestige.' Perhaps the reason why Oxford has prestige is because the College system has worked well for seven hundred years. No matter! It must go out of the window; *Red Mole* says so.

Mulling over my Creweian Oration, then, I have decided that it ought to reflect, in its small way, the actual state of the University, the things that have been going on, the issues that are being struggled over. By the rules of the game, any such

reflections have to be fitted into the *cadre* of thanks to benefac-
tors. A moment's reflection solves the difficulty. The relevant
passage from the Oration runs:

The University has been less fortunate, during the past year, in
evoking a corresponding love from hearts nearer at hand. Her
ways, her traditions, and some of the people who carry out her
work have met with impatient question and intemperate
criticism. The resentment flared over the issue of whether the
University should, or should not, provide a Central Students'
Union. In the large civic universities, such unions are essential,
for without them the students would be left on the pavement,
with – to quote a line of W. H. Auden's – 'Nothing to eat and
nowhere to sit down'. Oxford students, already comfortable in
their colleges and common rooms, could make no such argument
from necessity, and in fact it has been, for the most part, honest-
ly admitted that the demand for a Central Students' Union is
politically motivated. It would not be fitting to discuss the
matter here, nor even to narrate its unfolding history. The
Creweian Oration is intended to commemorate and thank those
whom the University recognizes as benefactors. But surely we
do so recognize the officers and functionaries of the University
who, in these strident and strife-ful months, have been called
upon to show, and have shown, unusual patience, unusual for-
titude, unusual self-control. From the three-man disciplinary
court presided over by Professor Barry Nicholas, to the Univer-
sity constables, porters, door-keepers, secretaries, cleaning ladies
who during these disturbances found their work impeded and
themselves insulted and even threatened, we offer them our
recognition and our thanks appropriately at this time: for you,
Mr Chancellor, who have presided over our ceremony once again,
whose experience of change and development in this University
goes back over so many years, and who have so wisely advised and
guided us, will surely agree that these good and loyal people are,
also, our benefactors.

So that is my Oration, and it is nestling in my pocket as I knock back a final glass of champagne and prepare to move off. 'Mr Chancellor' is of course Harold Macmillan. He is here, grave, myopic, very much the elder statesman; I am briefly introduced to him in the crush, and I don't blame him at all for registering me as one more face, not attached to any particular person. (He must register me, though, in another part of his mind; a few months later I have lunch with him at his request; he has been reading my book on Johnson, and has written me a letter about it.)

The time has come to move off. Outside, the rain is bucketing down. Normally, we would all go in procession; but it is clearly not right to expose Harold Macmillan, not to mention the more venerable dons and the distinguished honorands, to a chilling downpour followed by ninety minutes of compulsory sitting still. Cars are provided, umbrellas held up. I hear Mr Macmillan protesting gently about this; he wants 'to march with the troops'. He is shepherded, equally gently, into a car. So am I. My car contains two dons – proctors, I think – and John Betjeman, who is here to receive his D.Litt. Betjeman is humorous and deprecating; one sees why people like him so much. Wet photographers take pictures as we move off, and again as we arrive at the Sheldonian. The procession winds in. It is all rather like a dream, not at all an unhappy dream but slow-paced, unreal. I am installed in one of the two ornate boxes or pulpits that dominate the building from either side. Getting to my feet to deliver the Oration, I am exactly on a level with the corresponding box on the other side, which contains the young who have won prizes – the Newdigate, the Chancellor's English Essay, prizes for Latin verse and Greek prose – and with the gilded seat of the Chancellor, whose wise-old-elephant head gives no indication as to whether he is listening, dozing, or recalling some June day in the Oxford of sixty years ago.

As well as judging the Newdigate Prize for poetry (with two other judges, changed every year) I have to set the title. This first year, the title is one I have inherited; it was set by my predecessor Roy Fuller: 'The Death of a Poet'. There are several good entries, but one stands out, and when the names are known it turns out that the writer is Alan Hollinghurst of Magdalen.

His poem is clearly about Auden — a preference invited, of course, by the choice of that title in that particular year. A poised, humorous young man, he reads from his poem at Encaenia without a trace of nervousness. But behind that exterior there is obviously a very active imagination. This is how his poem runs:

Death of a Poet

Et le jour même la nouvelle de sa mort se répandit par le monde où elle fut accueillie avec une religieuse émotion — Mann

1
The poet sits in his chair by the fireside:
and it is already time to assess

his innovations and what influence he had.
Novel but not uncommon Alonso:

before you can help it the old sea-change
has had you; the sweets you gave to children

are gems; your agonised sex-life
and everything you said and made

are struck to a coral too hard and strong to snap.
Your mouth hangs open as if he suddenly saw

that the time to say the prepared words had come:
these unknown, let us case in ormolu caskets.

Let us make sure that all is planned —
that each moment is a crystal with its place in the
    crown —

that your life is a perfect and wrought emblem.
Let us find nothing that we cannot manage,

and make you stand for our skill at stones;
while I lurk ready, devious, the locksmith.

2

Those two images of childhood — were they with him
at the end? The sands and the mountains

suddenly focused, that had crossed his vision
at a sea-cove in the old time, where he had

sprawled or clambered in luminous adolescent
    dreams?
Those same peaks and moon-crossed beaches seemed

a passage of unguessed clarity and knowledge
in the landscape his poems fought over to the end.

Walking at dawn on the sands, pondering,
leaning by the sea-wall, where gulls beat off out

to the edge of sight, the man saw himself
with the rest of things — sometimes desolate, strong.

Then gasping, flung back on a mountain, he saw
triumph cast the world in his eye-ball;

there birds flew close, unused to men,
and could one live there? Different people,

different epochs, gazed inward and outward:
Petrarch climbed an Alp, peculiarly closed

the Middle Ages. At the end did these
two visions kiss, unite their periodicities?

The wide mouth at the extreme moment
may have admitted that it was not so.

3
He did not choose a fatal Polish boy
to lead him to the loggia at the world's end;

he did not select the uncertain glory of martyrdom,
to die on a beach, senseless with sunset, as the

incarnation of beauty ran and ran on the sandbanks
till he could no longer be seen. That was not

his training. Serious and ungodly he had not
eaten himself in a sauce of passion in any

café or garret that the end of a century
might have forced him into, wasting his pocket-
    money

on mystics or drugs or wasted women
that his friends could later have painted. No.

Have you missed out, sir, not having shared yourself,
in a Club? And what of the proper poetic masks –

personae that excuse you for your narrow experience
and your terror of naked flesh? It seems

that mouth might try to answer: 'I was myself,
even in games, I failed at the charade.'

Spittle hangs on the wing of the moustache:
'I never was a burglar or a mango-tree.'

Silence deepens. The proofs of his last labour
are nearly all corrected. Outside a glow falls

upon the window: almost invisible a tall boy
tosses his golden hair and smiles; then goes.

4

Those two morbid Victorian gentlemen, one
heavily moustached, with affected sageness, the other

unspeakably hungry, remorselessly eating small
    children —
a defenceless minority of Oysters. They were not for
    you.

You were after some modern charity and had
    eschewed
the grandiloquent, the greed of the affable affluent
    Walrus.

To you small children had some power greater
than that which laid railways over mountain passes

That dune where you seemed buried in shadow
or petrified in study of the minute, was really

a rockface as great and as sonorous as any
Bedivere might clatter round on for the good of the
    nation.

From there you saw that horrid expedition, where the
    sun
shone even at midnight — and you could not find

so extreme a distortion amusing, or approve
the minimal repentance of the waistcoated Walrus.

But you saw at the same time how the light fell
at midnight, how regardless of cause and concern

birds with comical motions ran on the sand.
Susceptible, you might have heard, too, the sound

of a girl's voice calling cattle, but you never
said so. You shewed us instead a page in your
    sketchpad,

how owls look in daylight, or on a winter evening
a full moon balanced on a frond of bracken.

5
Rain and night consume the back-garden: the fire falls
and dulls: in the dark hollow of the chair

the poet is slumped; the glow makes unaccustomed
highlights at ankle, ring-finger and brow.

The open mouth is filled with darkness — the eyes still
    open
do not see the sea of shadow. Watch and clock

tick on for one whose time means only nothing to see
and no work. There open infinite depths in a sitting
    room,

the one experience he may not describe.
No-one knows yet that the winter night

and a broken heart-beat have stopped the oracle
as children stop the mouth of a statue with stones.

The few who think of him or read him
at this moment do so as of a living man —

and see him still as a walking-companion
who might suddenly meet them at a gateway or
    ruined house.

The face has often gazed motionless, but never
with this involuntary stillness as a corpse

weighted with lead goes down and down
but says nothing and thinks nothing, and when it
    plumbs the bottom

stays there. Does the fire-glow pass beyond
those filmed-over eyes, reflect into a dimming inner
    chamber

a flicker of remembrance? Or does some sightless creature
at this unknown depth suck in his body with the rest?

6
What he has done and where he stood, are fixed now
by accumulative obituaries. Death

precipitates the assessments. Somewhere a colleague
inscribes a friendlier memoir – the Oxford days

seem a laugh on the lips of the past
and the War a sob at an immovable anguish.

The 50s volume of Collected Works
goes out of print: An American scholar

oils his machinery for the hermetic edition,
presuming that the encyclopaedic is the ultimate

and that no case should be left open.
Too weak to resist the plan, the dons

the friends, and the lover send in the letters
and the unpublic poems – surrender

to the predicted enemy. I too
will oil the hinges, sand the locks,

to cover a terror of chaos with craft.
And the unequal pulse of moments goes, and the eye

sometimes sleeping or failing; the man
unhappy or struggling or calm

goes out to come back stuffed and few notice
that its eye is glass, that a replica

is not the real thing. The rest
unknowing are no way affected.

The Carpenter was wise to doubt
if sandy quantities could ever be removed;

mountains stay still, for
there is no faithful man.

Your death, the slip you made
of dying, marks the change.

Another poet launched! God, or the Muses, or Good Luck, or
Dame Kind, or some other power if there is any other, keep him
away from all the shoals and sandbanks, all the things that wreck
poets before they have begun to carry cargo — the cheapjacks,
the bribers, the flatterers, the seducers who will try to turn his
rarest and most unique thoughts to profit and advantage, and
will hate him if he refuses. Help him to be equally indifferent to
their fulsome overtures and to their enmity. This we pray.

3
Teaching a Trade

> — I am Cinna the poet, I am Cinna the poet.
> — Tear him for his bad verses, tear him for his bad verses!
>
> *Julius Caesar*

Back to work. Early in 1974 I decided that my dramatic sequence of poems, *Feng*, was finished as far as it will ever be. Since I take the view that one of the things I am paid for as Professor of Poetry is to write poetry, I sent it to my publisher, adding one final detail: a dedication to Peter Levi.

Feng uses many forms to catch the central character's many moods. One of my deepest convictions about the poet is that he should possess all skills relevant to his craft, disdaining nothing, inventing new forms, reviving old, but always finding vehicles to embody the beat and flow of his imagination, never just pouring his thoughts loose on to the page.

This pragmatic effort naturally finds its counterpart in critical argument, and I make that argument the theme of my fourth lecture.

ON THE BREAKING OF FORMS

Near the beginning of Ezra Pound's Canto LXXXI occurs a line that has been much quoted by those who see E.P. primarily as the great innovator, the key-turner who conducted poetry in English out of the cell of an obsolete idiom. This line is enclosed in brackets and reads:

(to break the pentameter, that was the first heave)

The words have struck a particularly responsive chord among those who see the 'pentameter', or as they usually call it the 'iambic pentameter', as the main repressive instrument whereby poetry was held back and denied its birthright of a living speech rhythm. It is true that when one actually looks the line up it turns out not to be in a passage concerning the technicalities of verse, or the relationship of literature to language, except as part of a very general disquisition on 'cultural level'; but, then, I feel a proper hesitation in assigning 'subject' to any part of the Cantos, especially the Pisan Cantos, of which this is one. Confined in his prison camp, actually in his steel-mesh cage (ah, yes, that cage!), the poet had no access to books, and fell back on that most allusive and multi-dimensional instrument, the memory. The immediate context runs:

'You will find' said old André Spire,
that every man on that board (Credit Agricole)
has a brother-in-law
    'You the one, I the few'
    said John Adams
speaking of fears in the abstract
  to his volatile friend Mr Jefferson

136

(to break the pentameter, that was the first heave)
or as Jo Bard says: they never speak to each other,
if it is baker and concierge visibly
    it is La Rochefoucauld and de Maintenon audibly.

Perhaps the baker and concierge, so commonplace to the eye and so aristocratic to the ear, are meant to typify the stilted grandeur of an artificial metre; it all depends, I suppose, on whether it is meant to be a good thing or a bad thing that there is such a gap between how these people look and how they talk. Personally I have long since abandoned the search for a solution of these puzzles, which in the later Cantos meet one at the rate of about one every seven lines; to sort them out calls not only for an in-wardness with the Poundian Sacred Books, but also for a kind of mental hedge-hopping that I know, now, I shall never be able to cultivate. Still, we might as well assume that those people are right who flourish this line as a banner, and read in it one of the prime objectives of Pound's modernizing programme between about 1908 and 1920 when he left England for good. Such an assumption makes it even more interesting to turn over two pages and read, in that same Canto LXXXI, the famous passage:

The ant's a centaur in his dragon world.
Pull down thy vanity, it is not man
Made courage, or made order, or made grace,
    Pull down thy vanity, I say pull down.
Learn of the green world what can be thy place
In scaled invention or true artistry,
Pull down thy vanity,
      Paquin pull down!
The green casque has outdone your elegance.
'Master thyself, then others shall thee beare'
    Pull down thy vanity
Thou art a beaten dog beneath the hail,
A swollen magpie in a fitful sun,
Half black half white
Nor knowst'ou wing from tail

> Pull down thy vanity
>   How mean thy hates
> Fostered in falsity,
>   Pull down thy vanity,
> Rathe to destroy, niggard in charity,
> Pull down thy vanity,
>   I say pull down.

These lines are probably the best-known in the entire Cantos, certainly in the later ones; the average reader of modern poetry, if asked without warning to quote anything from the Cantos, would almost certainly produce some part of them; they stay in the mind as memorable and moving. It is impossible, of course, to separate them from one's knowledge of the poet's situation at the time of writing, and to that extent they are a personal utterance and even 'autobiographical'. But what particularly concerns me at the moment is that they are decasyllables; or, if you prefer the term, iambic pentameters. To be strictly impartial, when we quote

(to break the pentameter, that was the first heave)

we should not fail to add that the best-known passage in all Pound's later work follows almost immediately and is in flat contradiction or reversal of the 'heave'.

I have no doubt that among the flock of commentators who follow the Cantos like gulls following a ship there will be some who would describe these lines as parody. Pound's generally allusive and frequently satiric manner lends itself very easily to parody, and indeed is continually treading on its verge; some of his most celebrated passages have an undoubted tinge of parody, as in the famous lyric from 'Hugh Selwyn Mauberley' beginning 'Go dumb-born book', where the poet, in deciding to break finally with a certain tradition of romantic lyricism, pays that tradition the tribute of a last salute – exquisitely written (to show that he can bring off these effects if he chooses) and slightly overblown (to indicate which of its characteristic features make him uneasy). To my present argument it makes, of course, no

difference whether we decide that these particular decasyllables
have, or have not, somewhat the function of parody. What
matters is that, having arrived at a key passage, an emotional
and doctrinal node, the poet chooses to pick up the rhythm of
the classic English ten-syllable line which it was earlier his
dedicated 'heave' to get away from.

Parody or not, deadly serious or not, these lines convey their
meaning as much by their form as by their paraphrasable con-
tent. Put like that, it is a cliché. Every statement does so, from
the humblest fragment of conversation to the highly conscious
use of linguistic effect that we call literature. All the more reason
why Pound's lines should stand at the threshold of a discus-
sion of form in poetry and the imaginative arts generally. Form
is communication. It is a system of signals between writer
and reader. Immediately on approaching a poem, story or novel, the
reader recognizes the nature of its form, and that recognition
establishes a relationship. In the case of a poem, as soon as we
begin to read we see whether it fits in to a previously existing
form – sonnet, ballad, limerick – or whether it eschews form
altogether. In any event, the poet is aligning himself with all
those poets before him who have done the same. To write a
passage in end-stopped couplets is to stand in some relationship
with all the previous poets who have used that metre – or the
villanelle, or the canzone, or the alliterative line breaking into
two halves, or the *haiku*. It is, in practice, impossible to write in
a form without indicating some sort of attitude towards the
literary tradition, and therefore to the past generally. And, since
one's attitude to the past is a seamless fabric with one's attitude
to the present, the choice of form also signals a cluster of
opinions about the political and social realities of one's own day.
I do not propose to push the argument to absurd lengths – it is
not possible to deduce the whole range of a writer's beliefs from
his choice of form for one poem – but it remains true that a
writer's attitude towards form, which is inescapably the first
thing we notice when we approach his work, is a reliable guide
to his attitudes in general. And we should notice here – if it is
not too obvious to be worth pointing out – that non-form (free

verse, absence of punctuation, breakdown of normal word-order
and syntax) is merely, from this point of view, one of the pos-
sible choices of form. To adopt it is to align oneself with all the
previous writers who have made that particular choice. Talk of
'freedom' in such a case is bound to be to some extent illusory:
there is no avenue that leads to complete individualism, there is
only a choice of different categories of alignment.

The attempt to 'escape' from 'the confines of' form is
meaningless. Once a writer accepts this, and begins to explore
the possibilities of form as communication, he has come of age.
One of the most fertile of these possibilities is the use of form as
external reference, a means whereby the poem can point outside
itself. Kipling's 'Danny Deever' is a good simple example. Here,
for reminder, are the first two stanzas.

'What are the bugles blowin' for?' said Files-on-Parade.
'To turn you out, to turn you out', the Colour-Sergeant
    said.
'What makes you look so white, so white? said Files-on-
    Parade.
'I'm dreadin' what I've got to watch', the Colour-Sergeant
    said.
For they're hangin' Danny Deever, you can hear the
    Dead March play,
The regiment's in 'ollow square – they're hangin' him to-
    day;
They've taken of his buttons off an' cut his stripes
    away,
An' they're hangin' Danny Deever in the mornin'.

'What makes the rear-rank breathe so 'ard?' said Files-on-
    Parade.
'It's bitter cold, it's bitter cold', the Colour-Sergeant said.
'What makes that front-rank man fall down?' says Files-on-
    Parade.
'A touch o' sun, a touch o' sun', the Colour-Sergeant said.
They are hangin' Danny Deever, they are marchin' of 'im
    round,

They 'ave 'alted Danny Deever by 'is coffin on the
    ground;
An' 'e'll swing in 'arf a minute for a sneakin' shootin'
    hound –
O they're hangin' Danny Deever in the mornin'.

Two devices are used here. Each stanza begins with a
question-and-answer which intentionally recalls the use of
the same device in the late medieval border ballads such as
'Edward':

'Why dois your brand sae drap wi bluid,
        Edward, Edward,
Why dois your brand sae drap wi bluid,
    And why sae sad gang yee O?'
'O I hae killed my hauke sae guid,
        Mither, mither,
O I hae killed my hauke sae guid,
    And I had nae mair bot hee O.'

'Your haukis bluid was nevir sae reid,
        Edward, Edward,
Your haukis bluid was nevir sae reid,
    My deir son I tell thee O.'
'O I hae killed my reid-roan steid,
        Mither, mither,
O I hae killed my reid-roan steid,
    That erst was sae fair and frie O.'

'Your steid was auld, and yet hae gat
            mair,
        Edward, Edward,
Your steid was auld, and ye hae gat
            mair,
    Sum other dule ye drie O.'
'O I hae killed my fadir deir,
        Mither, mither,
O I hae killed my fadir deir,
    Alas, and wae is mee O!'

'And whatten penance wul ye drie for
    that,
      Edward, Edward?
And whatten penance will ye drie for
  that?
My deir son, now tell me O.'
'Ile set my feit in younder boat,
     Mither, mither,
Ile set my feit in yonder boat,
    And Ile fare ovir the sea O.'

'And what wul ye doe wi your towirs
      and your ha,
      Edward, Edward?
And what wul ye doe wi your towirs
  and your ha,
That were sae fair to see O?'
'Ile let thame stand tul they doun fa,
     Mither, mither,
'Ile let thame stand tul they doun fa,
    For here nivir mair maun I bee O.'

'And what wul ye leive to your bairns
      and your wife,
      Edward, Edward?
And what wul ye leive to your bairns
  and your wife,
Whan ye gang ovir the sea O?'
'The warldis room, late them beg thrae
      life,
     Mither, mither,
The warldis room, late them beg thrae
  life,
For thame nevir mair wul I see O.'

'And what wul ye leive to your ain
      mither deir,
      Edward, Edward?
And what wul ye leive to your ain
  mither deir?

My deir son, now tell me O.'
'The curse of hell frae me sall ye beir,
     Mither, mither,
The curse of hell frae me sall ye beir,
     Sic counseils ye gave to me O.'

That degree of concentration and dramatization – everything
that can be left out is left out, so that (for instance) we are not
told why Edward's mother made him kill his father – is an effect
that Kipling is both seeking to reproduce and also to recall by
allusion. Then, in its second part, his stanza breaks into the
rhythm of the regimental march. The juxtaposition is strikingly
successful because it brings together the two worlds whose ideas
and attitudes the poem straddles. A long-term volunteer army,
serving in a foreign country, breeds the same kind of remorseless
loves and hates as a static border feudal society, the same
vendettas and revenge-killings; to combine the world of
'Edward' (which is, *mutatis mutandis*, the world of *Macbeth*)
with the world of the parade-ground is already to convey much
of the poem's essential meaning. A contemporary protest-poet,
aghast at the horrors of militarism, would dwell far more on the
physical horrors of the hanging, but would scarcely equal the
frisson of Kipling's laconic exchanges, with their rich overtones in
poetic tradition.

' 'Is cot was right-'and cot to mine,' said Files-on-Parade
' 'E's sleepin' out an' far to night,' the Colour-Sergeant
     said.

Another use of form as external reference is of course the
ironic use of a form whose associations run counter to the
meaning that is specifically conveyed. The aubade, a love-song
from the lover to his mistress at dawn, is given a new slant –
part sardonic, part poignant, in William Empson's 'Aubade',
which begins

Hours before dawn we were woken by the quake.

Louis MacNeice, at about the same time, was giving the same title to his poem about waking from the illusory comfort of the thirties to the realities of Czechoslovakia and Poland.

> Having bitten on life like a sharp apple
> Or, playing it like a fish, been happy,
>
> Having felt with fingers that the sky is blue,
> What have we after that to look forward to?
>
> Not the twilight of the gods but a precise dawn
> Of sallow and grey bricks, and newsboys crying war.

The title of that poem – 'Aubade' – is only one word long, but it works harder than any other single word even in this characteristic specimen of MacNeice's terse lyricism. It relates the poem to a whole system of resonances. Another example would be Hardy's triolet, 'At a Hasty Wedding'.

> If hours be years the twain are blest
> For now they solace swift desire
> By bonds of every bond the best,
> If hours be years. The twain are blest
> Do eastern stars slope never west,
> Nor pallid ashes follow fire:
> If hours be years the twain are blest,
> For now they solace swift desire.

The triolet is so much associated with carefree, light emotions that Hardy's gleeful grimness peers through it with far more effect than would have been possible with a 'straight' choice of form. It is, I suppose, superfluous to point out the brilliant touches of detail; a line like 'By bonds of every bond the best', which is exactly in the vein of the medieval triolet as domesticated in Victorian English poetry, is a plank leading to the cold-water splash of 'If hours be years' (but they aren't). The poem's ominous note, conveying clearly that these two imprudent people are preparing many years of unhappiness for one

another, sounds so clearly because of the tension between the
wedding-cake prettiness of the form and the dourness of the con-
tent. 'Escape from' form and you escape from all such pos-
sibilities.

This is not meant to be an exhaustive list of the possibilities
of form, but even in such a rapid canter it would be fatal to leave
out the simple bedrock use: form as mimesis. This is so obvious
(everyone knows that the manner of a piece of writing must to
some extent mimic the matter, so that one doesn't express a
funereal lament in perky jog-trot rhythms or produce the verbal
equivalent of trying to do a Cossack dance to a pavane) that it
tends to sink out of sight. Yet how can we explain the perfection
of a poem like Chidiock Tichborne's 'Written the Night Before
His Execution' without pointing out the obvious, that the
prowling rhythm and echoing rhyme convey the sense of feet
pacing round a dungeon, and beyond that the intolerable con-
striction of death moving in on a healthy young life?

My prime of youth is but a frost of cares;
    My feast of joy is but a dish of pain;
My crop of corn is but a field of tares;
    And all my good is but vain hope of gain;
My life is fled, and yet I saw no sun;
And now I live, and now my life is done.

The spring is past, and yet it hath not sprung;
    The fruit is dead, and yet the leaves be green;
My youth is gone, and yet I am but young;
    I saw the world, and yet I was not seen;
My thread is cut, and yet it is not spun;
And now I live, and now my life is done.

I sought my death and found it in my womb,
    I looked for life, and saw it was a shade,
I trod the earth and knew it was my tomb,
    And now I die, and now I am but made:
The glass is full, and now my glass is run,
And now I live, and now my life is done.

The thought of mimesis brings with it, as of right, the thought of the dramatic. Most mimetic poems have at any rate a hint of attribution to a speaker. Take the brilliant pencil-sketch by Gwendolyn Brooks, 'We Real Cool'. It shows a group of delinquents in a pool-room.

We real cool. We
Left school. We

Lurk late. We
Strike straight. We

Sing sin. We
Thin gin. We

Jazz June. We
Die soon.

The pared-down vocabulary, echoing in rhyme as the click of the plastic balls echoes in the pool-room and as the frustrated young lives echo in the empty spaces of the city, conveys the in-articulateness of the young people, their narrow, thwarted violence. The result is a perfect marriage of form to content: dramatic, though not striking one directly as 'dramatic' because the dramatic element is perfectly organized into the whole.

When the dramatic element does take command, it does so either for conspicuous good or conspicuous ill. Those Victorian 'dramatic monologues', especially Browning's, which read like too-long speeches excerpted from an unwritten play, are un-dramatic in themselves and help to suggest reasons for the failure of Victorian closet-drama. The dramatic, in or out of poetry, is a matter of concreteness, of sharply focused time and place: nothing is dramatic that does not happen in a definable here and now:

Mark but this flea, and mark in this
How little that which thou deniest me, is.

In 'Sailing to Byzantium' Yeats has the old artist, seeking refuge

from the 'breathing human passion' as did Keats once, come
onstage with a gesture towards the land he has left behind:

That is no country for old men.

To begin so abruptly with 'That' is an effective way of begin-
ning the poem on a dramatic trajectory; he is placing both
himself and the country he has left, and, for that matter, the holy
city he has come *to*. Thereafter we see him looking round in
awestruck wonder and love at the city which is to be his life, his
justification and his element, taking into his possession all its
splendours.

O sages standing in God's holy fire
As in the gold mosaic of a wall,
Come from the holy fire, perne in a gyre,
And be the singing-masters of my soul.

This is dramatic, dramatic through and through with never a
dab of greasepaint. The only thing that comes near it is that
other soliloquy of an old man, 'Gerontion', which conveys so
perfectly the play of memory in a fading mind. (Fraülein von
Kulp, who paused in the hall, one hand on the door, is more
vivid than some characters who have had whole plays written
about them.) And that poem, too, speaks largely through its
form. Eliot managed to write a soliloquy in Jacobean blank verse
without suggesting any one specific Jacobean dramatist.

So far, I have been speaking of form as a signalling system
between the poet and his audience. So it is, but it is also an im-
portant channel of life-giving communication between one poet
and another. When one poet learns from another we call the
result an 'influence'. Sooner or later everyone who talks about
any art finds himself talking about influences, from the most
profound scholar to the cub reporter who comes round to inter-
view a writer and asks him which of his contemporaries has in-
fluenced him. So we should not be too proud to go along with
this universal practice. And as soon as we reflect on it we see
that the influence of one writer on another is always a matter of

form, whether there is an influence of theme and attitude or not. So that, in a literature which denies itself a variety and abundance of forms, it is that much harder for one poet to set another's bell ringing.

I distinguish three kinds of influence. First, the openly proclaimed influence, the conscious imitation of an original which has high prestige in the tradition ('Look at me writing like Aeschylus') or high cash-value among the populace ('Look at me writing like Ian Fleming'). Second, the sheer technical helpfulness of one writer's work to another. Literature is a difficult art, and one is often groping for an effect without being certain how to attain it; if, at such a point, one has the luck to come across another writer who has achieved the objective, his procedures can be assimilated to one's own idiom. Third, unconscious influence born of ignorance. Every writer is influenced by somebody; language is a social medium, learnt initially by listening to others and copying them; and, though a writer may attain originality in greater or less degree, he never starts with it. On the other hand, if he has no knowledge of the art of literature and no range of reading, he will be influenced by what is nearest to hand without even knowing that it is an influence. (A hundred years ago every English journalist tried to write like Macaulay, including the young novice trying to get into print in the village paper who had never heard of Macaulay and was simply trying to write in the way that was expected of him.)

The first category of influence – the proudly proclaimed reproduction of the style of some admired master – is to be seen everywhere and at all times. When the master's prestige is high enough, merely to reproduce the same effects is praise enough. There are poets writing today in English who would be nothing but flattered to be told that they had succeeded in imitating Mayakovsky or Paz or Neruda; and surely the young Stephen Spender would have felt the same if told that he wrote like Rilke.

When the language of the lofty model is very far removed from the language of the imitation, we often find a blend of the first and second kinds of influence. A. E. Housman, for instance, wanted to reproduce the lyrical terseness of Horace, that blend of lucidity and density; he succeeded, partly no doubt by direct imitation of Horace but also with the aid of the poems of R. L. Stevenson and, confessedly, Samuel Johnson's *jeu d'esprit*, 'Long Awaited One and Twenty'. Another example of this two-stage influence, more interesting still because it involves two languages other than English, comes to mind when we invoke the honoured name of Milton. When Milton set out to write an epic poem, he wanted to remind the reader of Virgil and to some extent also of Homer. (Influence, first category.) But, in his long search for a style that would achieve this, he got the most practical help from Italian literature. Certainly there are other elements in the finished style – direct imitation of his Classical models, instinctive prompting from the genius of the English language, probably some help from an English epic tradition running through Spenser – but the electric starter which made his own engine begin turning over was the Italian example: Tasso in the theory of *Discorsi del Poema Eroica* and the practice of the *Gerusalemme Liberata*, and behind Tasso the experimental sonnets of Della Casa, and Bembo's critical *Prose della Volgar Lingua*. All this was finely expounded twenty years ago by F. T. Prince in *The Italian Element in Milton's Verse*, a beautiful book and a show-case example of how to analyse the effects of a learned poet. Not only does Mr Prince indicate with delicacy and precision exactly what techniques Milton took from the Italian poems that were in front of him, he also distinguishes between the help Milton received from poetic practice and the help he received from critical discussion. In the case of the sonnet, Italian poets had already achieved perfection, and there were many masterly examples for Milton to follow; but, in the more important case of the epic, the theory had been elaborated but the greatest work had still to come; it did not arrive till the eighteenth century, with Parini's *Il Giorno*. But, Mr Prince adds,

> this eighteenth-century achievement, and the admirable blank verse of the Romantic period which followed it, had itself been prepared for by the experiments of the

Cinquecento: Milton in England did but develop the Italian epic tradition as it might well have been developed in Italy itself in the seventeenth century, had it not been for the failure of creative power which then came to Italian literature.

I find this an inspiriting thought. It is so perfect an example of how the torch of great art can be passed from one nation to another, just as long as there are original artists willing to take the trouble and undergo the discipline. By making himself so completely familiar with the Italian humanist discussion of what a modern epic could be like, Milton was in a position to put these hopeful theories into practice before the Italians themselves did so. (I am accepting Prince's account here, but I do not think it has been challenged.) It also seems to be wise to admit that there are some phenomena that literary history cannot explain. Prince makes no attempt to explain *why* 'a failure of creative power . . . came to Italian literature' in the seventeenth century. It just came, like the sudden access of power which came to English literature at the end of the sixteenth century, an epoch not notable for good writing until the sudden blaze of glory in the 1580s. There may well be social reasons for these phenomena, much as undersea earthquakes cause tidal waves; but it is not necessarily the business of the literary critic to find them. What does necessarily concern the critic is the impressive way in which power flows through the forms, so that to study them is to plug oneself into a source of imaginative strength. Great poetry results when the poet who receives this strength is able to match it with his own native vitality. Neither will do without the other. At certain times in the past, too many poets have relied too much on the vitality of the forms and been unable to match it with vitality of their own; today, too many poets ignore the latent vitality in form and try to get by on their own vitality alone.

How did this come about? Given the variety of strengths and advantages that the strategic use of form can give the poet, how did the whole notion come to be thrown aside? For thrown

aside, very obviously, it has been. The result is a poetry heavily
under one single influence, the influence of prose. Literary
history can show us, in many languages, examples of prose in-
fluenced by verse; with English poetry, at the moment, it is the
other way round. Since it is not given to any human artist to be
so original that he breaks free of *all* influences and still remains
an artist, a poet who throws away all the aids designed for him
by his predecessors in poetry ends up leaning on one crutch
alone, the crutch of prose. I was forcibly reminded of this when
reading the issue of *Encounter* for August 1973. 'R', in his
column, was engaged in bestowing high praise on a new book by
D. J. Enright, *The Terrible Shears*, poems recalling his boyhood
in Leamington during the thirties. High as it is, I am sure R's
praise for this book is merited ('irony and wit are at one with
deep feeling, and a highly complex and sophisticated personality
finds expression in a deceptively natural and simple language' –
personally I would outlaw 'deceptive' as a critical term, but still).
The passages quoted, however, are interesting for our present
discussion because of their complete abandonment of any verse-
technique at all – except, of course, for the chopping-up which
makes it look like verse to the eye. The first of R's extracts,
taken out of a connected sequence, reads:

> The wife of a teacher at school (she was
> Mother of one of my classmates) was
> Genuinely enraged when I won a scholarship.
> She stopped me in the street, to tell me
> (With a loudness I supposed was upper-class)
> That Cambridge was not for the likes of me, nor was
> Long hair, nor the verse I wrote for the school mag.
>
> Her sentiments were precisely those of the
> Working class. Unanimity on basic questions
> Accounts for why we never had the revolution.

Of course this is highly effective writing – Mr Enright is too
professional a writer to blur or stutter, and always makes his
points with satisfying neatness. But the question I cannot

repress when I read verse like this, or like the poems in R. S. Thomas's recent collection *H'm*, is: why is this in verse? Or, more precisely, since it so obviously isn't in verse, why is it offered as such? After all, there is nothing to be ashamed of in writing prose, especially when one writes it as well as Mr Enright or Mr Thomas. But is that really what the art of poetry has come down to – a typographic convention, allowing a certain kind of essayist to be classified as a poet?

'Somehow', 'R' goes on, 'Mr Enright has managed to combine a flat Midlands accent with rhythms of an almost Chinese subtlety.' With due respect, I don't believe it. If the book did not happen to be concerned with Leamington I don't believe 'R' would have detected a Midland accent in it and, as for the bit about almost Chinese subtlety, it means nothing without some supporting demonstration that 'R' knows what the rhythms of Chinese poetry are. (From what period? What region?) Perhaps it is time we all came off it and decided to call verse verse and prose prose.

R. S. Thomas, by the way, is a particularly depressing example of the damage caused to a poet's work by the flight from form; his subject-matter has always been rather lowering (depopulation of the countryside, depopulation of the human heart through the decay of beliefs, etc.). But there was a time when the depressing nature of what Mr Thomas conveyed was irradiated and made bearable by his beautiful sense of rhythm and sound. The poems in *H'm* offer no such consolation. Here is one of them, 'Via Negativa':

> Why no! I never thought other than
> That God is that great absence
> In our lives, the empty silence
> Within, the place where we go
> Seeking, not in hope to
> Arrive or find. He keeps the interstices
> In our knowledge, the darkness
> Between stars. His are the echoes
> We follow, the footprints he has just
> Left. We put our hands in

His side hoping to find
It warm. We look at people
And places as though he had looked
At them, too; but miss the reflection.

This is undeniably a fine poem. A fine piece of writing, on se-
cond thoughts. And that is always something to be grateful for,
in our rubbish-clogged age. But – to say the least – the lowered,
daunted quality of the subject-matter is matched by the same
characteristics in the expression. Why complain? Isn't that what
writing is all about – getting the two in line?

Not quite. There is a contrapuntal quality about most good
writing, a creative tension between opposites, that is itself an
important element in the 'meaning' to be communicated. In the
days when Mr Thomas made graceful, lyrical poems about being
daunted, he was telling us that the negative experience was
being contained in a mind, and expressed by a sensibility, that
was reaching beyond, attaining something positive. Perhaps, in
the deep night that now faces the faltering human race, this at-
titude should be given up. But, in that case, so will the very idea
of art. Because art has always sought to contain chaos and
failure in a tensile web of the ordered and the achieved.

In the modern arts, as has often been remarked, novelty is
the uncomfortable norm. That this has led to a flight from
the formal vessels associated with a tradition is therefore
not surprising. But that flight, which has now reached its
ultimate boundary and has brought us to the verge of non-
communication, will, unless it changes direction, take us out of
art altogether. Is this what we want?

In some quarters, the answer would probably be Yes. That
corruption of the democratic ideal which asserts as a dogma that
what all can't attain no one must – a corruption that would
make high achievement impossible in physics as in politics, in
basketball as in cooking, in engineering as in acting – infallibly
leads to an impatient dismissal of craftsmanship and knowledge
as 'élitism'. Not thinking so ill of democracy, which has always
seemed to me a noble ideal, I cannot see why it should not be

part of the richness of human life that many, or most, skills and
crafts should be within the reach only of people who were born
with a gift and have laboured to develop that gift. One can, of
course, imagine a bad élite, an élite based on privilege and
money, admitting no one to its ranks who had not been to the
right schools and been elected to the right clubs. This élite
would be bad because it would exclude people of imagination and
integrity, on irrelevant grounds, and thus impoverish itself;
and, if it were in a dominant position within the culture, would
impoverish the whole culture. But I can see nothing wrong with
a élite that can be joined by anyone who is prepared to do his
homework, take trouble, be self-critical. The tragedy of our pre-
sent situation is that gifted young artists are being ruined by the
all-pervading impression that art is easy. I once had a letter from
a youth, enclosing a sheaf of his poems for criticism, in which he
informed me that he had decided to go in for poetry as a career
because it was, as far as he could see, the easiest thing to make a
reputation at. This unfortunate lad was probably no loss to the
world of literature, but in his simple way he reflected an attitude
that is doing harm to genuinely gifted people.

On a more positive note: since I have named two contem-
porary poets who to my way of thinking do not, despite their
splendid gifts, make a satisfactory amalgam of form with con-
tent, it is right that I should if possible name two who do. First,
Philip Larkin. The delicacy of Mr Larkin's eye and ear for form
is something I hope to demonstrate in the lecture I intend to
give on his work, the next in my series. Next, John Heath-
Stubbs. Mr Heath-Stubbs is a contrasting type. Squarely within
the poetic tradition of the learned man who makes use of his
learning, he makes of his poetry a coat of many colours, and the
reader's response is enriched by − though never totally depen-
dent on − the range of these colours he is able to recognize and
trace to their source. His epic poem *Artorius* (1973) draws to
one centre a wide spread of references and a wide range of styles.
In the course of it he modulates from alliterative verse to rhymed
lyrics to decasyllabics to prose to the formal ode. The main
burden of the narrative is borne by a loosened blank verse which

I would trace to the Arthurian poems of Charles Williams; but virtually every age of English poetry is laid under contribution, and the result is a poem entirely of the 1970s, since all the elements have been simmered in the cauldron of the poet's imagination and his life is lived in the here and now.

These two examples, one that I glance at here and one that I reserve for a fuller treatment later, may give us heart. For a full and creative use of form will not come back unless form is conceived of as something vital, a source of strength, of subtlety, of awareness. Sixty years ago there was every reason for taking the contrary attitude. The generation of great artists who came to maturity in the years about 1914 – the generation of Picasso, of Gertrude Stein, of Stravinsky, of Pound – had all been born and brought up in the Victorian era, when children were seen and not heard. Any form of self-expression had been rigorously denied them by the prevailing *mores* of their society. The result was an urgent need for liberation from social and aesthetic restraints. Putting such a high value on self-expression, they made it the backbone of their work, becoming the great self-expressers of all time. (Eliot's continually proffered theory of objectivity concealed from his admirers, for thirty years, the basically idiosyncratic and personal nature of his work. The others scarcely tried to conceal it; more often, they gloried in it.) But no artist now living can remember a time when self-expression had to be won at such cost. Our memories are of flux and transience.

In conclusion, it seems to me possible that the throwing away of form in contemporary poetry and the arts generally is the result partly of that jelly-bellied democratization (in a mass society, only the lowest level of finesse is acceptable) and partly of sheer mental confusion. The birth of modern art was attended by an impulse to escape from form, so its maturity must be true to the same impulse. The implications are not thought out. How, otherwise, can we explain the pitiful arguments brought forward to justify shapeless and sinewless expression? Take, as a concrete example, the frequently voiced opinion that traditional rhythmic patterns (the 'iambic', for instance) are no longer true

to the way the language actually flows on people's tongues. We
can't write iambics because people don't speak them any more.
This fallacy can be nailed simply by keeping one's ears open.
Here are three of the scores of perfectly formed iambic pen-
tameters I heard uttered in ordinary speech during a couple of
days' listening out:

Two men speaking of a third: *You never know with Harry, what
he'll do.*

Mother to child: *Your face is dirty. Do you ever wash?*

Journalist, interviewing politician on the radio: *How would you
like to see the system changed?*

Nor is the iambic the only one. All the metrical patterns that
have served poets faithfully are still serving ordinary speakers.
The rhythms of the Anglo-Saxon alliterative metre are so per-
vasive that one cannot talk in English for two minutes without
running through the whole repertory of them. And rhythms from
outside English, such as the Alexandrine and the hexameter, are
very apt to occur in speech. W. H. Auden's last collection,
Thank You, Fog, contains interesting evidence that, having gone
along for some years with the idea of shuffling prose-influenced
verse, he was becoming drawn to the rhythms of Latin poetry;
there are poems that seem lightly based on the hexameter, and
there are one or two direct forays into the Ovidian elegiac
couplet, pentameter and hexameter – for instance:

> Policy ought to conform to Liberty, Law and Compassion
> But, as a rule It obeys Selfishness, Vanity, Funk.

Auden was always alert to the rhythms of the spoken
language, an alertness probably forced on him by his change of
habitat in early middle life. And anyone who listens to the
spoken language will see where the Classical metres, and all
other metres, came from. A few minutes before coming out to
deliver this lecture, I was in my study hunting for a letter I had
mislaid, and called to my wife, 'There isn't a cache of letters that
I don't know about, is there?' Which is a hexameter, though the
fact would probably not be noticed if we were not playing the

metre game. So much for the idea that the more unformed one's verse is, the more it fails to rise to any strong rhythmical pattern, the more it resembles 'living speech'. A selection from the real language of men is always, among other things, a selection of prosody.

The painter Victor Neep, who like most painters has to do a certain amount of teaching to make ends meet, went in to his class one day and was greeted by one of the students with 'We've been discussing it and we've decided that no painting is worth anything that doesn't make its protest.' 'Exactly,' said Mr Neep without hesitation. 'Like – *that*,' and he pointed to a still-life of some apples by Cézanne. 'What's that protesting about?' asked the student. 'Sloppy thinking,' replied Mr Neep.

*

That anecdote about Victor Neep reminds me of how much deep nourishment I have drawn from personal contact with artists of every kind, writers, painters, composers. Without for a moment undervaluing all those people who love and follow the arts without being tempted to make a contribution to them – the encouraging, discussing, cash-paying public without whom the whole caravan of the arts would be frozen into immobility in an instant – the real vibration comes from those who face the endlessly renewed challenge of making something exist where nothing existed before. Even in a free society where no slit-eyed commissar is going to vet your work for political heresy, it takes a certain amount of courage to be an artist; at the very least, it means accepting insecurity and also being a target for endless criticism, some of it very wounding; and I know that in my own life that courage would have failed, many a time, but for the companionship of people who had made the same decision, who spend their lives *making* things.

This, of course, is what draws young artists into the cities. High rents, bad food, lack of peace for working are easily outweighed by the mere presence of fellow-artists actual and poten-

tial; yes, even the phonies, the burnt-out cases, the camp-
followers are better soil for the seeds than those communities
where there is not a single person who has produced a work of
art and precious few would recognize it if he did.

It is also the reason for the movement outwards of artists in
early middle life. The general pattern seems to be a few years in
the capital city, the gathering of a circle of friends, enemies and
alliances; then the move to quieter surroundings, cleaner air,
more peace and quiet for concentration. After all, once you have
friends among your fellow-artists, you can always ask them
down for the week-end.

In my case, Oxford took the place of the metropolis. Though I
am grateful for what London has done for me, and still does, it is
nevertheless true that London has always been more on the
periphery of my life than in the centre. Oxford claimed me very
young. When I was a Sixth-Former, in the middle of the war, we
were always told that we must get admission to university as
soon as we possibly could, so that we would be sure of a place
after returning from war service. Accordingly, I fixed up to enter
St John's College in 1943, when I was seventeen. A few weeks
after arriving there, I took my medical and was turned down for
defective eyesight. This left me in a by-term (I had gone up in
January), a full year younger than I ought to have been as a
freshman, and generally at sixes and sevens. It turned out,
however, that all this was a blessing in disguise. If I had waited
till the autumn of 1943 to enter Oxford, I should never have met
two men whose example has made an enormous difference to my
life. I should say whose two very different examples, for Philip
Larkin and John Heath-Stubbs resemble each other only in their
dedication as poets, their consummate craftsmanship. I have
described elsewhere (in *Sprightly Running*) my personal impres-
sion at that time of Larkin and Heath-Stubbs. Both have
remained very important to me; and, since both went down at
the end of June 1943, and for some years thereafter were seldom
seen in Oxford, I might never have met either of them but for
my premature arrival on the academic scene. (Not that the
'meeting' was in any sense a meeting of minds, since I had

nothing but tongue-tied admiration. Still, we were introduced.)

Deeply as I admire Heath-Stubbs's work, with its incantatory power and its restless search for material in myth, legend and history, it is Larkin's that has involved me the more personally. It is he, plainly, who must be the subject of my next lecture on a living poet. So, amid the first buds of spring, I go along to Brasenose hall and pay my tribute.

THE POETRY OF PHILIP LARKIN

Let us begin by looking attentively at one of Mr Larkin's poems – not 'a typical poem', since his range is too wide to allow of such a thing, but one whose texture and tempo will give us some idea of what kind of poet we are dealing with. For this purpose it is better to avoid the brilliant show-pieces and pick out an unspectacular success; 'How Distant', for example, from the most recent volume.

How Distant

How distant, the departure of young men
Down valleys, or watching
The green shore past the salt-white cordage
Rising and falling,

Cattlemen, or carpenters, or keen
Simply to get away
From married villages before morning,
Melodeons play

On tiny decks past fraying cliffs of water
Or late at night
Sweet under the differently-swung stars,
When the chance sight

Of a girl doing her laundry in the steerage
Ramifies endlessly.
This is being young,
Assumption of the startled century

Like new store clothes
The huge decisions printed out by feet
Inventing where they tread,
The random windows conjuring a street.

The subject of this poem is emigration. That, at least, is the
take-it-or-leave-it description. During those years − 1870 to
1910, say − when so many people left the British Isles to settle in
the vast and still-empty spaces of America and Australia, what
did it feel like to be one of them? And especially to be one of the
young men, dissatisfied with the little of life that had gone by,
full of large imprecise hopes for the much that remained,
sometimes purposeful, sometimes merely slipping away from a
strangling environment? 'Married villages' is an expression
typical of Larkin's sharply focused economy of language: in
those villages, every relationship was fixed; everybody was
somebody's father, mother, cousin, bride, sweetheart, friend or
enemy, with no room for those tangential and evanescent
relationships that the young need. Another Larkinian feature
(though all these things are features of good poetry, generally, no
doubt) is the precise and telling selection of physical detail − the
tiny decks, the fraying cliffs of water, the salt-white cordage; the
experience of a long voyage by sailing-ship, or sail-assisted
steamship, is brought home in a way that would take a novelist
ten pages, to say which is no disrespect to the novelist.

But the poem has a wider subject than 'what was it like to be
an emigrant?' and that is − once again, in a take-it-or-leave-it
description − the nature of an epoch. It is a historical poem.
That time when anyone who could scrape up a few pounds could
emigrate without passport and visa, those days when huge new
territories were waiting to be explored, lived in and domesti-
cated (one thinks of Louis Simpson's line 'And grave by
grave to civilize the ground') are now as remote from us as the
top-hat and the hansom cab, which is the reason for the poem's
title. These far-off people, seen as in a sepia photograph, are
making a world, though to themselves they are only getting on
with their lives. Hence 'The huge decisions printed out by

feet/Inventing where they tread'. (Try saying as much as that, or half as much, in as few syllables.) People arrive in a place, be it Borroloola, Northern Territory, or Deadwood, South Dakota, and put up a few houses; then a few more; then another and another. To themselves, they are just making houses to give the new arrivals a roof over their heads; they put in windows where it suits them to put them in; but to the next generation, growing up, that is the village street, immutable, one with the natural order of things, not to be changed without a pang. It has been 'conjured' with the same unconscious power that has 'printed out' the huge decisions that underpin a civilization.

I apologize for the ponderous shredding-out of this beautifully lucid poem; my excuse must be the monumental thick-headedness with which Larkin's poetry is so often approached; there is no explanation, however otiose, that is not needed by *somebody*.

In any case, it is as well to get on to terms from the beginning with the fact that the main thrust of Larkin's poetry is towards an increase of consciousness. These facts, this situation, which we have for so long 'known' in the sense that we have carried their dimensions in our heads – what are they like when seen from the inside? What would it be like not merely to 'know' these things but to possess them, to *understand* them, to perceive their *haecceitas*? So often, Larkin takes a situation we have all experienced, or might perfectly well have experienced, and by his luminous meditation and sharply lyrical language makes us possess it in its fullness. For instance, the experience of listening to a concert on the radio, and knowing that among the audience is someone you love, so that the applause evokes as much feeling in you as the music. A commonplace experience, though not one that seems to have inspired a poet before; but there is nothing commonplace in the imaginative delicacy that Larkin brings to it.

Broadcast

Giant whispering and coughing from
Vast Sunday-full and organ-frowned-on spaces

Precede a sudden scuttle on the drum,
'The Queen', and huge resettling. Then begins
A snivel on the violins:
I think of your face among all those faces,

Beautiful and devout before
Cascades of monumental slithering,
One of your gloves unnoticed on the floor
Beside those new, slightly-outmoded shoes.
Here it goes quickly dark. I lose
All but the outline of the still and withering

Leaves on half-emptied trees. Behind
The glowing wavebands, rabid storms of chording
By being distant overpower my mind
All the more shamelessly, their cut-off shout
Leaving me desperate to pick out
Your hands, tiny in all that air, applauding.

This poem has no simple subject, any more than 'How Distant' has, but it is certainly, among other things, a love poem. Larkin has no poem that could be described as erotic, but the theme of sexual love appears often in his work, and his restrained, almost glancing treatment is often more moving than the full-frontal treatment of those who come on strong as erotic poets.

The difficulty of saying what Larkin writes 'about' will by now have become apparent. Still, we shall hardly get a grip on his poetry unless we succeed in bringing into relief its principal themes. One of these is certainly choice, the act of choosing. I would not expect Larkin's poetry to be popular – or, more accurately, permitted to be popular – in a totalitarian country whose citizens have no alternatives but to work, fight, breed and cheer the Leader. But in the still-free parts of the world, to the extent that they are still free, the individual is constantly being faced with choices, and these choices, large and small, add up to the large multiple act of choice that we call a life-style. Choice of a life-style is one of Philip Larkin's recurrent themes. What kind of person am I, and how is my kind of person best fulfilled and expressed in how I live? All life, from trivialities to grave momentous decisions, finds itself included in this collective choice, for 'how we live measures our own nature'. Very often, the poet compares his life-style with that of others; sometimes the others are people who seem to reap all the advantages of life with very little effort or sacrifice, even such effort and sacrifice as is exacted by 'the toad Work':

> Lots of folk live on their wits:
> Lecturers, lispers,
> Losels, loblolly-men, louts –
> They don't end as paupers.
>
> Lots of folk live up lanes
> With fires in a bucket,
> Eat windfalls and tinned sardines –
> They seem to like it.

At other times the compared life-style is, on the surface, more generous, more responsive to others' needs – but is it really so? Arnold, the much-married man whose spare time and spare cash are remorselessly swallowed into the maw of domesticity, seems a paragon – 'To compare his life with mine/Makes me feel a swine' – still, even Arnold

> . . . was out for his own ends
> Not just pleasing his friends;
>
> And if it was such a mistake
> He still did it for his own sake,
> Playing his own game.
> So he and I are the same,
>
> Only I'm a better hand
> At knowing what I can stand
> Without them sending a van –
> Or I suppose I can.

One way or another, the life-style is chosen; and, within it, the poet still worries away at the theme. How was the choice arrived at? Did 'I' choose? And, if so, with what elements in my personality? The poem 'Dockery and Son', which opens so amusingly, moves through the heart of this perplexing question and finishes with sober daunting reflections.

> ... To have no son, no wife,
> No house or land still seemed quite natural.
> Only a numbness registered the shock
> Of finding out how much had gone of life,
> How widely from the others. Dockery, now:
> Only nineteen, he must have taken stock
> Of what he wanted, and been capable
> Of ... No, that's not the difference: rather, how
>
> Convinced he was he should be added to!
> Why did he think adding meant increase?
> To me it was dilution. Where do these
> Innate assumptions come from? Not from what
> We think truest, or most want to do:
> Those warp tight-shut, like doors. They're more a style
> Our lives bring with them: habit for a while,
> Suddenly they harden into all we've got
>
> And how we got it; looked back on, they rear
> Like sand-clouds, thick and close, embodying
> For Dockery a son, for me nothing,
> Nothing with all a son's harsh patronage.
> Life is first boredom, then fear.
> Whether or not we use it, it goes,
> And leaves what something hidden from us chose,
> And age, and then the only end of age.

Still, the 'something hidden from us' has made its choice and thenceforward we have a life-style which we must labour to make workable. To do this involves fending off the uncomprehending criticism of people who see our life-style from outside – and also our own discouragement and self-undermining.

The blend is perfectly conveyed in 'Vers de Société' with its progression from the comic exasperation of the opening lines to the sombre reflections of the closing.

Another of Larkin's themes is history. He is a historical writer in the sense which I attach to the term, one who places in the forefront of his work the effect of time on individual lives. All thoughtful writers give this theme a place in their work, but the historical writer makes it specially prominent. The world is different from what it was when I was a schoolboy; I also am different; part of the difference in the world is the result of the passage of my generation through it; we have acted on the world and been acted on by it in an endless ramifying reciprocity. As the poet says,

> Truly, though our element is time,
> We are not suited to the long perspectives
> Open at each instant of our lives.

Here, as so often with a good poet, Larkin himself has found the words to describe one of his major themes: 'the long perspectives/Open at each instant of our lives'. It is the saturation of his work in this awareness that gives it its historical quality; among English writers, the one he most strongly recalls to me is Arnold Bennett (if this seems an odd judgment, reread 'Afternoon'), and Bennett's best novels owe their emotional and imaginative power to his compassionate sense of the ordinary human being trapped within time, and to his perception that a historical epoch is vested in individual human lives more than in stone or paint or clay or printed words; when John Baines the draper dies, mid-Victorian England dies with him:

> Mr Critchlow and the widow gazed, helplessly waiting, at the pitiable corpse, of which the salient part was the white beard. They knew not that they were gazing at a vanished era. John Baines had belonged to the past, to an age when men really did think of their souls, when orators by phrases could move crowds to fury or to pity, when no one had learnt to hurry, when Demos was only turning in his sleep,

when the sole beauty of life resided in its inflexible and
slow dignity, when hell really had no bottom, and a gilt-
clasped Bible really was the secret of England's greatness.
Mid-Victorian England lay on that mahogany bed. Ideals
had passed away with John Baines. It is thus that ideals
die; not in the conventional pageantry of honoured death,
but sorrily, ignobly, while one's head is turned.

Larkin has this same sense of the organic relationship of the
human being with 'our element', time. Sometimes he expresses it
in overtly historical poems like 'MCMXIV' or 'The Less
Deceived' with its theme from Mayhew. At other times an unob-
trusively placed detail will reveal that his imagination is playing
on a scene from the past. 'The Explosion' (one of his finest
poems, incidentally) is about a mining disaster, and this is a
possibility in any age that mines for coal; but the universality is
not diluted by the fact that the poem evidently refers to a world
that has now passed away. These are miners out of the world of
D. H. Lawrence's boyhood.

The Explosion

On the day of the explosion
Shadows pointed towards the pithead:
In the sun the slagheap slept.

Down the lane came men in pitboots
Coughing oath-edged talk and pipe-smoke,
Shouldering off the freshened silence.

One chased after rabbits; lost them;
Came back with a nest of lark's eggs;
Showed them; lodged them in the grasses.

So they passed in beards and moleskins,
Fathers, brothers, nicknames, laughter,
Through the tall gates standing open.

At noon, there came a tremor; cows
Stopped chewing for a second; sun,
Scarfed as in a heat-haze, dimmed.

The dead go on before us, they
Are sitting in God's house in comfort,
We shall see them face to face –

Plain as lettering in the chapels
It was said, and for a second
Wives saw men of the explosion

Larger than in life they managed –
Gold as on a coin, or walking
Somehow from the sun towards them,

One showing the eggs unbroken.

The sense of a historical setting is conveyed not only by surface details (modern working men don't wear moleskins; in 1900–14 they were conventional), but also by an interior illumination, a light switched on inside the object; the women hear the words of the memorial sermon 'plain as lettering in the chapels' – the inscriptions in nonconformist chapels, mostly gold on dark wood, have a special severe plainness like Victorian typefaces. Larkin picks out and focuses this kind of detail because he is imagining the situation intensely and identifying with these obsolete working-class women, not patronizing them or using them as a text for a sociological sermon.

A more overtly historical poem, a poem whose actual subject is the difference between epochs and their attitudes, is 'Posterity'. The *persona* of the research student who is writing a thesis on Larkin, Jake Balokowsy, typifies that world (already arrived, in great measure) in which Larkin's way of looking at the world will have become irrecoverably obsolete, only to be studied from the outside. The poem is ironic and funny but without bitterness; Jake Balokowsky is not a particularly unsympathetic figure; he has some ideal for which he is prepared to work and perhaps even suffer ('I wanted to teach school in Tel-Aviv'). Under the joking, a serious historical point is being made, and it is made with tolerance and understanding.

Since we have spoken of time and history, this may be the place for a glancing mention of Larkin as a satirist. He does not thrust forward as a satirist, any more than he thrusts forward as a 'love poet', but the element is there, unobtrusively but powerfully. Only two of his poems that I can think of are straight satiric pieces — 'Naturally the Foundation Will Bear Your Expenses' and 'Homage to a Government'. Both, not surprisingly in view of Larkin's general stance, are aimed at opinions and attitudes associated with trendy academia and the *New Statesman* left. (Notice, in the former poem, the cool effrontery of the pronunciation of 'Berkeley'.) Not unnaturally, people who share these attitudes are quick to dismiss both poems as marginal and unsuccessful; to some of us, they seem highly effective and all the more welcome because they attack positions which are very much mandatory within a powerful in-group. Who, within that group, would think it anything but a reactionary folly to maintain 'a military presence' in far-flung parts of the earth? Or anything but a salutary expedience to cut defence budgets and spend the money on the Welfare State? As for the statues in the square, which are mostly of generals and statesmen, who that cared for his progressive reputation could use them as in any way a yardstick of England's deterioration? Larkin does so use them, signalling here as elsewhere his quiet independence of fashion; 'Homage to a Government' is remarkable not only for that independence but for the superb tailoring of form to content. The poem is clinker-built; its timbers are designed to overlap. Each six-line stanza has three rhyme-words, each repeated twice, closing in to a tight centre and then opening out: *Home – right – orderly – orderly – right – home.* The purpose of the poem is to convey disapproval and contempt; the self-enclosed pettiness and lack of imagination, which the poet sees in the government he is satirizing, have got into the texture of the verse; it enacts its content.

Satire, of course, is a matter of positive and negative; when a

poet writes satire, he does so because, in the immediate matter
in hand, he feels confident that he is right and the people he is
satirizing are wrong; this in turn means that most satirists con-
cern themselves with relatively small-scale issues, or at least
limited, concrete ones, usually matters of political and social
procedure. At the other end of the scale lie those large, un-
answerable questions which shade into other questions and
others beyond that, questions at whose frontiers the satirist
halts. These, too, are within the range of Larkin's poetry; he is
as well able to make a poem out of what he doesn't know as out
of what he does. One is always apt to come up against this kind of
unanswerable question in any of Larkin's poems, as one does
in 'Dockery and Son'. One of the few that devote themselves
simply and solely to the topic of mystery, the permanent ques-
tion mark, is the brilliant and ungraspable 'Days':

> What are days for?
> Days are where we live.
> They come, they wake us
> Time and time over.
> They are to be happy in:
> Where can we live but days?
> Ah, solving that question
> Brings the priest and the doctor
> In their long coats,
> Running over the fields.

I call this poem ungraspable because, while perfectly clear as
to content, it is scarcely paraphrasable; it offers an image which
conveys a very clear metaphoric message, but (except by writing
many lines of diluting prose) it is not possible to put it into other
terms. All one can do is to describe the mental picture that the
poem gives one, a picture chillingly direct in its implications.
The substance of the poem is of course in the last four lines; the
first six are simply a launching-pad. What do the last four lines
make you see? To me, the picture is of a cluster of houses on the
outskirts of a village, where the street runs out into fields. It is
evening; the lights are just coming on; and in one of the houses

somebody is dying. Across the dusk-laden fields, two figures are approaching; they wear long overcoats and are bearded and side-whiskered like characters out of Chekhov or Alphonse Daudet; the doctor, I think, is a doctor of philosophy but he might conceivably be a physician. What gives my mental picture the obsessional character of a nightmare is that the two figures are *running*. If they were merely walking sedately towards the dying person's house, deep in consultation, the scene would be terrestrial; in fact, it is metaphysical.

So much, then, for a brief sketch of the range of Larkin's poetry, the kind of terrain it covers. As the range of content is wide, so is the range of form. He can, with unobtrusive skill, write virtually any kind of verse, from traditional to free. '*Vers de Société*' demonstrates what one wouldn't have thought possible, that the decasyllabic couplet, technically no different from that which we find in the narrative poems of Leigh Hunt and Keats, can be handled today with freshness and vigour; while the free verse of poem like 'Days' is free without wilting; it has a backbone. (If I had to describe the prosody of 'Days', I should say that each line is like one-half of a classic Anglo-Saxon alliterative line, with two heavy stresses surrounded by a variable number of light syllables. It is free verse written by a poet who, however he may have since forgotten it, at one time knew enough Anglo-Saxon to read *Beowulf*. Larkin's rhymes are a study in themselves; according to the needs of the moment, he can make them precise ('Cut Grass') or off-rhymes of the kind pioneered, I suppose, by Wilfred Owen. Usually, though not always, he uses off-rhymes in the poems that have some ironic or satirical overtones; they are ideal for a rueful-funny effect:

> For something sufficiently toad-like
>> Squats in me, too;
> Its hunkers are heavy as hard luck
>> And cold as snow. . . .

Hard luck and *toad-like* is a beautiful off-rhyme; so, in a more restrained, straight-faced way, is *lives* and *perspectives* in the

passage about time I quoted a little earlier; a rhyme can be dis-
tanced, muffled, by being moved slightly away from its fellow
either in sound or in rhythm. One poem, 'The Building', uses
rhyme in a delicately cadenced but unstructured pattern; each
seven-line stanza has rhymes which make it chime and cohere,
but the rhymes do not occur in the same places. Etc., etc. The
delight in form, the supple finesse with which form is adapted to
matter are endless; the texture of the poetry changes as restlessly
and subtly· as the marks made by the wind on a calm sea or a
field of corn. Is there a rhythm that other poets have long since
thrown aside? Larkin is just as likely to pick it up, if it suits a
particular poem. 'The Explosion' is written in the rhythm of
Hiawatha, after which one can hardly be surprised at anything.

   What else is there to say, that might lead people towards an
appreciation of this quiet, strong, piercingly perceptive verse?
(Not that they don't appreciate it already, if the sales figures are
anything to go by; one of the few really encouraging signs in the
present-day literary scene.) Would it help to point to his
recurrent images? Like most poets, he has a mild obsession with
certain images that recur again and again; anything to do with
water (the middle panel of the triptych 'Livings' must surely be
the best verbal description of the sea in recent poetry); the bride,
a very important symbol; perhaps above all, trees. Larkin's
image for contentment and repose seems to be trees seen through a
window ('The gas fire breathes, the trees are darkly swayed'),
though sometimes this sight underlines a restless tension, as in
'Broadcast', and in 'Going', the poem that seeks to imagine the
human consciousness at the point of death, the tree seems to
represent nothing less than life itself.

   Where has the tree gone, that locked
   Earth to the sky?

And in Larkin's novel, *Jill*, when the central character lies in a
fever, the trees outside the window echo his delirium and
perhaps re-enact the invasion of reality by fantasy, the severance
of the normal links with experience, that make up the book's

theme:

> He was watching the trees, the tops of which he could just
> see through the window. They tossed and tossed, reckless-
> ly. He saw them fling this way and that, throwing up their
> heads like impatient horses, like sea waves, bending and
> recovering in the wind. They had no leaves. Endlessly, this
> way and that, they were buffeted and still bore up again to
> their full height. They seemed tireless. Sometimes they
> were bent so low that they passed out of sight, leaving the
> square of white sky free for a second, but then they would
> be back again, clashing their proud branches together like
> the antlers of furious stags.

Mention of *Jill* reminds one what an accomplished writer
Larkin already was in his undergraduate days. When I first
knew him in wartime Oxford, he was working on two books at
once, besides studying English literature effectively enough to
get a First in the Schools: *Jill*, and the collection of poems
published in 1945 as *The North Ship*. Both have been re-issued
and both will stand, and better than stand, rereading. The hero
of *Jill*, a working-class boy who has been dragooned into taking
examinations and winning scholarships largely to gratify the am-
bition of his careerist schoolmaster, is pitchforked into the
Oxford of 1940, finds himself entirely unable to adjust, and
retreats into a fantasy life and thence, finally, into anarchic
behaviour and illness. The initial fantasy is that he has a sister
called Jill who is away at school in Yorkshire; he begins a cor-
respondence with her, writing both sides of it, of course, and
then, finding this insufficient to round out his imaginative por-
trait, writes about five thousand words of Jill's diary, im-
aginatively living her school life from day to day. In 1943, it had
leaked out that Larkin was engaged on this part of his novel;
sources close to him reported with amused awe that 'Philip's
writing a schoolgirl's diary.' This seemed right; it had the cor-
rect ring of decadence. (Young people like decadence in
literature; they take the line that there is enough wholesomeness
in real life without reading about it as well.) In fact, 'Jill's diary'

does reveal, even thus early, Larkin's Richardsonian gift for
illuminating the female mind from within, as he does in his only
other novel *A Girl in Winter* and to some extent in poems like
'Maiden Name', 'Love Songs in Age' and 'The Less Deceived'.

The chief reason why *Jill* maintains its importance, though, is
that it is Larkin's first treatment of a theme that has remained
constant with him — dream versus reality. Oddly enough, after
this first large-scale treatment, the subject retreats to a fairly in-
conspicuous place in Larkin's work over the next fifteen years
or so, re-emerging strongly in *The Whitsun Weddings* and *High
Windows*, where it is a major ingredient. The human being sees
experience in the mirror of dreams, and sorting out the objective
from the subjective has always been too much for most of us.
One of the most moving poems in *The Whitsun Weddings*,
'Essential Beauty', is about advertising: even the crude false coin
proffered by the ads can deceive us; even the visions we see at
solemn moments, such as the moment of death, might be the
cheap commercial mirage of 'the good life' we have seen on some
hoarding:

... There, dark raftered pubs
 Are filled with white-clothed ones from tennis-clubs,
 And the boy puking his heart out in the Gents
 Just missed them, as the pensioner paid
 A halfpenny more for Granny Graveclothes' Tea
 To taste old age, and dying smokers sense
 Walking towards them through some dappled park
 As if on water that unfocused she
 No match lit up, nor drag ever brought near,
 Who now stands newly clear,
 Smiling, and recognising, and going dark.

Another poem in that same collection to take up the theme is
'For Sidney Bechet'. This poem, which I have found by inquiry
to be opaque to people who (1) know nothing about jazz and (2)
do not remember the forties and early fifties, concerns not jazz
itself but the effect of jazz on the Anglo-Saxon middle-class
record buyers who, outside his immediate earshot, were the

public for a musician like Bechet. Such people found that his
music fed their dreams, those dreams which grew in the soil of
the Mississippi Delta as richly as the Western-addicts' dreams
grew in Texas and Nevada. In rapid, economically presented
array, the pardonable illusions pass in front of us, until – this
being, after all, an address from one artist to another – the poet
has to say what Bechet's music suggests to *him*; and the poem's
conclusion measures up nobly to the assignment:

> On me your voice falls as they say love should,
> Like an enormous yes. My Crescent City
> Is where your speech alone is understood,
>
> And greeted as the natural noise of good,
> Scattering long-haired grief and scored pity.

The last line repays attention, not only rhythmically but for
the neatly stacked multiple meanings in the words: the jazzman
of the 1930s and 1940s referred to his classical confrère as a
'longhair'; similarly, 'scored' music occupied a low place in the
jazz hierarchy of values, since by definition it could not have the
spontaneity that was the pride of jazz and its chief contribution
to music. When Bechet's natural noise of good scatters long-
haired grief and scored pity, we think of something natural and
fresh dispersing something stale and predictable; but there are
other strong suggestions too, for the visual association of long-
haired grief is with a tradition of statuary – all those women
with long weeping hair, collectively suggesting some tragic
character from Classical mythology such as Niobe. And 'scored'
pity is not only written down and rehearsed, but also deeply
scratched, showing the claw-marks on brow and cheek.

> I see a girl dragged by the wrists
> Across a dazzling field of snow,
> And there is nothing in me that resists.
> Once it would not be so;
> Once I should choke with powerless jealousies;
> But now I seem devoid of subtlety,
> As simple as the things I see,
> Being no more, no less, than two weak eyes.

There is snow everywhere,
Snow in one blinding light.
Even snow smudged in her hair
As she laughs and struggles, and pretends to fight,
And still I have no regret;
Nothing so wild, nothing so glad as she
Rears up in me,
And would not, though I watched an hour yet.

So I walk on. Perhaps what I desired
— That long and sickly hope, someday to be
As she is — gave a flicker and expired;
For the first time I'm content to see
What poor mortar and bricks
I have to build with, knowing that I can
Never in seventy years be more a man
Than now — a sack of meal upon two sticks.

So I walk on. And yet the first brick's laid.
Else how should two old ragged men
Clearing the drifts with shovels and a spade
Bring up my mind to fever-pitch again?
How should they sweep the girls clean from my heart,
With no more done
Than to stand coughing in the sun,
Then stoop and shovel snow onto a cart?

The beauty dries my throat.
Now they express
All that's content to wear a worn-out coat,
All actions done in patient hopelessness,
All that ignores the silences of death,
Thinking no further than the hand can hold,
All that grows old,
Yet works on uselessly with shortened breath.

Damn all explanatory rhymes!
To be that girl! — but that's impossible;
For me the task's to learn the many times
When I must stoop, and throw a shovelful:

I must repeat until I live the fact
That everything's remade
With shovel and spade;
That each dull day and each despairing act

Builds up the crags from which the spirit leaps
– The beast most innocent
That is so fabulous it never sleeps;
If I can keep against all argument
Such image of a snow-white unicorn,
Then as I pray it may for sanctuary
Descend at last to me,
And put into my hand its golden horn.

This poem, striking and memorable in itself, is even more so in view of the trajectory of Larkin's poetry during the thirty years that followed. How could it have been more deeply and strongly expressed, the poet's conviction that his individual path was through prose to poetry, through the habitual to the unique, through dailiness to the irrecoverably precious?

Another poem in this early collection that points forward is 'To write one song, I said':

To write one song, I said,
As sad as the sad wind
That walks around my bed,
Having one simple fall
As a candle-flame swells, and is thinned,
As a curtain stirs by the wall
– For this I must visit the dead.
Headstone and wet cross,
Paths where the mourners tread,
A solitary bird,
These call up the shade of loss,
Shape word to word.

Just as in 'I see a girl dragged by the wrists' the poet is acknowledging his acceptance of ordinary routine experience, the many times he must stoop and throw a shovelful, as his own

personal route to exaltation and ecstasy, so here he affirms a
belief that joy is to be sought through sadness – not by turning
one's back on grief, or skirting round it, but going straight
through the middle of it. Only when he has accepted the stark
necessity of visiting the dead, walking those paths where the
mourners tread – and done these things for their own sake, not
as an avenue to something else – does he discover that locus of
joy where 'Hamlet and Lear are gay'.

Neither of these poems is the most beautiful in *The North
Ship* – that honour, I think, must go to No. X, 'Within the
dream you said' – but we are looking at the moment less for the
perfectly achieved than for the forward-pointing. In this connec-
tion No. XIII, 'I put my mouth', is important.

> I put my mouth
> Close to running water:
> Flow north, flow south,
> It will not matter,
> It is not love you will find.
>
> I told the wind:
> It took away my words:
> It is not love you will find,
> Only the bright-tongued birds,
> Only a moon with no home.
>
> It is not love you will find:
> You have no limbs
> Crying for stillness, you have no mind
> Trembling with seraphims,
> You have no death to come.

The water and the wind will not find love because they lack
the qualities needed in a being that is to experience love. (One
readily forgives the youthful solecism of 'seraphims' – the word
'seraphim' is already the plural of 'seraph', but in any case the
poet needed a rhyme for 'limbs'.) What strikes one is the
catalogue of essential qualities, prerequisites for love and

therefore for life. And these are 'limbs/Crying for stillness',
'mind/Trembling with seraphims', and the knowledge of death
waiting up ahead.

Moving forward from *The North Ship* to *High Windows*
twenty-nine years later, one finds the same themes worked out,
not with wearisome repetition but with a richness of develop-
ment that reveals new wealth in them with each poem. 'Livings',
for instance, is a celebration of duty and function; how we live
measures our own nature, and we all spend a major part of our
time at work, as a man of sixty has spent twenty years in bed.
And in all, or nearly all, the poems in *High Windows* there is that
same grateful celebration of the quotidian; what astonishing
things, after all, these familiar sights and sounds are!

> I listen to money singing. It's like looking down
>   From long french windows at a provincial town,
> The slums, the canal, the churches ornate and mad
>   In the evening sun. It is intensely sad.

Poetry, the amazing, the piercingly unique, exists within the
shell of ordinariness – even, as in 'The Card-Players', obviously
based on some oafish-beautiful Flemish interior, of uncom-
promising ugliness. This is the coral-insect activity that builds
up the crags from which the spirit leaps. And, if we view it in
the suddenly right, suddenly breathtaking perspective, this
ordinariness is irretrievably lovely, as the poets and painters have
always told us it was. That perspective comes at heightened – or
perhaps drastically lowered – moments: when we are sitting in
the waiting-room of a hospital ('The Building'), perhaps, an-
ticipating the examination that will either license us to walk out
free or condemn us to 'join/The unseen congregations whose
white rows/Lie set apart above'. Through the window we catch
a glimpse of the normal, unexciting life of every day, and the
poet selects half a dozen gleefully prosaic images because, in this
framework, their very ordinariness will catch at the heart.

. . . Outside seems old enough:
Red brick, lagged pipes, and someone walking by it
Out to the car park, free. Then, past the gate,
Traffic; a locked church; short terraced streets
Where kids chalk games, and girls with hair-dos fetch

Their separates from the cleaners – O world,
Your loves, your chances, are beyond the stretch
Of any hand from here! And is, unreal,
A touching dream to which we all are lulled
But wake from separately. . . .

Ordinary life, Toad-land, is a touching dream. And also a
dazzling vision. And intensely sad. And an empyrean where
stones shine like gold above each sodden grave. This is the
Larkinian imperative, the point at which his poetry assumes its
authority and speaks out. Into this dailiest of daily lives come
the priest and the doctor, running, in their long coats; into this
most prosaic of prose chronicles come the limbs crying for
stillness, the mind trembling with seraphim.

Jean Cocteau said, 'Victor Hugo était un fou qui se croyait
Victor Hugo.' Philip Larkin is a creatively sane man who
acknowledges the possibility that he may be Philip Larkin.

*

A new poet has appeared in the streets of Oxford. The title-page
of his book, *Somebody Like You*, names him as 'T. Carmi', but I
have no idea what the T. stands for and I have never heard
anybody call him anything but 'Carmi'. He is like a Welsh bard
in having just the one name. Even his wife, the artist Tamara
Rikman-Cherny, calls him 'Carmi'.

Carmi is a Hebrew poet; said by many to be the most impor-
tant poet writing in that language. He was born in New York in
a Hebrew-speaking household – his father was a Rabbi – and
went to Israel at an early age. Tamara was, I think, born in Tel-
Aviv. Her stock is Eastern European. So between them they are

the diagram of an Israeli couple, except that not every couple is so original and powerfully creative.

I don't suppose it is possible to write down a description of Carmi that will bring him to life for anyone who has never seen him. But I have to try. He is of medium height, lean and strong of build, with a shock of wiry brown hair just beginning (he is the same age as I am) to be shot through with grey. His skin is browned by years of Mediterranean sun and his eyes are brown too, warm and luminous. His accent in English is that of his native New York; he is inclined to dismiss the influence of New York on his nascent mind, but it certainly formed his speech and I often think I can hear New York in his quick, ironic humour. Though of course the humour, and the speech, of New York is very Jewish in any case.

Carmi has a beautiful voice, gentle but resonant; on the telephone, when one cannot see his quick play of expression, the smile that comes and goes quickly, and the continual responsiveness of his eyes that gives liveliness to the whole face, it sounds melancholy, elegiac. It is true of anyone, but especially of him, that to get his full flavour you need to see as well as hear him. His laugh, in particular, is unforgettable. It comes very quickly, surging up from his belly and shaking his whole frame, and emerges as a comical goose-like honk. It seems to tear itself out of him in pain; I have seen people in hospital, with fresh abdominal stitches, laugh like that. Yet he obviously enjoys mirth.

Once, when he was lecturing on Hebrew poetry, and in particular on the problems and opportunities of a literary life spent moving between two languages, an aggressive questioner, clearly with the intention of being rude, got to his feet and started, 'Well, I only speak and write in one language. . . .'

'Oh, yes,' said Carmi, 'which one is that?'

In the chuckle that followed, the steam went out of the man's attack and he subsided.

Peter Levi and Sally Purcell have made an English translation of 'Amorgos', by Nikos Gatsos. It is a poem full of leaping and flowing imagery. I don't 'understand' it, any more than I can construe the elegant Greek characters of the original, but it communicates an untamed strength, an urgent response to life. It makes me think intensely of Greece, that country I have never visited, but which has a hard, clear reality in my imagination. It brings to my mind a people materially poor but proud and ample in the depth and colour of their feelings.

Gatsos says – at least, Peter and Sally make him say, he speaks to me through them –

Lamentation is useless
Everywhere life will be the same, with the flute of the
    serpents in the country of ghosts

With the song of the robbers in the spice groves
With the knife of a sorrow in the check of hope
With the grief of a springtime nesting in the heart of the
    young owl

It is enough if a plough is found and a sickle sharp in
    a happy hand

Enough if there should flower only
A little grain for festivals, a little wine for remembrance,
    a little water for the dust. . . .

Every day I meet in the street poets who write in languages I have never learnt. Carmi writes in Hebrew, Bruno Tollentino writes in Portuguese, Kamal abu Deeb writes in Arabic, and they are all my neighbours. When I go into the Bodleian, I know that I am in the same building with thousands of poems I shall never read in the original. But the presence of these hosts of veiled poems does not depress me: on the contrary, I feel up-buoyed by the presence of so many unheard melodies. All those poets serenely encased in the golden amber of their beloved languages, they help me just by being there, 'the singing masons building roofs of gold'.

A note from the poet Anne Stevenson. She has just written a review of *Feng* for a weekly paper. Her interest being seriously engaged, she criticized it in detail, listing all her misgivings and everything she thought wrong with it, before ending with a paragraph saying that it was an important poem and ought to be read. When the piece appeared in print she saw that the editor, without a word of consultation with her, had lopped off the positive ending of the article, leaving it merely as a list of complaints, misrepresenting entirely her attitude to the poem.

She is gracefully apologetic. I know this editor: he is always very genial with me when we meet, but never loses a chance to do me harm with the reading public.

I reflect, for the thousandth time, that literary London has not changed at all since the notes to the *Dunciad* were penned.

Kamal abu Deeb is sitting with me beside my study fire. A Syrian poet, bringing his region of the earth into the room with him, importing it with his black hair and dark liquid eyes: a large, gentle, soft-spoken young man who smiles and laughs easily; in the five years I have known him I have never found a flaw in his easy, courteous geniality. Now we are sitting together, on a blistering-cold January night, beside my roaring study fire and he is expounding to me, as far as he can through the opaque curtain of my ignorance, the *rubá'iyàt* of Nizam al-Din al-Isfahani. (*rubá'i* means a quatrain, and *rubá'iyát* is the plural, a term made familiar to English readers by FitzGerald's masterpiece.) Kamal has unearthed a collection of over 550 *rubá'iyát* by this thirteenth-century poet, and prepared an edition; both of us are interested in exploring the possibility of a translation, versification by me on the basis of a literal translation by him. And so on this northern winter night we drink wine by the fire and think of Nizam al-Din al-Isfahani.

The quatrains turn out to be either untranslatable or very nearly so. Language alone cannot really bridge the gulf between entirely different cultures, entirely different philosophical predicates, entirely different ways of approaching life. Linguistic commerce is like money; it will buy this or that isolated object, but in the end each currency represents its own nation and society.

What look on the surface like love poems, of much the same kind as we are used to in our own literature, the Arabic tradition reads as radiating from two centres — sexual love and religious mysticism. The longing of the lover to unite himself with his beloved finds expression in the same language as the longing of the wandering human soul to merge its identity in the Divine. Hence his highly wrought, dense, allusive poetry is quite capable of expressing both yearnings at once, and making a seamless fabric of the two. As we have, indeed, already seen them doing in the poetry of Emily Dickinson.

The more one contemplates this poetry, the less surprising such a union seems. If God exists, our sexual longings, like all our others, are implanted by Him: and why should not the craving of the lover to possess his beloved, to strip off the burden of his individual identity in the ecstasy of fusing it with hers, be the terrestrial counterpart of a yearning for one-ness with God? The urge to mate, the rage to procreate and keep life in motion, is too deep and irrational to be encompassed within the neat bounds of any merely reasonable, hedonistic, logical view of existence; it involves us in suffering as readily as in pleasure, it leads us to make efforts and face odds far greater than anything we would attempt in the mere interests of security or comfort. Of all our normal experiences, 'love' — taking the whole range of compulsions covered by that word as it relates to the sexes — is the only one that habitually takes us beyond the familiar range of our natures: makes us behave better, or worse, than we had thought ourselves capable of, heaps on us joys and miseries we are hard put to it to bear. So that here, within the realm of our normal, expectable experience, is something that already takes us into the strangeness and intensity of the numinous.

When, as a young student, I first read that the Song of Solomon was commonly interpreted by Christian divines of the Middle Ages and later as a religious allegory expressing the love of the soul for God, I assumed with youthful insouciance that

what was at work here must be hypocrisy, conscious or un-
conscious: these passionate, sensual strains had to be given some
doctrinal coating before they could be received as the Word of
God. Now, thirty years later, when both the interpretation of
poetry and the love of women have lost their novelty but not
their difficulty or fascination, I am not so sure. If we are not to
image the journey towards God in terms of the journey towards
a woman, how else are we to image it?

Meanwhile, the Arabic quatrains are lying there on the page, and
Kamal is courteously willing to help. But –
    I find that every time I make a rough shot at one of these
quatrains, I have to heap up so many explanatory notes that I
am writing four lines of verse and then a two-page essay. Which
means that I am attempting the impossible. Quite apart from the
deeper issues of mystical religious emotion and a philosophical
tradition, there is the straightforward matter of vocabulary.
Arabic words, any more than European words, do not pull up
cleanly out of the ground with no soil sticking to their roots;
they bring with them associations, exploitable ambiguities, all
the organic life of a civilization. Take a fairly innocuous
example:

> Dove, when you sing, to whom are you calling?
> Whom do you trust with the secrets of your longing?
> Unfailing flow the tears of my eyes
> Over your lyrical, love-pursuing cries.

That – as I don't need to be told – is not very good as a quatrain
of English verse. But to labour over it, to try over in one's head
dozens of different phrases and rhythms and rhymes and then
balance them up into a whole, would be wasted labour because
the final product would not convey, any better than this rapid
sketch does, those qualities that give pleasure to the Arabic
reader. The first two lines are fairly straightforward, but in the
third and fourth insuperable difficulties occur. The word I
translate as 'lyrical cries' (the plural, actually, is a licence, to

rhyme with 'eyes') is *saj'*, a word meaning rhymed and cadenced prose, a form that exists in Arabic but not in English. The word for 'shed tears', more literally 'scatter', is also a word that means writing prose. My eyes, sharing your grief, make their prose statement even as you make your more elaborate and musical prose statement.

When we say that a certain kind of poetry is untranslatable, this is what we mean. It is difficult enough to provide an equivalent as between two languages with neighbouring cultures, such as France and England; but when irreconcilable traditions, irreconcilable histories and geographies, are involved there is just no substitute for learning the original language.

4
A Little Touch of Harry

Well, sir, at last the rehearsals begin; then, sir, begins another scene of trouble with the actors, some of whom don't like their parts, and all are continually plaguing you with alterations. At length, after having waded through all these difficulties, his play appears on the stage; where one man hisses out of resentment to the author, a second out of dislike to the house, a third out of dislike to the actor, a fourth out of dislike to the play, a fifth for the joke sake, a sixth to keep all the rest in company. Enemies abuse him, friends give him up, the play is damned, and the author goes to the devil: so ends the farce.

Henry Fielding, *Pasquin*, Act IV sc. I

All poetry smacks of the drama. It is fined down, honed to a point, divested of padding, in a way that prose fiction does not seek to be. Exactly what constitutes the dramatic is as difficult a theoretical question as what constitutes the poetic. But one thing they certainly have in common. Each is rooted in its particulars. The theatre, however it may bring us into the presence of lofty transcendent issues, must begin with a here and now: it must have a place, and a time, sharply and concretely established. Some poetry is intensely dramatic, with a place and time and physical setting that are positively thrust into the reader's face; I noted as much in 'On the Breaking of Forms'; but even poetry that is not overtly dramatic is never far from the dramatic concreteness, the dramatic selection of a point in time and space.

I should have been doing less than my duty, then, if as Professor of Poetry I had not tried to make some kind of meaningful statement about the links between poetry and drama, the dramatic content that is normal to poetry and the rich effects that are possible when the two arts embrace each other. On the face of it, this could have been most conveniently done by giving a lecture, or more than one, on Shakespeare. It is no accident that the foremost poet in the English-speaking world is also the foremost playwright; and, if my competence had extended to criticism of literature outside English, I should have before me the cases of Racine, Calderon, Sophocles, Goethe, the Noh Plays. To Shakespeare, then, I might reasonably have turned. But it so happens that I incorporated my thinking about Shakespeare into a book that came out in the 1960s. Having treated the subject as fully as I was able to, and on the whole still agreeing with what I said in that book, I found myself with not many new ideas to offer on Shakespeare; and, lacking the bland effrontery, which academic life teaches those who stay in it long enough, to stand up on a platform and retail my remaindered stock as if it were new, I decided to leave him alone.

The obligation to speak of dramatic poetry, and the dramatic element in poetry, remained. And so did the other obligation I consistently acknowledged: to share with the University such lessons as I learnt in the course of my work as a practising writer. In 1975 I was writing a play, for a specific theatre and a specific director. The play included songs, and I was collaborating with a musician. When I looked round for a work within classical English literature to which this experience seemed more or less relevant, I thought first of Yeats; but it so happened that Yeats himself put into my head the idea that *Comus* would be the really perfect example. The result was my lecture for the summer term.

REFLECTIONS ON THE FIRST NIGHT
OF COMUS

One of W. B. Yeats's last plays, *The Death of Cuchulain*, begins
with 'a bare stage of any period', on to which enters 'a very old
man looking like something out of mythology'. The old man,
who is a surrogate for the author, opens the play with these
words:

> I have been asked to produce a play called *The Death of
> Cuchulain*. It is the last of a series of plays which has for
> theme his life and death. I have been selected because I am
> out of fashion and out of date like the antiquated romantic
> stuff the thing is made of. I am so old that I have forgotten
> the name of my father and mother, unless indeed I am, as I
> affirm, the son of Talma, and he was so old that his friends
> and acquaintances still read Virgil and Homer. When they
> told me that I could have my own way, I wrote certain
> guiding principles on a bit of newspaper. I wanted an
> audience of fifty or a hundred, and if there are more, I beg
> them not to shuffle their feet or talk when the actors are
> speaking. I am sure that as I am producing a play for
> people I like, it is not probable, in this vile age, that they will
> be more in number than those who listened to the first per-
> formance of Milton's *Comus*. On the present occasion they
> must know the old epics and Mr Yeats' plays about them;
> such people, however poor, have libraries of their own. If
> there are more than a hundred I won't be able to escape
> people who are educating themselves out of the Book
> Societies and the like, sciolists all, pickpockets and
> opinionated bitches. Why pickpockets? I will explain that,
> I will make it all quite clear.

191

The burden of the speech (it goes on for about as long again) is clear enough, the familiar Yeatsian preference for the 'dream of the noble and the beggarman' as against the world of 'Book Societies and the like'. What pulled me up, when I was looking at the play again recently, was the reference to the first night of *Comus*. Obviously this is not fortuitous; it takes its place with all those references in Yeats to a lofty art produced for the few who by birth and training are fit to receive it, all that talk of 'Duke Ercole, that bid/His mummers to the market-place', and the great gazebo, and the wondrous blade of the Japanese sword. It might be interesting, I thought, to conjure up the first night of *Comus*, to see it as Yeats might have seen it, and as we see it now.

I

Comus was not called *Comus* until the eighteenth century; Milton's own name for it was *A Maske, Presented at Ludlow Castle, 1634: on Michaelmasse Night, before the Right Honourable John Earle of Bridgewater, Viscount Brackly, Lord Praesident of Wales, and one of His Majesties most honourable Privie Counsell*. And within that *cadre* it must be judged. This, of course, applies to all Milton's work. He was a highly social poet. His notion of poetry was not one of unbridled self-expression, but of personal utterance within recognized forms. These forms, though 'discovered, not devised', had something of the authority found in venerable objects in nature; they were, at the very least, dignified and ancient buildings, whose making was the result of collaborative effort by the European literary community of whom he knew himself to be one. Every one of Milton's works, from his earliest efforts to his most mature masterpieces, is consciously aligned to a particular tradition within the over-arching tradition of European letters, and in each case he has studied the form he is using until he inhabits it naturally, at ease with its history and its nuances. By the same token he demands always to be judged by a jury of those who have made a similar effort. Thus the preface to *Samson Agonistes*, while offering a sketch of Classical tragedy which will at any rate suffice to fill in the gaps of the unlearned reader, adds pointedly that when it comes to his handling of the story ('the disposition of the fable') 'they only will best judge who are not unacquainted with Aeschulus, Sophocles, and Euripedes'. To take Milton's collected poetry in one's hand, and fairly claim to understand and be in a position to judge every poem, calls for a very comprehensive knowledge of European literature. The Victorian critic Mark Pattison remarked that 'an appreciation of Milton is the last reward of consummate scholarship', and has been a good deal laughed at for his pains, but what Pattison doubtless had in mind was not the mere spotting of every reference as if one were a walking dictionary, but the reading and meditation required to see each of Milton's poems in its appropriate landscape.

So we will try to see *Comus*. A masque is not a play, and does not grow from the same root. Drama is a narrative art, telling a story not by means of direct recounting but by representative action. A masque, though it has some tenuous narrative or situational thread, is much closer to ritual and celebration. Its origins are very ancient, and take us into anthropology. The most satisfying general study of the subject, Enid Welsford's *The Court Masque* (1927), lays down the guide-line in its very first paragraph: 'Curiously enough, the Court masquerade, that very sophisticated amusement of Renaissance society, was more primitive than the drama of the rough Elizabethan playhouses.' The masque is a celebration, and everywhere shows the marks of its origins in that basic stratum where magic and religion meet, where the human being demonstrates his eternal need to signalize and memorialize the pivotal events of existence – change of season and harvest, death and rebirth, marriage, conflict. As soon as any society emerges out of the fog of prehistory we find it busy with these rituals. The refined seventeenth-century court masque has many direct links with the festivals of some primitive settlement, and two in particular: the lavishing of resources, and the notion of salvation by touching. The first is too obvious to need much comment. Primitive agricultural peoples, who lack the resources to keep their animals alive during the winter, have to slaughter and eat them in the autumn, so even people who live flat on the subsistence level have a week or so in which they gorge themselves like bears preparing for the winter, and for the same reason. The masque, right up to its final blaze of magnificence in the early seventeenth century, retains this atmosphere of abundance. Considering that a masque was always a one-off performance, the amount of money and effort that went into the staging is nothing short of astounding. We can remind ourselves of this extravagance, this conspicuous consumption run amok, by a glance at the stage directions of a typical Whitehall masque, Carew's *Coelum Britannicum*, which was put on only two years before *Comus* and numbered some of the same performers.

> When this Antimasque was past, there began to arise out of the earth the top of a hill, which, by little and little, grew to be a huge mountain, that covered all the scene; the under-part of this was wild and craggy, and above somewhat more pleasant and flourishing; about the middle part of this mountain were seated the three kingdoms of England, Scotland, and Ireland, all richly attired in regal habits, appropriated to the several nations, with crowns on their heads, and each of them bearing the the ancient arms of the kingdoms they represented. At a distance above these sat a young man in a white embroidered robe; upon his fair hair an olive garland, with wings at his shoulders, and holding in his hand a cornucopia filled with corn and fruits, representing the Genius of these kingdoms.

And again:

> The dance being past, there appears in the further part of the heaven coming down a pleasant cloud, bright and transparent; which, coming softly downwards before the upper part of the mountain, embraceth the genius, but so as through it all his body is seen; and then rising again with a gentle motion, bears up the Genius of the three kingdoms, and being past the airy region, pierceth

the heavens, and is no more seen; at that instant, the
rock with the three kingdoms on it sinks, and is hidden
in the earth. This strange spectacle gave great cause of
admiration, but especially how so huge a machine, and
of that great height, could come from under the stage,
which was but six foot high.

Another feature that links the court masque with its primitive
ancestor is the notion of salvation by touching. Primitive
societies, and perhaps all of us in the primitive reaches of our
being, have a rooted belief in contagious holiness. When an
animal is ritually slaughtered or hunted down, its blood is often
flung out over the bystanders so that as many of them as pos-
sible may be touched by the blood (i.e., the life) of the beast on
whom the survival of the people depends. And when the ritual
culminates in a dance the dance winds through the village, in
and out of people's houses, so that the greatest number of in-
habitants may be touched by its powerful magic. The ceremonial
hunter dons the skin and horns of the animal, to take over its
sacredness by contact; and as with animals, so with plants. I
was among the crowd in the streets of Oxford at six o'clock last
May morning, and there among them was Jack-in-the-Green,
with his framework of freshly leaved branches, moving among
the thickest of the throng, touching them, sharing with them the
sacred power of vegetation. In the masque this survives in the
convention that ends the entertainment with a general dance:
not just a dance in which the performers take themselves
offstage, but a dance in which the performers and audience com-
bine, in which the rehearsed and acted emblematic narrative
becomes one with the general and spontaneous celebration, the
audience become performers and the ritual gathers up everyone
present.
The masque has yet one more mark of its celebratory origin,
one that we who are reared in a modern bureaucratic state will
find hard to understand. Feudal society – and the heyday of the
masque coincided with the final self-consuming blaze of
feudalism – is already hieratic, structured, symbolic, already
half-way to being like a lofty ceremonial entertainment in itself.

The masque unites many arts in the celebrating of a person or persons of high estate, royal or noble; the performers are not usually professionals, but other members of the same aristocracy, offering their skill in singing, dancing and reciting poetry, in an act of homage between equals; the effect is to restate and confirm those values by the grace of which the aristocracy exists and performs its function, which is to govern.

In other words, the masque celebrates those virtues which, by a legal fiction, are supposed to be inherent in an aristocracy – a ruling caste that perpetuates itself by a mixture of heredity and training. This legal fiction is not, any more than another, believed in literally – everyone knows that an aristocracy includes within its ranks many who are stupid, weak or depraved – but it is enacted in the masque, and the one symbolic enactment matches the other. The king or nobleman, seated with his retinue about him in their descending order of function, is the apex of a structure that matches the structure he is watching, and when the masque culminates in a general dance the two structures blend into one, which in a sense they have been all along. We, who live in societies in which a democratically elected (if we are lucky) executive expresses its (sc. our) will through an elaborate bureaucracy, can only understand this notion of power and authority if we go right back and take a bearing from Fustel de Coulanges in *The Ancient City*. 'Ancient law was not the work of a legislator; it was on the contrary imposed on the legislator. It had its birth in the family.' Similarly, the structure of laws in feudal Europe was the expression of qualities that were supposed by a legal fiction to inhere in the feudal pyramid. So that a masque celebrating some event in the life of a great aristocrat was, by definition, a celebration and a demonstration of those qualities by which the aristocrat justified his power.

II

So much, by way of rough diagram, for the general nature of the masque. Now to the particular nature of *Comus*. John, Earl of Bridgewater, had been appointed President of the Council of

Wales, and Lord Lieutenant of Wales and the border counties of England, in 1631. This was a formidable responsibility. The Council of Wales, about eighty in number, included men high in the service of Charles I and also English and Welsh gentlemen who held estates in that part of the world and could administer the law at local level. That Bridgewater was given this high office indicates that he was held in great esteem. It involved residence in Ludlow Castle, and the Earl, who normally resided at Ashridge in Buckinghamshire, took his time about making the move. Not until the summer of 1634 were he and his wife installed at Ludlow, and their three youngest children, left behind during the summer at Ashridge, joined them some months later. Milton's masque was presented on the evening of the day on which Bridgewater formally took office.

This was the basic situation for which Milton had to devise a framework. The story he hit upon was obvious enough, yet completely appropriate. By a pardonable foreshortening of time, he imagines that the three children, journeying from Ashridge to Ludlow, are arriving that very evening; that they undergo trials and dangers on the way, which they surmount by showing the aristocratic virtues of courage and self-command, and that at the culmination of the masque they step out of the picture-frame and are presented as real children to their real father and mother. It is a charming plan, and Milton carries it out charmingly. *Comus* is, of course, lightweight by comparison with most of Milton's work. It has not the piercing beauty of 'Lycidas', let alone the volcanic power of *Paradise Lost* or the granite authority of *Samson Agonistes*. But it is a perfect example of Milton's lifelong ability to take an established genre and, without bending it into an unrecognizable shape, put his signature firmly on it. *Comus* has all the features of a masque, yet it is Milton's masque and no one else's. And of all extant masques it is the most literary. A large proportion of its energy is pumping through the language.

But now we shift focus again. In the background is the masque tradition; in the middle ground is the official occasion for which *Comus* was written. But in the foreground is a real

family, living a real life with its attendant problems, and there
are signs that in writing *Comus* Milton may have felt himself
very closely meshed in with the situation. To get a grip on it, we
must go back a couple of generations.

Many years earlier, in the days of Elizabeth I, Edmund
Spenser dedicated one of his poems, *The Teares of the Muses*, to
his young kinswoman and friend Alice, Lady Strange. Her hus-
band, Ferdinando, Lord Strange, was a man of letters in his own
right, and took besides a deep interest in the theatre, main-
taining a company of actors, Lord Strange's Players. On the
death of his father in 1593, Ferdinando Strange became Earl of
Derby; and Alice retained the title of Countess of Derby
throughout her subsequent widowhood, remarriage and second
widowhood. The couple, who resided at their country house in
Harefield, on the borders of Middlesex and Buckinghamshire,
had three daughters. Ferdinando died, one year after succeeding
to the title, and in 1600 Alice married Sir Thomas Egerton, a
man who had served the Derby family for some years as their
legal adviser. In that same year, Alice's second daughter married
Sir Thomas Egerton's son John: so that the children of that
marriage were simultaneously the grandchildren and step-
grandchildren of the senior couple.

Another of Alice's daughters, Anne, was widowed, and in
1624 this Anne married Mervyn Touchet, alias Lord Audley, the
Earl of Castlehaven. Touchet/Audley was a widower with six
children, of whom the eldest, James, in 1628 married Elizabeth,
one of Anne's four children by her first marriage. A family tree
will make all plain:

Alice, Countess of Derby (widow) = Sir Thomas
                                     Egerton (widower)

Mervyn Touchet = Anne   Elizabeth   Frances = John (Earl of
(Earl of   (widow)   Bridgewater
Castlehaven)   1617)

  James   =   Elizabeth
                  (married at   Alice   John   Thomas
                  11 or 12)   (actors in *Comus*)

Once again the loose ends were neatly tucked in, and if any children resulted from this latter union, they would be both great-grandchildren and step-great-grandchildren to the redoubtable old lady at Harefield.

Sir John Egerton was a man of importance. He was created Earl of Bridgewater in 1617; still higher honour was destined for him, but for the present he and his family lived semi-privately at Ashridge, not far (some sixteen miles) from Harefield.

We have therefore to think of these two aristocratic households, within easy reach of each other, populated by one of those intricately interconnected families that abound in the English ruling class: everybody was everybody else's cousin, niece, uncle, step-grandson, etc., etc. John Egerton and his wife produced four sons and eleven daughters. Four children died in infancy, but eleven remained, and quickly grew up to the age at which they could form fresh alliances with nobility and wealth.

All this amounts to a formidable power-structure, but it was an intellectual and artistic structure as well. John Egerton's children were musical. To encourage their gifts he took on as music teacher to the household no less a musician than Henry Lawes; when, we do not know, but it was before 1627, because Lady Mary Egerton, who had been one of Lawes's charges, got married in that year. Through Lawes, the family had an open avenue to the world of music and drama. It was the heyday of the masque, and Lawes had been much involved in masques, with their equal demand on composer, poet, actor, scenic designer, painter, singer, instrumental performer. He not only wrote music for masques, but also performed in them. He had been seen in two masques by Ben Jonson, two by Aurelian Townshend, and one each by Shirley and Carew. In some of these masques he had acted alongside his young charges of the Egerton family. They had a friendly relationship – not merely master and pupils, but collaborators in dashing and stylish (if somewhat improvisatory) works of art.

All, then, was reasonably sunny on the Harefield–Ashridge side of the family. On the Castlehaven side there were deep shadows. Mervyn Touchet was a bad lot. His sexual tastes were

200   PROFESSING POETRY

decidedly seamy and he had no hesitation in gratifying them by
the use of every kind of power, including violence. He compelled
not only his wife but also her twelve-year-old daughter, bride of
his own son, to take part in group sexual activities, of just about
every imaginable kind, involving the servants and anyone else
who happened to be on the scene, including a whore calling
herself Blandida, who took up residence in his house for some six
months. Finally the whole matter was dragged to light. In April
1631 the Earl of Castlehaven was tried, convicted of rape and
sodomy, and forthwith executed.

Naturally these events were much talked of, and naturally also
the effect on the families concerned was painful in the extreme.
Each branch of the clan reacted in its own way. The Castlehaven
family made an unavailing effort to get Touchet pardoned. The
Bridgewater family maintained a dignified silence. Though John
Egerton was a member of the Privy Council and therefore
wielded exceptional influence, he seems to have made no attempt
to intervene on Castlehaven's behalf. Evidently he accepted his
kinsman's guilt. During the relevant period he is not on record as
having attended any Privy Council meeting, nor was he present
at Castlehaven's trial. Doubtless he was licking his wounds in
private, the wounds to his family pride and aristocratic code of
behaviour.

The Earl of Bridgewater and his wife could take refuge in
silence. Not so the old lady at Harefield. On her, the effect of the
Castlehaven revelations was one of deep grief and shock. She
gathered her other three granddaughters by Anne into the
protection of her household, but she would not take Elizabeth,
the girl who had been involved in the scandal, nor would she take
her own daughter, the girl's mother. The King had not yet par-
doned them. In any case, the girl ought to go back to her hus-
band and start life with him anew. One thing was certain: after
such experiences, Elizabeth was no fit companion for the
children she, the Countess, was looking after. To Viscount
Dorchester, His Majesty's Secretary of State, Alice wrote several
letters in 1631, describing herself as one 'whose heart is almost
wounded to death', and discussing with him the question of

what should be done with Anne and Elizabeth Audley. The old
Countess still had hopes of their reclamation, praying that
'neither my daughter nor she will ever offend either God or His
Majesty again by their wicked courses, but redeem what is past,
by their reformation and newness of life'.

But as for letting Elizabeth Audley join her sisters in the house
at Harefield, that would not do at all: 'I am fearful lest there
should be some sparks of my grandchild Audley's misbehaviour
remaining, which might give ill example to the young ones
which are with me.'

In November of that year, the King pardoned Anne Audley
and her daughter Elizabeth. The old Countess at Harefield could
take some comfort from that fact. But the shock had been
grievous, and her family must have wanted to do what they
could for her.

John Milton now enters the story. One summer evening, the
Countess was presented with an entertainment by 'som Noble
Persons of her Family'. These scions paid homage to the old
dame in her seat of state by means of a procession interrupted by
a speech from 'the Genius of the wood', and by two exquisite
lyrics. Both lyrics and speech were by the young Milton, who
printed them in his *Poems* of 1645. The verse is light and
delicate in rhythm, agreeably sonorous with vowel-music, in
every way fitting for a summer evening, a beautiful garden and a
family celebration. The 'song' that concludes the entertainment
shows that Milton could imitate Shakespeare while remaining
his own man.

> O're the smooth enameld green
> Where no print of step hath been,
>   Follow me as I sing,
>   And touch the warbled string.
> Under the shady roof
> Of branching Elm Star-proof,
>   Follow me,
> I will bring you where she sits,
> Clad in splendor as befits
>   Her deity.

> Such a rural Queen
> All *Arcadia* hath not seen.

> Nymphs and Shepherds dance no more
>   By sandy *Ladons* Lillied banks.
> On old *Pycæus* or *Cyllene* hoar,
>   Trip no more in twilight ranks,
> Through *Erymanth* your loss deplore,
>   A better soyl shall give ye thanks.
> From the stony *Mænalus*,
> Bring your Flocks, and live with us,
> Here ye shall have greater grace,
> To serve the Lady of this place.
>   Though *Syrinx* your *Pans* Mistres were,
>   Yet *Syrinx* well might wait on her.
>   Such a rural Queen
> All *Arcadia* hath not seen.

We do not know the date of *Arcades*. Milton's modern biographer W. R. Parker assigns it on grounds of probability to 1630 or even 1629. Both dates put it well before the catastrophe of the Castlehaven scandal. I could wish for the unearthing of some document that would put it a year or two later, after the storm had broken over that venerable head. The fullness of compliment, the assurance that she was unshakeably a 'rural queen', most fit to rule over the realms of pastoral, would take on a beauty, if they were intended as consolation and support, that as merely formal tribute they necessarily lack.

   Still, whatever the date, *Arcades* was clearly the occasion of Milton's relationship with the family of John Egerton. Doubtless the intermediary was Henry Lawes. Since Milton's father was a connoisseur of music and something of a composer, it need not perplex us that Lawes knew the Milton family. It is also quite possible that John Milton's budding fame as a poet, a fame that took root first in Cambridge but might easily spread to a circle of acquaintances in London, had come to Lawes's ears independently. In any case, we may take it that Lawes invited Milton to collaborate on *Arcades*, and that Milton went to Harefield to see (or even take part in?) the entertainment. There

he would meet and work with the 'noble Persons of her family'
who were the actors and singers. Would the party include Anne
and Elizabeth Audley? Or were they at this time immured in
Castlehaven's lair, acting out his fantasies with Blandida and the
rest of the crew?

The Countess of Derby died in January 1637. Whatever the
trials of her life, it is a pleasant thought that she was the object
of tributes by both Spenser and Milton. (If it could only be
proved that somewhere along the line she was the subject of one
of Shakespeare's sonnets, the triangle would be complete.) And
in the year of her death Milton was once more drawn into the
circle of her family. Lawes, needing to put on something much
more elaborate than *Arcades* and to put it on in Ludlow Castle,
remembered the beautifully polished verse Milton had turned in
on the former occasion. He invited him once more to write
something for the Egerton family and to share to that extent in
its life. There would be consultations, rehearsals, and beyond all
doubt a visit to Ludlow.

The circumstances, however, were different. Even if *Arcades*
was well before the Castlehaven scandal, *Comus* was after it.
Elizabeth Audley, who had been eleven years old when all this
happened to her, was fifteen now. And her cousin and exact con-
temporary, Alice Egerton, was to be the main female performer
in the masque Milton and Lawes were devising.

It is this, surely, that explains the emphasis Milton decided to
put on the virtue of chastity. To most of us nowadays, his deci-
sion would not need to be explained. We think of him as the
austere, not to say grim, poet of Puritanism, very suspicious of
pleasure and self-indulgence of any kind. But the young Milton
had not yet so decisively adopted this stance. He was, certainly,
a serious and studious young man, and of blameless life. (In
boyhood, he had been destined for Holy Orders, and he had not
yet renounced that intention. He never did, indeed, formally
renounce it; his view would be that the Church left him, rather
than that he left the Church.) But as a poet he delighted in the
rich sensuousness of the Renaissance, the lust of the eyes and the
pride of life. His favourite poets were the Latin elegiac love

poets, who entertained no high opinion of chastity. He was a
musician, a swordsman, a good dancer, handsome, attracted by
female beauty. The Milton we see in our mind's eye wrote
Paradise Lost and *Samson Agonistes*, not *Comus*.

The three young people he imagines making their adventurous
journey, to be played by the fifteen-year-old girl and her brothers
of eleven and nine, face dangers and temptations. But, out of the
wide variety of dangers and temptations they might have met
with, Milton specifically chose the sexual. It may be that he went
a little too far for the tone of the occasion. Certainly the cuts in
performance seem to have been, mostly, the removing of
passages which would be too openly sexual to be spoken by a
young lady in such a setting.

Any reader who knows 'the literature of' Milton will see by
now that I have been convinced by Barbara Breasted's article
'*Comus* and the Castlehaven Scandal'.* The text of *Comus* exists
in three forms, each slightly different. There is a manuscript at
Trinity College, Cambridge; there is the 'Bridgewater manu-
script', still in the possession of the family; and there is the printed
version, first published by Lawes in 1637 and substantially
repeated by Milton in the collection of 1645. What concerns us at
the moment is that the Bridgewater manuscript is the shortest of
these variants (908 lines against a printed 1023), which alone would
point to its being the acting copy, and that these cuts seem to have
been made for a reason. At this reason, Dr Breasted appears to me to
guess convincingly.

In the story, the two brothers leave the lady alone in the wood
while they go to explore. Comus and his followers have been
whooping it up in the forest, but the enchanter suddenly senses
the approach of someone very different, and interrupts the wild
dance with

> Break off, break off, I feel the different pace
> Of some chast footing neer about this ground.
>   . . . Some Virgin sure

* *Milton Studies III*, ed. J. D. Simmons (University of Pittsburgh Press, 1971).

(For so I can Distinguish by mine Art)
Benighted in these woods. Now to my charms. . . .

His plan is to seduce the virgin and enrol her in his gang. He
and they hide, the Lady enters, and she speaks.

This way the noise was, if mine ear be true,
My best guide now, me thought it was the sound
Of Riot, and ill manag'd Merriment,
Such as the jocond Flute, or gamesom Pipe
Stirs up among the loose unleter'd Hinds,
When for their teeming Flocks, and granges full
In wanton dance they praise the bounteous *Pan*,
And thank the gods amiss. I should be loath
To meet the rudenesse, and swill'd insolence
Of such late Wassailers; yet O where els
Shall I inform my unacquainted feet
In the blind mazes of this tangl'd Wood?
My Brothers when they saw me wearied out
With this long way, resolving here to lodge
Under the spreading favour of these Pines
Stept as they se'd to the next Thicket side
To bring me Berries, or such cooling fruit
As the kind hospitable Woods provide.
They left me then, when the gray-hooded Eev'n
Like a sad Votarist in Palmers weed
Rose from the hindmost wheels of *Phoebus* wain.
But where they are, and why they came not back,
Is now the labour of my thoughts, 'tis likeliest
They had ingag'd their wandring steps too far,
And envious darknes, e're they could return,
Had stole them from me. . . .
I cannot hallow to my Brothers, but
Such noise as I can make to be heard farthest
Ile venter, for my new enliv'nd spirits
Prompt me; and they perhaps are not far off.

She then sings the delicate lyric to 'Sweet Echoe'. Being a
well-brought-up young lady, she cannot make her voice carry by
shouting and yelling, but she can and will make it carry by
singing. But of course any reader who knows *Comus* tolerably

well will have realized that I have missed out a large chunk of that speech; quoting it, in fact, as the Bridgewater manuscript has it. The full text runs:

> And envious darknes, e're they could return,
> Had stole them from me, els O theevish Night
> Why shouldst thou, but for some fellonious end,
> In thy dark lantern thus close up the Stars,
> That nature hung in Heav'n, and fill'd their Lamps
> With everlasting oil, to give due light
> To the misled and lonely Travailer?
> This is the place, as well as I may guess,
> Whence eev'n now the tumult of loud Mirth
> Was rife, and perfet in my list'ning ear,
> Yet nought but single darknes do I find.
> What might this be? A thousand fantasies
> Begin to throng into my memory
> Of calling shapes, and beckning shadows dire,
> And airy tongues, that syllable mens names
> On Sands, and Shoars, and desert Wildernesses.
> These thoughts may startle well, but not astound
> The vertuous mind, that ever walks attended
> By a strong siding champion Conscience. . . .
> O welcom pure-ey'd Faith, white-handed Hope,
> Thou hovering Angel girt with golden wings,
> And thou unblemish't form of Chastity,
> I see ye visibly, and now beleeve
> That he, the Supreme good, t' whom all things ill
> Are but as slavish officers of vengeance,
> Would send a glistring Guardian if need were
> To keep my life and honour unassail'd.
> Was I deceiv'd, or did a sable cloud
> Turn forth her silver lining on the night?
> I did not err, there does a sable cloud
> Turn forth her silver lining on the night,
> And casts a gleam over this tufted Grove.
> I cannot hallow, etc.

This cut cannot have been made on grounds of literary quality. The writing is excellent, some of the best in the work, and it is also dramatically appropriate. Too appropriate, perhaps. The emotional temperature rises steeply: the girl is disturbed, feeling the vibration of the enchanter who is hiding nearby and lustfully watching her. Obviously whoever cut these lines was not so much out to improve the text as to cool it.

A similar cut occurs in lines 697–700. After Comus has presented himself to the Lady in the guise of a humble swain, and offered to lead her to a humble but safe habitation, she puts herself in his hands and we next see her not in a cottage but in 'a stately Palace, set out with all manner of deliciousness; soft Musick, Tables spred with all dainties'. The Lady, surrounded by Comus and his rabble, is powerless to rise from her enchanted chair. This is already quite strong symbolism; he has power over her body, and it is up to her mind to resist him. In the course of the exchange that follows, she says to him:

> Hast thou betrai'd my credulous innocence
> With visor'd falshood, and base forgery,
> And wouldst thou seek again to trap me here
> With lickerish baits fit to ensnare a brute?

The Bridgewater manuscript gives only the first of those four lines. Perhaps the other three laid too much emphasis on the precise nature of Comus's intentions. 'Lickerish', in particular, had the specific meaning of 'lecherous'. Somebody (we can only conjecture who) decided that Lady Alice had better not speak so openly of what they were all thinking. For everyone present must have thought, as the action unfolded, of that real-life Comus, lurking in the dark forest of family history, who had had his way with just such a girl as this, a girl of the same age and the same family as she whom they were watching.

III

At this point, conjecture takes over; but the kind of conjecture that no imaginative person can help making. Dr Breasted, as a scholar should, confines her essay almost entirely to ascertaining the facts. But even she cannot resist, at one point, wading into the water of conjectural interpretations. 'By idealizing these last

three unmarried Egerton children and their relationship with
their parents,' she writes, 'Milton invites us to regard the
masque as a ritual purification of the entire family.' This is
cautious; the words 'invites us to regard' keep the question
within the normal bounds of literary criticism; yet it conveys, to
me at least, that Dr Breasted thinks of Milton, pacing the
country lanes and meditating a theme for *Comus*, saying to
himself, 'The Bridgewater family, eh? What that lot need is a
good ritual purification.'

What, indeed, were Milton's feelings about the Castlehaven
scandal? Did he breathe a sigh of relief when Mervyn Touchet
went to the block, thinking that from now on England would be
a cleaner place? Did he feel a deep pity for the old Countess at
Harefield in her affliction? Or did the experience, on the con-
trary, sow the seeds of doubt and suspicion in his mind? Was
Elizabeth Audley invited to Ludlow? After all, if the King had
pardoned the girl, it would not be seemly for a member of the
Privy Council to ostracize her. Did Milton meet her and, if he
did, what did they find to say to each other? What thoughts
went through their minds? (This seems to me better material for
a historical novel about Milton than anything that went into Mr
Graves's little anti-Miltonic phantasmagoria, *Wife to. Mr
Milton*.)

Be all this as it may, in any attempt to reconstruct the life of
Milton, *Comus* provides a vital hinge. Before it, Milton is a
gifted schoolboy and undergraduate, already widely read,
already conscious of superior powers and exceptional gifts; a
child of the comfortable middle class, living (materially) a rather
sheltered life within an approving and admiring family circle; his
father, indeed, was worried about the son's decision to give his
life to poetry, and some friction arose between them, alluded to
with frankness in 'Ad Patrem'; but, on the whole, it had been a
boyhood and youth devoted to learning, amassing information
and ideas and enjoying the arts, within the security of a family
circle. Ahead lay the black and stormy seas, the agonizing
decisions, the lonely toil, the tragic disappointments and dis-
illusions. But for this moment the sun shone warmly. Milton had

emerged from his comfortable but rather limited *milieu*; he was mixing with people of importance, people who made momentous decisions, which to a young man is wonderfully interesting and stimulating; he was also mixing with people whose artistic sensibilities were as cultivated as his own – whereas at Cambridge, we may well conjecture, he had mixed chiefly with men who had plenty of reading but not much else. As a developing artist, young enough to be growing very fast, he must have felt warmed and encouraged by the knowledge that his prowess at his chosen art had won him a place in this larger, more magnificent, more important world.

Not that this kind of support was then, or is now, essential to the producing of great art. The greatest art can grow in loneliness and sorrow. But surely every artist needs one period in his life, even a short one, when he can feel that he is in the right place at the right time. The Milton of *Samson Agonistes* is a greater poet than the Milton of *Comus*. (The post-Romantic doctrine that poets do their best work in youth and then 'go off' was unknown to him as it was unknown to Shakespeare.) But the poet of *Samson* must often have thought back to the young man who wrote *Comus*, and thought of him as someone exceptionally fortunate, a gifted and protected being on whom life had so far rained only gifts. 'He plays yet, like a young prentice the first day, and is not yet come to his task of melancholy.' To this young man, standing in the sunshine, the deep and tragic questions had not yet presented themselves: Whose hands are fit for power? How shall a nation govern itself? How far should conscience trim itself to a legitimate authority, and when does authority cease to be legitimate? All these questions met Milton head on before many more years had passed, and he did not flinch from them. The struggle cost him eyesight, health, leisure, friends, everything except life itself. For twenty years he was silent as a poet – he, who had spent his first three decades in preparation for the writing of poetry. When the Restoration came, and his hopes of a theocentric republican form of government were finally overthrown, we can only be glad that Restoration England was not the kind of place where, once a political faction is put down, its adherents are rounded up and shot in batches. Milton's life was evidently in the balance for some time, but it was spared, and as a result we have *Paradise Lost* and *Samson*. (There is a political moral here. A regime based on the slaughter-house loses a lot of art as well as a lot of everything else.)

IV

When the young Milton enjoyed the shelter of Ludlow Castle and the society it housed, he was assenting to, and co-operating with, an *ancien régime* that was fated not to last much longer. Indeed, he, with his wholehearted support of the Commonwealth, was to be one of the people who brought it down. That decision was a dark and tragic one, and what it cost Milton is not to be lightly conjectured, unless we have the arrogance to believe ourselves qualified to plumb the mind of a great poet with ease. And such thoughts naturally bring us round to Yeats again. When Yeats spoke of writing for people he liked and therefore having an audience about the size of that for the first night of *Comus*, he was consciously aligning himself with the Milton who wrote for the Egertons. Not that Lady Gregory had that kind of importance or that kind of wealth! Coole Park was not a notable estate, even by Anglo-Irish standards; there was never much money there, and its closing years were a sad struggle, against hopeless odds, to keep it together.

At the time Yeats met Augusta Gregory, he was exhausted and ill from years of toil and frustration. She took him to Coole Park, nursed him back to health, and provided him with a home there as long as she ran the place. Further, she helped him by bringing him into the cottages of her tenants, and plugging him in to a source of tradition and folklore that Yeats, whose own background was mainly urban, would probably not have found for himself. He repaid her friendship in some of his finest work. It was a loyalty that never wavered; Yeats did not, like Milton, have to face the crisis of an ideological parting of the ways. To him, the social and political set-up which produced families like the Gregories was in line with his views on society generally. On the other hand, he had to endure the slow agony of watching everything he loved go down. After the Republican government took over, the social function of the landed gentry was no more; they could survive only with large independent resources, and these the Gregories did not have. Coole was poor soil, the house was quite an ordinary house, and the only feature of the estate that made it valuable, in material terms, was that Lady Gregory's husband had been a great planter; he had grown many trees, including some rare species, and when finally the estate had to be sold a government department bought it for the sake of the trees, and let the house fall down.

Yeats, of course, had seen it coming, had looked ahead to the time

When all those rooms and passages are gone;
When nettles wave above a shapeless mound
And saplings root among the broken stone.

All this leaves problems that are still unsolved, problems of the social relationships of art. The modish view nowadays is that such a tradition as Yeats found, and cherished, among the Anglo-Irish country gentry is useless and worse; it isolates the artist and cuts him off from communion with the One True God – namely, Demos. This view is as unsatisfactory as modish views generally are, especially since most of the theorists who worship Demos most shrilly are essentially nurslings of bureaucracy who have no sympathy with the common man and wouldn't know how to talk to him. And yet, one has a certain sympathy with the young poet of middle-class background who tries to dress, talk and generally act like 'a worker' and is always looking for barricades. At least he feels, obscurely, that some need in our present culture is not being satisfied. He wants to be in touch with some source of power that he feels to be lacking in the bureaucratic structure of the modern state. Who can blame him? If Milton and Lawes were collaborating today, they would be putting on some colossal top-heavy production at Covent Garden, and the money would come from the Arts Council. Does anyone genuinely feel that this would be as good as the arrange-

ment they actually had? And if Yeats's relationship with the
Gregories was already obsolete in his time and more so in ours,
where is the relationship with a trade union or a commune or a
writers' workshop that is enabling a poet to do work of anything
like that quality now?

Politics, and not only direct governmental politics, is the art of
the possible. Living as we do amid a fury of egalitarianism, it
would be useless to try to canvass any support for the idea that a
poet's work could actually be *improved* by mixing on equal
terms with a social class that admitted art into its way of life,
one with enough leisure to cultivate the arts and take an interest
in them. All we could hope to establish, and that grudgingly,
would be that the poet might, in some circumstances, escape
being fatally flawed by such contact. So it is probably for my
own pleasure, rather than in the hope of convincing anyone, that
I quote the wise remarks of C. S. Lewis on the situation of the
courtly poet (*Studies in Words* (1960), p. 23):

> The court takes from the class below it talented individuals
> – like Chaucer, say – as its entertainers and assistants. We
> ordinarily think of Chaucer learning his courtesy at court.
> And no doubt he did; its manners were more graceful than
> those of his own family. But can we doubt that he also
> taught courtesy there? By expecting to find realised at
> court the paradigm of courtesy and nobility, by writing his
> poetry on the assumption that it was realised, such a man
> offers a critique – and an unconscious critique – of the
> court's actual *ethos*, which no one can resent. It is not
> flattery, but it flatters. As they say a woman becomes more
> beautiful when she is loved, a nobility by status will
> become more 'noble' under such treatment. Thus the
> Horaces, Chaucers, Racines, or Spensers substantially en-
> noble their patrons. But also, through them, many graces
> pass down from the aristocracy into the middle class. This
> two-way traffic generates a culture-group comprising the
> choicest member of two groups that differ in status. If this
> is snobbery, we must reckon snobbery among the greatest
> nurseries of civilisation. Without it, would there ever have

been anything but wealth and power above and sycophancy or envy below?

Something of this ideal, albeit turned upside down, may underlie the modern young poet's emotional need to blend with the working class: the ideal of a culture-group that takes in the most gifted individuals from two contiguous areas. If so, it is another mark of that deep need to identify with, and draw strength from, something more vital, more organic, more instinctual than a merely bureaucratic structure. Indeed, everywhere I look I see this need. 'The Tip, Burnley, Lancashire', is the address of a group called 'The Welfare State', who describe themselves as 'Civic Magicians'. Their aim is to bring back a sense of ritual into our lives; they will supply festivals to order; their manifesto draws on the kind of ideas made familiar in Frazer's *Golden Bough*, just as *The Waste Land* did half a century ago.

So the first night of *Comus* turns out to be a rich theme for meditation, as one suspected it would, even though it was an entertainment put on in one place for one night, celebrating an event in the history of one family, and for only as many people as could get into one large room. Some of the conditions were present, it seems, that go to make great art. And, in the cement warren of our bureaucracy, the search for those conditions goes on, because the need for something more living persists: for the personal relationship that enriches art, for the roots going down into the instinctual and primitive, for a victory of the men over the machines.

*

So much for theory, historical conjecture, homiletics. But these things are the shavings from a workshop. For me, 1975 is theatre year. My play, *Harry in the Night*, is put on at the Victoria Theatre, Stoke-on-Trent. The locale is important to me; I was born near here, played as a boy in these streets, came past the theatre on my way to school. (It was a little flea-pit cinema then.) The audience will be the people I know so well, even though nowadays I know very few of them individually: Peter Cheeseman, who commissioned the play and is directing it (*le Vic, c'est lui*) has made an imaginative and emotional identification with Potteries people, and his love of them is an important help to me, always, in keeping that tap-root open. But, if writing a play for the Vic is *à la recherche du temps perdu*, it is also an important new starting-point in my life. My professional pride is involved: there are many instances of writers who have written poetry and plays, rather fewer who have written novels and poetry or novels and plays, but I cannot think of anyone who has scored a triple, who has been poet, novelist and playwright.

(No, wait a minute. G. K. Chesterton wrote a vast amount of verse and fiction, mostly journeywork but sometimes shot through with that careless brillance; and he wrote at any rate one successful play, *Magic*. Chesterton and I! A strange conjunction.)

Taking the train to Stoke, staying in Peter's house so often that it becomes a second home, walking those so-familiar streets (but thirty-five years ago I never drank in the pubs), sitting in the theatre for the read-through and then for rehearsals, rewriting the scenes that the company have difficulty in bringing to life, rewriting them again, then again ... for a week of that glorious summer weather, each day is tripartite: in the theatre all afternoon, break for a meal (the length of the break is laid down by Equity − it must be two hours), then back to the theatre all evening, finally drinks and more talk before bed. And in the morning? Every morning I go to my typewriter and rewrite the scenes that did not come off the day before. In the end, I have written the play three separate times from the first word to the last; and the last act, which carries the burden of the rather difficult things the play is trying to say, I have written ten or a dozen times.

In solitude, one simply could not force oneself to drudge like this: two or three rewritings of a chapter, possibly the jettisoning of a third of a book when the instinctive alarm-bells keep signalling that it is going wrong; but not the endless recasting and shifting of the same few basic materials that theatre seems to require. But, slavery as it is, one never grudges it. The euphoria of making a work of art with other people, the miracle of seeing a flower growing out of the soil of our collective effort, keeps one going through all discouragements. These actors and actresses are serving me, and I am serving them: they take hold of the words I produce, eagerly absorb them into their own imaginative metabolism, and give them back radiant with light and shade and movement.

So much for the general experience of play-writing. Where this experience comes close to my life as a poet is that Peter Cheeseman specifically asks for the action to be interspersed and illuminated by songs. His style of production is closer to revue than to the kind of theatre I grew up with: short scenes, with songs to signal the mood and to move the action from one plane to another. All his actors and actresses have to be able to sing; if they cannot read music when they join the company, he speedily has them taught. I accept all this; as a novice, I am ready to do it his way, and in any case I see no reason why the drama should deny itself the aid of such a powerful sister-art. I write lyrics, tentatively, keeping the words simple, using open vowels, making the verse as singable as I can, and Peter Cheeseman engages Michael Garrick to set them to music.

I have run into Mike Garrick a few times before – as a jazz-based composer, he has been interested in working with poets – but I have never worked in harness with a musician until now. His quick, fertile mind moves much faster than mine; a neat, dapper man, his intent face suddenly breaking into laughter above that trim goatee, his hands incredibly agile on the keyboard. He comes to Stoke for a working session; we are grouped round the piano, and my role is mainly to listen. Peter Cheeseman, tirelessly intent and alert, his head moving quickly on his neck like a bird's, his stocky body restless with energy, seems to know exactly what the music ought to sound like, and Mike catches his ideas by E.S.P. I hang about, my participation limited to a dutiful promise, every now and then, to rewrite some lyric that does not fit their purposes.

In the end, we are left with a sheaf of songs that will be put
in, taken out, shifted from one part of the play to another, and
finally performed to a paying audience. The numbers all fas-
cinate me: two of them, in particular, seem to me to deserve an
independent life, not to die with the show. Mike Garrick's
favourite is a song for Mary, Harry's wife, a generous woman, a
lover and giver; because Harry is wrapped away from her in
overwork and personal problems, and her glowing warmth and
love have nowhere to go, she has an affair lasting for years with
his brother, in whose drab life her love is the only brightness.
She sings for him and for herself:

> I want your needing
> I need your wanting
> asking is granting
> loving is feeding
>
> I'll sing you to sleep
> or I'll kiss you awake
> I'll do the giving
> for giving's sake.
>
> Bring me your aching
> bring me your craving
> thirst is for slaking
> and love is for having
>
> I'll sing you to sleep
> or I'll kiss you awake
> I'll do the giving
> for giving's sake.

Mike has given this an enchanting setting. He has a superb
woman singer with his Quintet, by name Norma Winstone, and
he tells me he is thinking of putting Mary's song into the Quintet's
repertoire as a vehicle for her. I hope he will, but as far as I am
concerned Mike's masterpiece here is the setting he has made
for Kitty's song. Kitty, Harry's daughter, is a sweet, pensive girl
who works as a schoolteacher: she is pregnant, though since

becoming so she has decided that the man in question is im-
possible for her to live with, and she is going ahead as a single
mother. But the baby inside her makes her soft-eyed towards her
infant-school charges, and she sings:

Children, children,
the dull and the clever
like a tide coming in
for ever and ever.

Children, children
ugly ones and pretty ones
Children, children,
country ones and city ones.

Each of them someone's son or daughter
leaping and shining like restless water
mouths and noses, eyes and ears
ready for laughter, ready for tears:

minds and bodies always moving:
where do they come from? They come from loving.

All those heads
and all those faces
they come from loving
in secret places:

from heat of love
all were begotten:
from love still burning
or love forgotten.

Mike Garrick's music for this song is enchanting, and as Jenny
Howe sings it in her pure, soft voice she *is* Kitty. Words,
music, voice flow into one whole: Jenny, Mike and I have put
our three individualities together and made something that none
of us, alone, could have made. These are trite words, this is a
trite description, but what other is there? Listening, in the dark
cavern of the theatre at rehearsal, or amid the audience in perfor-

mance, I feel humble and grateful: humble, because of the extent of my dependence on others; grateful, because the most fortunate of all human destinies is to be an artist, however flawed, however struggling.

And in the dark winter days, when *Harry* is no more than a memory, Eirian plays Kitty's song on the piano, and sings it, and it blossoms again in a different soil. Am I writing too many words about a little song? I shall print the music at the end of this book. Judge it, musical reader, for yourself, and agree with me.

Back in Oxford. An evening drink in the Plough at Wolvercote with another Oxford poet, David Winzar, a tall, gentle creature like a giraffe. Not having lived long enough to grow a leathery skin, he carries his poet's vulnerability on the surface, but immediately beneath it there is strength. His shy, humorous manner is a door ajar on the fiercely burning imagination within. Once again that bell rings in my head.

POEMS BY DAVID WINZAR

A Dead Spider

> There's beggary in the love that can be reckoned
> *Antony and Cleopatra*

Soggy still,
But stiffening up a bit,
A skull and cross bones on the grill,
A homeless, hopeless squatter joining hands against the law,

My spider
Sits with legs stuck round the compass,
And fingertip body mashed,
But whole.

I'd seen it before, quick as a laser,
Running wild, as shiny white
Cliff sides beat back its terror,
And packed its head foursquare with fear.

A clockwork purpose couldn't cope with this.
The four white walls of the stadium
Grinned like God; and hooked on his enamel lip
Two taps beat Chinese time.

My spider raced the bath's banked track,
And lost. A bullet-head led nowhere,
But hid at the last, zeroed on the pipe,
And crouching, was crushed.

The beggar bobs about now,
A gashed aquatic mine.
Its spines, fine triggers once,
Are broken.

                    . . .

I'd tried to save the thing,
Had thrust a paper ring at it.
It scuttled back in blank mistrust,
So I left it to its fate.

The Racing Tyre
For Mike Burns

Slick, bald, and black,
It sits, squat and fat,
An ogre's dumpling,
Waiting to be used.
As malleable as moral choice,
Its softness is insidious.

Steely-eyed, omnipotent, the machine sits still,
Big amidships, purposeful, coming to a point,

Its red heart worn all over, inside out.
Beyond this torso's militant heat, both beak
And brain, the nosecone and the helmet, wait,
Hungry for the cool of thunder.
Hatched in an open dome, each pack of cells,
Hawkeyed, in fancy, gapes,
Eager to bolt a hole clean through
The heart of the informal atmosphere,
The indifferent air, that's nowhere, and weighs tons.

The bright machine is useless for a while;
As rubberware is ripped away
To be refilled with air,
It's jacked up on a scaffold, impotent.
Then compensation fiddles on the wings.
Their metal fingers,
Stretched to skim the air as though
They're eager to decapitate
That passive weakling, sky,
Are trained to take a dive,
To ease the rubber's drifting from the level, narrow
    straight.

At last, the engine barks.
The car starts past on squat new slicks,
Its voice a howl of purity.

Perfectible intensity of purpose
Rolls by on soft black compromise.

For Ivor Young

'Huntington's Chorea: An hereditary type which may
occur in adults. Choreic signs (irregular and involun-
tary contraction of muscles) are marked and the men-
tal powers may be affected, leading to dementia. The
disease is progressive.'

Hung out to jerk on broken strings, he's cured
In his sickness like a kipper – salted, smoked:
His disinfectant blent with sour tobacco.

Limbs pinned in an arbitrary body
Staccato like fish in a box,
Bashing their fatuous tails

On the sensible slats.
Frenetic gulls rotate about the catch,
Gutting sprats and rubbish.

The salt sea air will hose down everything
Until it's clean – or so it seems.
Deposits gather slowly, white as time.

Last summer, it was my duty for the first time to think of a title
for the Newdigate Prize Poem. I came up with 'The Tides'. What is
needed, it seems to me, is a title that could trigger off any kind of
poem the writer feels able to offer. 'The Tides' could be taken
historically, scenically, philosophically, analogically. In the event,
the entries that come do in fact cover that kind of range. Mulling
over them with my two fellow-examiners, I find that we all three
pick the same winner, and it turns out to be by Andrew Motion, a
poet I have known for a couple of years and whose work I respect.
His poem, which he subsequently publishes under the title 'Inland',
is a beautifully thought-out blend of the historical and the symbolic.
Certain East Anglian villages in the early seventeenth century fell
prey to rapacious landowners who enclosed their common land on
the grounds that it was liable to flooding and therefore useless to the
villagers and in need of reclamation. This technique was pushed es-
pecially hard in those villages that lay nearest the sea, and could be
flooded by high tides as well as rising fen water. So that 'Inland' has
a social and historical dimension as well as being a highly ac-
complished piece of scene-painting and a general statement about
life. Short of printing the whole, which I have no space for, the

poem's range cannot be represented, but here is a chunk that has its own unity within the whole:

Disembarkation

Sun flicked round the bay,
binding the outline of farms
to their reflection in grey
bands of light. The marsh
always survives. Always.

Cattle stirred in their shed,
uncoiling sweet whisps
of breath over my head;
fresh shadows spilt down
their flanks and spread

across water to flake
into shrinking fragments
over the strangers' wake.
Their boat put down
some men; one staked

its prow into our land,
waded towards us
over the grass, and
lifted one arm. Our world
dried on his hand.

An Ultimatum

I waited in silence, weighing a stone in my pocket,
    on our green beach;
a low boat swerved from the other's shadow
    and moored out of reach.

We saw nothing exactly; a stranger hunched
  in the stern
studied our silence, then stood. In the village
  behind us, quietly, locks turned.

Even his words were blurred by distance;
  we pressed to the shore,
thinking if this was the danger we feared,
  there must be more.

But when we stared at his elegant silhouette,
  into the sun,
we heard a tiny ripple of syllables claiming
  the village, then run

underwater over our fields until we were strangers
  in our own land,
watching our shadows circle on memories
  we could no longer lose, or understand.

An Appeal Refused

In the church it was cold:
we knelt by the altar
waiting for fields to unfold
indoors the scent from flowers
of tamarisk, marsh marigold.

How could I leave that place?
I could imagine nothing except
its imperfect, stubborn grace,
– but from the shadows
no saviour unveiled his face.

Did we want miracles? Signs?
I only saw light,
piercing the window, define
a forbidden landscape where
water and earth entwined.

We knelt until sunset burned
it to dark. Below us, as lamps
in the village returned,
out of the dark a thickening
silence smothered the love we earned.

Jesse Sease

Jesse Sease walked hunched, head weighed down
to take in the flat parish he lived for.
At noon on our last day, crossing the crown
of dry land, he stooped into his stone church

and knelt until evening, below his high shadow
hardening in the glass. When he came out
he walked to our yard: 'Go on up. I'll follow.'
One hand with its heavy ring picked at some cloth

on our cart; hens clucked through a dark door.
We could not meet his look, or anyone's,
but travelled inland towards our new law,
hoarding familiar, fragrant dust on boots and hair.

He must have stood by his church
watching our tense backs thinning in twilight,
then turned to the silver water, and lurched
in. We only hear our rough wheels grin uphill.

Searching next morning, we found him
drowned in the salty grass. He lay
with his head bending the water's rim,
the ring embedded in his swollen hand.

Towards the middle of August, *Harry in the Night* goes on at
last. I suppose nothing can quite equal the excitement of having
one's first play open its doors to a paying audience. Yet my
excitement, everyone's excitement, is to some extent smothered
and drained by the heat. For weeks, England has been broiling in

a southern European summer. Frequently, the temperature in London has been higher than in Athens. The paving-stones bake, the tar melts, the streets shimmer. Only in the evening, sitting in pubs with the doors wide open, rejoicing in the coolness and bitterness of deep glasses of beer, does one seem able to manage coherent thought.

The Victoria Theatre, that old converted cinema, has very little defence against weather. In the mornings it is often freezing cold; with a full house and the lights on, it becomes startlingly hot. This first night of *Harry*, the audience are sweating and fanning themselves with their programmes. The cast seem to be acting under water. In the thick, drugged heat they move their agile limbs with an unnatural slowness. A short hesitation while memory assembles a line becomes a long, languorous pause. The whole experience is dream-like, though this is good too because it means that one has no difficulty in entering the imaginative world of the play. Being half-asleep to begin with, we dream the more readily. On this first night, the dream scenes in the play, when Harry in delirium acts out his conflicts in surreal emblematic situations, seem to me to come over with a special force.

At any rate, I can at last sink back in my seat and watch the play with a relieved sense of detachment, of being just another spectator. It is on, it will have thirty-two performances whether anyone comes or not, it is all there with words and gestures, music and sets and costumes and lights shining down and people serving coffee in the interval. I am a playwright.

Harry in the Night is not, in the end, a resplendent success in the eyes of the world. It doesn't go to any other theatre, doesn't make anyone rich. But I am content and better than content. My play is acted by a first-rate company; it pulls in interested, responsive audiences quite up to the Vic's average attendance; for all the weeks I inhabited the theatre I have collected a pay-packet, plus £180 in royalties at the end; and the intensive training in stagecraft, given me by one of England's most creative directors, is free of charge.

This first night, the sensation of living in a dream is heightened by the fact that all the sections of my life seem to have come together in this one building. Oxford friends have come up in a mini-bus; Sally, Andrew, Jill represent poetry; my wife and children, my father, various cousins and nephews and nieces, all share with me in the enactment of this piece of my imaginative world.

Next morning, everyone is eagerly reading the notices. When I publish a book, I never read any reviews or in any way acknowledge the public reception. This is self-protective; in matters regarding my work, I take orders only from myself. If I had taken heed of the things that have been said about my work I would have given up writing long ago. But now I read the notices like everyone else, because it is all sharing in the corporate experience. The notices are 'mixed'. Some are appreciative, even generously encouraging; one or two are vicious. The most dismissive of all is uttered over the radio by the big-hat girl, she who appears next to me on all the photographs taken on the day of my election as Professor of Poetry. From that humble beginning in our back garden, she has in two years clambered to the commanding heights of the media, and perhaps the zeal with which she belabours my play is part of some personal need to kick away the ladder. Whatever the reason, she shows no mercy to poor *Harry*, even informing her listeners that I must be patronizing my native town, showing a badly veiled contempt for its citizens by offering them this tasteless dish. A bad guess, Missy. I am giving them a slice of the truth as I have learnt it by living for fifty years, and it is the same as their truth. Harry, when his life crumbles about him, finds new strength not from some spectacular fresh beginning, some road-to-Damascus religious vision, but simply from usefulness and productive work, from the sense that he has skills and knowledge that are needed and so can respect himself. He makes his new freedom out of the sober, industrious habits of his old slavery. The mental attitude changes, but not the willingness to undertake the world's practical duties. This is something I learnt by growing up among these people and realizing what keeps them alive in their often monotonous and drab surroundings — alive, and full of zest and humour and courage. Patronizing them? Is that how it looks from Knightsbridge?

I have been corresponding with a French poet, Michel Velmans. I say 'French', and he is indeed a Frenchman and writes in that language, but his imagination appears to be entirely Celtic. He runs something called Les Rencontres Poétiques du Mont Saint-Michel du Cercle d'Études Poétiques Celtes et Vikings de de l'Université Européenne de la Poésie. (Yes, really.) Very much a man of the Atlantic coastline, living in Granville and with his face turned towards the stormy, mist-hung western sea with its islands and legends, towards Cornwall, Wales, the Hebrides; in a country whose literary culture is so decisively Mediterranean, he is very much a man of Brittany and Normandy. We have had a desultory correspondence, and now suddenly he is here, sitting in the garden. Externally, there is nothing to mark him out as anything but a solid, reliable country lawyer: dark-suited, thick-set, spectacled, with a short iron-grey beard. Nothing, that is, except his torrent of talk about poetry, Celtic legends, magical beliefs, and the gleam in his eye which accompanies it. 'Je vis le mythe,' he remarks with total unself-consciousness. I am not quite sure what myth he is living, but I am not in the least disposed to contradict him.

Knowing him to be a *Celtisan*, I parade Sally Purcell with her deep and wide-ranging knowledge of Celtic stories and beliefs, and Eirian to talk Welsh to him in case he wants to break suddenly into Breton. In the event, it turns as usual into another drinking-party. Velmans departs, breathing enthusiasm, and turns up again a couple of months later when we are in north Wales; he has just landed from a sailing expedition among the Hebrides, and looks like a slightly fey version of Neptune. He is marvellously good company, devouring everything, interested in everything, finding everything *sympathique*. We take him in a fishing-boat piloted by our friend Mons Bevan; on the warm misty swell, all of us floating on a thick summer tide of dreams, we sway gently past the granite cliffs and the purple humps of north Wales. Mons sets course for Llanddwyn; he finds a cove with delicious clear water, and everybody swims. Michel Velmans lies face down in the water and drives his strong, stocky body through it with the power of a walrus.

Meanwhile this is still the summer of the theatre, and my involvement with it continues in one way and another. Partly, I am an intermediary between the two worlds. Jill Haas has written a work called *The Winds*, a sequence of poems, songs and piano music; since it must obviously be heard rather than read, she wants to make a recording of it and see if that will result in a radio production. This in turn involves two verse-readers, male and female, a pianist (herself) and a singer (female), all brought together in front of good recording equipment. The theatre is the obvious place: Jill comes up to Stoke, the young sound engineer gives up some free time to make the recording, and Katherine Iddon with her strong and beautiful voice is willing to read verse and sing. I read the man's part.

In September I am back at the theatre again, this time on salary as 'textual adviser' for a Shakespearian production. It is *Much Ado about Nothing*, not a play I have ever known very thoroughly, and I am glad to be paid to study it carefully; glad, too, to work with actors and actresses, to know that any insight one manages to bring them will have immediate results in performance, helping to make the play alive and heart-warming to an audience. Working with students is pleasant and can be rewarding, but working with these players is vividly exciting; they concentrate so fiercely on their roles that giving them ideas is like throwing coal into a furnace, to be consumed instantly into heat.

Peter Cheeseman's method when producing Shakespeare is to begin with a detailed study of the text – the whole text, however much it will be cut in production. The cast spend a week reading the play slowly and carefully, at music-stands. My task is to explain any difficulties as they come up: obsolete words, textual difficulties, allusions. Because I have the title of Professor (which Peter Cheeseman impishly insists on using whenever he addresses me) I am supposed to know everything. In fact, as usual with Shakespeare, there are difficulties that not all the learned commentaries in existence can settle. For instance. After Benedick has challenged Claudio to a duel in Act V, scene I, and has abruptly left him and Don Pedro together, rejecting with cold anger their attempts to involve him in verbal horse-play, they are left wonderingly looking after him; then comes this exchange:

> *Don Pedro:* What a pretty thing man is when he goes in his doublet and hose and leaves off his wit!
> *Claudio:* He is then a giant to an ape; but then is an ape a doctor to such a man.

Since something is expected of me and I am not paid to say I don't know, I come up with a kind of explanation. A few minutes earlier, Claudio (not realizing that Benedick is now his enemy) has been appealing to him to amuse them out of their boredom, and has asked him, 'Wilt thou use my scabbard; shall I draw it?' Now that Benedick has shown icy disdain, issued his challenge, and swept off, Don Pedro says ruefully that it is a strange sight to see a creature dressed like a human being but behaving like a fierce animal. Claudio replies that such a being is larger and more dangerous than an ape; but, in so far as he is a man, he is less intelligent by the standards of his own *genus* than apes are by the standards of theirs; compared with such a man, an ape is wise and learned (a doctor). The poor little crestfallen quip seems hardly worth such a dragged-out explanation; but the actor must have confidence that he knows what it means, so the Professor must be ready with elucidation.

At another point we make a polite bow to the benevolent shade of Samuel Johnson. When Beatrice says in bitter-sweet self-mockery, 'Thus goes everyone to the world but I, and I am sunburnt,' she evidently means that she is the odd one out; all the other girls have mates, and she is avoided like one who is browned by the sun and has lost her peaches-and-cream complexion, so essential to an Elizabethan ideal of beauty. Johnson checked at the expression 'go to the world'; he was not content to take it in a loose general sense, 'go along with the world', 'accept the world's usages', 'do as everyone else does'; he emended 'world' to 'wood', thus substituting a precise metaphor: 'Everyone else goes into the cool shelter of the wood, and I stay

outside in the lonely field and am sunburnt.' Caroline Harington,
who is playing Beatrice, looks inquiring at the same point, and I
tell her to change 'world' to 'wood'. So we incorporate a little bit
of Johnson's Shakespeare, as a Staffordshire playhouse should.

Bill Coleman is in London, one of the great pillars of my life,
marvellous jazz trumpeter, musician's musician, Bill of the
flashing smile, the warm geniality that is never unmixed with
dignity, the emperor, the man who among other things helps me
to understand *Othello*. I once went on a pilgrimage to his
birthplace, Paris, Kentucky; a strange town, built to be the
capital of Bourbon County, its very name acknowledging the
help given by the Bourbon dynasty to the American settlers in
their War of Independence. An imposing court-house, two or
three beautiful eighteenth-century mansions, and then ... a dirt
road, a few run-down shops, the typical forgotten rural village of
America. Bill's memories of his childhood, which I have so often
eagerly pumped out of him, go back to an era as totally in the
past as Sally's Middle Ages. The life of a black child in Kentucky
before 1914 ... it bears the same relation to present-day life as
that of a child brought up in rural poverty in the Wessex of
Thomas Hardy. Once, when we were eating a superb meal cooked
by Bill's Swiss wife Lily, we talked of food, and with no trace of
bitterness or even under-privilege, just with his natural dignity and
benevolence, Bill recalled how there would sometimes be a hog-
killing, in that country district, at which, when the best meat had
been taken away by the white farmers and their families, the
remainder would be given away free to the Negroes—hence the ac-
cumulated lore, how to make a delicious meal from hog-jowl and
turnip greens, or chitterlings, or pig-foot; and I, with a background
among the English poor who for generations had kept themselves
alive on tripe and black pudding, faggots and trotters, had identified
totally, just as my non-musician's soul identifies with Bill on this
rainy evening, at the Seven Dials Community Centre. He goes on
to the tiny platform, to head an ensemble of London jazz musicians,
all brilliant but the brilliance of the rest overshadowed by the
warm, emotionally appealing virtuosity of Danny Moss on tenor

saxophone, and the moment Bill appears the atmosphere becomes
charged in that special way that I remember at so many of his per-
formances in Paris. Tall, commanding, yet hospitable, never up-
staging the other musicians but unfailingly sustaining and up-
buoying them, he holds his trumpet loosely by his side until it is
time to put it to his lips, and then – the high urgent clarion, the deep
dragging melancholy, the meditation, the personal statement
carried up from those depths of experience, the memories of Django
Reinhardt, of Fats Waller, of Coleman Hawkins, of hanging around
Boudon's in the thirties, of New York in the twenties, of Armstrong
. . . it all comes out, unforced, spontaneous, and I lean against the
wall in the crush of spellbound jazz-listeners, a minority by this
time no longer drawn from the young, taking in the sixty-year-old
face as well as the twenty-year-old, marvelling at this man: over
seventy years of age, under medical treatment for a failing heart. It
is now November and I happen to know that he has not seen his
home since July, living out of a suitcase for the whole intervening
time, meeting a different audience every second or third night,
giving, always giving. As I listen to Bill I suddenly realize how deep-
ly I love and admire people who perform, who give to an audience
out of the fibres of their existence, who find the energy and the
generosity to go on giving beyond the frontiers of exhaustion. Soon
afterwards, my poem 'Performers' gets itself written; I put into it
my feeling about Bill, about the actors and actresses I have been
working with, about everyone who chooses to accept a life founded
on communication with an audience.

   At almost exactly the same time – either the evening before
Bill's concert or the evening after, I don't remember which – I
take the chair at a reading by Yevgeny Yevtushenko at the
Wigmore Hall. Here again I recognize the presence of a per-
former. Yevtushenko may not be the finest of contemporary
poets, though a genuine poet he certainly is, but he is certainly a
performer to the core, giving himself to an audience and com-
municating with them on a deep level, emotional and instinctual.

   Quite possibly Yevtushenko has developed into more of a pure
performer than he would have under normal circumstances. But his
circumstances have not been normal. Poets in the Soviet Union
are in any case encouraged to give public readings of their work,

as a means of sharing it with the people, but Yevtushenko has
been particularly led to channel his energies into this kind of per-
formance. For years, he was an official export. Having expressed
with courage some opinions critical of the policies of the Soviet
Government, particularly its all-pervading anti-Semitism, and
got away with it, he became 'our dissident', paraded abroad to
show the liberality of Soviet institutions. He toured the world,
attracting large audiences in every capital city, first out of
curiosity and then, increasingly, because he spellbound them.
This went on for something like five years, but as time went on
it must have been felt in Moscow that he was in some way not
coming up to expectations, and he was withdrawn as the official
export; his place was taken by Vosnozhensky, who also did not
last long. This visit in 1975 is his come-back: older, not quite the
teenage idol of the early sixties, but with undiminished flair and
showmanship and still a very likeable and decent human being.

I have been asked to chair his reading, and to read the English
translations, by the Great Britain–U.S.S.R. Association, his
sponsors, and I have agreed on condition that I can do it my
way. A brief introduction, just the two of us on the platform, a
straight reading, no discussion. Above all, no discussion! In any
poetry reading that is followed by 'questions', the questions tend
to vapour on and on until all that anyone remembers afterwards
is the questions and not the poetry. And, in this particular case,
to invite questions would unleash such a torrent of irrelevances,
idées fixes, ancient grievances, such a demented swarm of bees
released from bonnets and bats from belfries, as to swamp the
literary nature of the occasion and quite probably lead to a
fracas into the bargain. I have sympathy with all the people who
would try to air their point of view, even with the monomaniacs
and paranoiacs who have probably been made like that by in-
justice and ill-treatment, but this is a poetry-reading, not a
political meeting in disguise.

So, no questions. And as I am to meet Yevtushenko first in
Oxford, then drive to London and repair to a flat that someone is
lending us as a greenroom, I bargained for adequate time in
which he and I can hole up, with a crate of beer, and discuss the

programme, rehearsing and timing the items.

We do and all goes well. The proceedings begin with an excellent lunch-party at Anne Shukman's house in Park Town. The guests are hand-picked, the atmosphere relaxed, the food and drink up to the best Oxford standard ('No emperor does himself so well'). Nevertheless, when I first enter and catch sight of Yevtushenko, he is looking slightly tense and hunted. It must, after all, be a dreadful life, this of touring superstar poet: the hotels, the airports, the official entourage, the meetings with distinguished foreign colleagues, the interviews, the food and drink taken at times to suit other people's convenience. On seeing me, he brightens, obviously because something tells him that here is an animal of the same kind, someone with the same interior diagram as his own. We talk; he has excellent English. At lunch we are on opposite sides of the table, but we signal to each other with understanding. Towards the end of the meal he leans across the table to me. 'John,' he says, 'you are a very juicy man. You know what is a juicy man? It is my dialect: Siberian.' Since from his expression I see that this is a compliment, I assume he means that I am the opposite of a dry stick.

The lunch-party breaks up. We drive to London. A flat has been kindly lent for the occasion by a young man whose name I never catch but whom everyone addresses as 'Rupert' and whom I vaguely understand to be a member of the aristocracy; here, Yevtushenko and I settle down and rehearse. He chooses the poems he wants to make up the programme, I look up the translations in the stack of books we have brought with us, and we read them, carefully timing ourselves. We approach the evening frankly as show-business. We are to entertain a paying audience, and we will take that obligation seriously. Between bouts of intense concentration we empty glasses and joke and exchange scraps of autobiography; though I empty my glass much more often than he does, for he is, like many performers, very abstemious before working. Once or twice he cautions me against drinking too much, as if afraid that I shall fall off the platform. I assure him that everything will be all right.

We walk round to the Wigmore Hall, getting lost twice on the

234 PROFESSING POETRY

way, and he and I wait in the artists' dressing-room while the audience assembles. The place fills up rapidly; the audience is narrowly watched by stewards, for anything to do with the Soviet Union brings out cranks of every hue, and just recently there has been particular indignation among the Jewish population at the plight of the Soviet Jews. Yevtushenko is nervous, pacing the carpet, but it is the nervousness of a racehorse capable of winning the Grand National. Everything is planned; he has asked me to read three of his poems in English first, to establish the mood, before he begins. After that, each poem will be preceded by its English translation. (This, at my suggestion. I have always found that when listening to poetry in a foreign language I get much more out of it if I hear the translation first.)

It is time. We go on. I have not described Yevtushenko yet, preferring to wait and let the reader see him at the same moment as the audience. He is tall, long-skulled, high-cheekboned, with expressive eyes and mouth, rapid movements, fiery glances. He wears a corduroy suit in brilliant green. He has a look of the North; he could be a Finn or a Laplander. The audience devour him.

After the briefest possible chairman's remarks, I explain that Mr Yevtushenko has asked me to begin by reading three of his poems in English, and proceed to do so. Half-way through the second, a woman with a strong Slavonic accent shouts out, 'Why don't you let Mr Yevtushenko read his own poems?' I do my best to reassure her, and grind on. At last the juicy man is replaced by the lithe, coiled-spring man. The audience sighs a little and settles back; fringe inattention subsides. I listen with the rest. As soon as Yevtushenko begins to read I am back in the theatre; not the theatre of Peter Cheeseman, but something closer to the Moscow Arts Theatre with its tradition of more rhetorical delivery. He uses the full range of his voice, extracting every drop of tonal value from every word, varying his pauses like an orator. Oratory, indeed, is what it comes across as. I listen in vain for any skeletal faithfulness to the rhythms of the verse, the shape that the poem has on the page. He reads them as speeches, and very effective speeches they are too. After each poem there is applause, I rise and read the translation of the

next poem, and he is into it again. I try to keep my reading plain and
rhythmical, content if I can be heard on the back row and give some
sense of what the poem is about and what is its dominant mood.
The emotion, the *frisson*, will come from the poet. And he does not
fail them.

During the interval, we are left in peace in our greenroom,
with a tray of drinks. Once again Yevtushenko scarcely wets his
lips, and the juicy man drinks for two. We have one visitor, a
middle-aged Russian woman poet, evidently an old friend of
Yevtushenko's, for she greets him with quiet, sincere affection
and they talk calmly, enjoying each other's presence. Afterwards
I learn that the quiet of the greenroom was in contrast to a
violent scuffle in one of the gangways of the hall, when someone
was trying to get at Yevtushenko with a parcel, though whether
the parcel contained a bomb, a bouquet, a message for relatives
in Russia, or merely the person's collected poems in typescript, I
shall never know, nor even whether the frustrated intruder was a
man or a woman.

Afterwards, we go back to Rupert's, but the magic has gone,
the entourage is thick, and I escape, glad to have met this man
whose name has been familiar to me for so long, glad to have
shared a few hours of his wandering life, glad to have struck a
chord of response from him. One thing I know for certain:
Yevgeny has vindicated his mother. That brave, unfortunate
woman, struggling along in poverty and hardship, had some
small talent as a singer – a talent that might have blossomed if
the circumstances of her life had been less desperate – and she
tried to scratch out a living by entertaining the troops during the
war. But exposure to the freezing air had ruined her voice, and
Yevgeny has movingly described her final defeat, when she tried
to sing to the soldiers and her voice came out as a piteous, un-
musical screech. Going home afterwards with her son, she told
him she knew how bad she had sounded, and the two of them
shared her agony. Well, he has avenged that agony now, paid for
it in jewels time after time, buried it under a mountain of golden
leaves. His mother, battered down by the hardship of her life,
failed to hold an audience, so Yevgeny holds them for her, forces

them to listen, to applaud, to bring him back time after time.

The next morning I read the notice of our evening in *The Times*. Their august critic has been wowed like everyone else. Never, in his opinion, has the Wigmore Hall resounded to a sound so 'mellifluous' as this poet's voice. Mellifluous! Trust *The Times* to find the faintly literary *mot juste* with which to wrap up the occasion! The critic must have been in generous mood, because even I get a mention. Well, not I but my clothes. I am described as 'wearing a blue denim jacket', which is about like saying that I came on to the platform in my braces. It was split cowhide, Reverend Sir.

Harry in the Night is over, but the Victoria Theatre sees me once more before the season dies. The Michael Garrick Quintet are visiting, and I am invited to read from my poetry round the edges of the music; not poetry-and-jazz as understood in the sixties, but poetry and jazz without the hyphens.

It is a Sunday afternoon. I go into the theatre to find the musicians sitting about in a state of gloom, tired by a long tour, cast down by the fact that at some places they have had poor audiences. Jazz, as they practise it, is undeniably a minority art; played by conservatory-trained musicians, it has lost its roots among the people, and it takes as much effort on the part of the listener as Cage or Stockhausen. (Though, in my opinion, with more to offer as reward for the effort.) I am introduced to them through a veil of indifference and reserve; they register me, at first, as just another poet who is going to act as performing flea during their breathing-spaces. But as the hours go by we are cemented into a kind of friendliness by the mere fact that we are all in it together. If the evening is a frost, we shall all be depressed and all in the same way; if things go well, we shall be similarly lifted up. We begin to speak each other's language. We test equipment, discuss the sequence of items, make a few muted jokes. Then come the beer and sandwiches, and the faint but perceptible electric current that moves through everyone's bones as the first customers arrive. They are here, money is changing hands, the evening is really going to happen, we are performers.

We go into the dressing-room; those of us who have performing-clothes put them on. Norma Winstone, Mike's celebrated and really remarkable singer, gets into her sequined dress. Out in the auditorium, the lights are gleaming on the drums, the saxophone, the big electric guitar. Too late to get out now; it's really going to happen. The theatre fills up, the time comes, Peter Cheeseman announces us, we're off.

All goes well. This, at least, is one concert the Quintet will look back on with solid satisfaction. They play with incredible flair and invention. Norma Winstone is everything she has been cracked up to be; her voice is small, so that before the era of the microphone she would have been confined to *salon* work, but her musicianship and imagination are wonderful. Even so, the show comes close to being stolen by Bryan Spring, the drummer, whose performance is lyrical, demented, brooding, sombre and humorous, sometimes by turns and sometimes all together. Towards the end of the evening, my great moment arrives. The Quintet are going to play some of the numbers from *Harry*. Norma will sing the lyrics; but, since one of the numbers is a straight twelve-bar blues, with choruses shared among the characters, it will sound absurd if she sings the chorus that should come from Harry. (With all her virtuosity, she cannot make herself sound like a middle-aged man.) So Mike Garrick decides that, since I am present, I must sing it. The musicians play, and Norma sings. I have never heard the blues sung with so much invention and feeling. As she plays with the twelve-bar form, soaring above it, digging beneath it, sabotaging it and then returning to put everything right, I realize that I am in the presence of pure genius. Then, at the appropriate moment, she holds out the microphone to me. I sing. Wonder of wonders, the effect is passable. My hoarse shout, which after thirty years of listening to the blues does at least put the right sounds in the right places, makes a contrast with her lyrical delicacy.

Afterwards, as I go to my seat, I feel one of those waves of elation that make life worth living. After all those years as a mere uninstructed consumer, I have made a contribution, I have sung the blues to a paying audience and they have liked it. My happiness is compounded by the fact that the theatre's electronic

technician is making a recording of the whole concert. My voice
will be on record! With Norma Winstone! With the Michael
Garrick Quintet!

Afterwards, Bryan Spring has nowhere to stay the night, so he
comes back to Peter Cheeseman's house. We eat bread and
cheese and drink beer. He is a strongly built man in his thirties,
crop-haired, articulate in a Cockney idiom, in many ways a classic
East Ender. I like him enormously. He is totally clear and un-
compromising about his values, certain what he is interested in
and cares about. He makes me happy by telling me that he liked
my poetry and it said something real to him. Presently he
fumbles in his grip and produces a well-used paperback copy of
W. B. Yeats's poems. He never goes anywhere without it, ap-
parently. He searches for a moment, finds a certain poem, and
hands it to me with a request to read it. I do; he approves; he
burrows again and produces another paperback, an anthology of
religious verse. This time it is a passage from *Paradise Lost* he
asks me to read. I didn't need to be told, of course, that lovers of
poetry do not fit into the same pattern or necessarily resemble
one another at all; still, Bryan is a man you might talk to for
quite a long time without guessing that he was an avid reader of
Yeats and Milton. The lesson to be learnt is one I had learnt
already, but it is always cheering to have it confirmed: poetry is
a universal art, and the love of it can flower anywhere, not just in
the carefully tended flower-beds.

Altogether it is a memorable evening, this last visit of 1975 to
the Victoria Theatre. I look forward with child-like eagerness to
getting my copy of the tape-recording that will immortalize my
singing. It comes; I avoid the egotistic temptation to spin it
backwards and forwards till I find my precious minute or two;
having fitted the tape on the machine, I sit reverently listening to
the whole evening, including the announcement of the intervals,
Mike Garrick's jokes, everything. Just as I judge that my own
piece will be coming up next, the tape finishes. Evidently
the engineer decided that he had recorded enough and went
for a drink. My moment of glory, my one piece of jazz
professionalism, is lost for ever.

5
Case-Histories

One September day, our old stone house is permeated by the

Sound of a stick upon the floor, the sound
Of somebody that toils from chair to chair.

Isabella Fey is visiting – a woman I met through Eirian and have known twenty years; then living in New York, subsequently in Australia, now a citizen of Tel-Aviv. With her white face topped by a shock of dark hair, her deep dark eyes, she seems to me like a Jewish Colette. In the grip of some cruel rheumatic disease, still she bravely launches herself on long journeys. With the poet's openness and vulnerability, she has the poet's tensile strength.

She tells me of a strange journey of the mind which has dominated her imaginative life for over a decade. I press her for details. I want to trace the steps of this journey. Soon after she returns home, a bulky file arrives through the post: 'Poems by Isabella Fey and Anthony Cam'. They are the same person. Each lives his/her independent poetic life, being accepted or rejected by editors and publishers as two distinct people; naturally so, since each is a credible, independent artist.

Cam started as a satirical joke. Isabella Fey, some time at the beginning of the sixties, had to face the unpalatable fact that her work as a poet would meet with more success in the world if it were not so good. (Many poets have had to face this fact.) Isabella Fey's work is imaginatively delicate as well as bold; it is lyrical, shaped, conscious of tradition. Without these qualities it would of course fit in much better with contemporary fashion. If

241

only her poems were unformed, crude, obscene! So, 'with a friend' (I picture the two of them dreaming it up over a long liquid lunch), she conceived the notion of a young male poet who should be all these things. She concocted some poems in the 'Beat' manner and sent them to the appropriate magazines. They weren't all published, but the response of editors was respectful and interested. Cam was producing the kind of poetry they wanted.

So far, the story is like dozens of others. But what happened next was interesting. Isabella began to be aware of Cam as a real presence, his maleness a real counterpoint to her femaleness; the two of them sang together, but in recognizable voices. The sexual difference, the sharing of all life between male and female, had always fascinated Isabella Fey. She had written a poem on the subject at the age of eleven, mused on it all her life, confronted it as woman, wife, mother of a son. From this point on, parody was forgotten, scoring off editors a dead issue; a whole element in her nature became articulate through a male *persona*.

Some difficulties of management remained: Cam had no independent address; his poems had to be sent out from the Fey house, nor could he ever go to lunch with editors or show up at literary parties. Isabella made up a history for him, a personality, a physique. Anthony Cam has a powerful body (his hands in particular are immensely strong), a taste for low life and alcohol, an English background (this explains why his grip on the American beatnik jargon is not always secure). He appeared out of nowhere (jumped ship?), and lives intermittently in an attic in the Feys' house, disappearing for long periods and consistently avoiding company. He reads in Isabella's library, but only late at night when she is in bed.

All these details flowered naturally out of Isabella Fey's imaginative symbiosis with Anthony Cam; she did not consciously set out to spoof anybody, yet because of the clarity of her vision of Cam she was able to look people in the face and unblushingly give them her fellow-poet's life-history. One editor, sympathizing with the difficulty she sometimes had in coping with such a *mauvais sujet*, offered her the consoling thought, 'There is a point beyond which no woman can understand a man's psychology.' The remark, though under the circumstances hilarious, is innocent and even, in its way, true. As a middle-aged woman led step by step into writing the poems of a young man, she was drawn towards the heart of the sexual mystery. There are realities here that one doesn't 'understand'; one's only object is to coexist with them and to recognize them as sources of joy and suffering and enrichment.

Isabella Fey intends to publish the poems of Fey and Cam with an introductory essay by Fey, containing her reflections on these matters. The folder she sent to me gave no attributions; it was simply a joint collection of poems by two authors, who were named on the title-page but nowhere else. Reading through them, I found it possible in most cases to apportion them between Cam and Fey (she has since sent me a key, against which I have checked my guesses); but sometimes, when Cam adopts a more formed and lyrical style, he swings closer to Fey.

POEMS BY ISABELLA FEY

Day of Wrath

Sweet death, unite us with all executed men!
Let these our dearest comrades be.
Give us our victims for our soldiery
And knit us into steadfast ranks again.

Though live men fail, we crave their love once more;
Worn with betrayals, we trust the thief and liar,
Nor does the blade-thrust underneath a rib
Amaze the startled heart, nor disowned sib
Love less that treacherous brother he denies.

We are bound by such sacred and such murderous
    ties,

Kindled so readily by the self-same fire:
Then marry us, sweet death, to those we shall betray —

If they be dead, and we be dead as they
What shall men fear upon the Judgement Day?

The Letters

Though they were long seas apart
He wrote often to his dearest love,
Word by word he sent her half his heart.
His letters reached her in the beaks of birds —
The sky was full of eastward messengers.

Then, 'I will go now myself to her I love,' he said,
'Over the waters I will follow my words.'
He summoned eagle, owl, dove,
He set out over the long seas
On wings of strength, wisdom, love,
And halfway there they faltered and fell down
And he and his riven heart were dropped and
    drowned.

The Fox

(After a Japanese painting)

I slept on the shore of a tigerless world
And woke to see an upright fox
Dancing towards me on two brown-nailed feet,
Yet leaving no footprints on the moon-clear sand.

From under a huge nasturtium-blossom hat
The beast regarded me with pointed smile.

Live animal or witch, my split tongue tried to say!
But flower-bonneted, lean-footed, shadowless,
It smiled, and danced towards me without sound.

POEMS BY ANTHONY CAM

Stiller, Who's Dead, Damn Him

Hunchbacked friend,
Stiller was friend, swine, hunchbacked teacher to my
   youth
Together we frothed in the swill of our sick appetites,
Stole, defiled each other's women,
Knifed cops, rolled drunks
And claimed each other's sacred poetry.

Stiller my friend, you fell reciting into Lake Michigan
   one November,
My best sonnets in your foul right hand,
Your left hand taking a leak
Heroic enough to raise the Great Lakes six inches
As you explained
And sank yackety-yack from my sight
Piss, poetry, friendship and all.

Second Poem to Stiller

That friend, who was closer than a brother,
Slight, light, witty trembling man
Who savaged my brain
Roughed my syllabic art
And finicked my bear's stroke to a leopard's lightning,
Friend all frailest bones and hudibrastic tongue –
In some of the many and not unhappy nights
Since the evening of your ambiguous death,
I have reviewed with tightfisted and parsimonious
   truth
My share, my guilt, my shame, my cowardice.
You were the noblest animal my ugly fist let drown.
Was it my invincible yet hesitating arm
That did not snatch you like the sacred salmon

And draw you safely from the watergrave?
What crueller and unsaid loyalty paralyzed this hand?
This hand — you saw it often
Tear Samson heads from off the shoulders of the
    Philistines —
Was this hand drunker than the brain that loved you?

Once more tonight, this hand
Idly moves the pen you gave me
(Old saved memento)
And writes, answerless:
Friend, did I do it, or the gods, or you?

More

There are always more martyrs than saints,
More fornicators than martyrs,
This being so, and finding myself in such a filthy
    majority,
I shall think about my salvation while fornicating,
And perhaps she
Who bears the burden of my loving ill-will
May bear me to that paradise
Where we were all once children, smiling.

Behind Bars

O she was jimp and sly,
She had an unfaithful eye;
    She stabbed me through and through
With her hot indifferent eye.

She would not love me true
    So I knew that she must die.
And I did what I had to do.

Now she's jimp but no longer sly,
Now her love is mine and true,
    I'm a man the whole night through
By the gleams of her faithful eye.

Creator Mundi

Out of my brains a hawk
Raging riving stooping for the kill;
Out of my lungs and liver and heart
A million million wingless creatures crawled;
Wolves snarled from my hair;
Ivory women
Rose from my teeth,
Walked, and were loved;
My killing thighs made men;
Out of my knotted ankles and my warrior feet
Sprang mountain lion life;
My skin sank into earth and returned as windswept
    grass;
Out of my right hand, summer;
Out of my left hand, galling dreams,
Seas, clouds, shelving lands and death.

And do not forget,
Love also
Out of my two great forgotten, but unforgetting eyes.

And now the summer of the theatre is finally over and normal
life, Oxford life, resumes as the dominant reality. It is autumn,
that time of the year when I have determined to attempt a
general statement. The involvement with a social art and a
ticket-buying audience, the long revisiting of my roots among an
industrial society have left my head full of social thoughts. I try,
accordingly, to address myself to thoughts of the artist's social
role.

POETRY AND SOCIAL CRITICISM

I want to make this lecture an exercise in ground-clearing. There cannot ever have been a subject about which so many contradictory opinions are expressed as this of the social involvement of imaginative art; and, though my brief is to talk about poetry, most of the conclusions I have come to could be equally well applied to painting or theatre or prose fiction (even, with some adjustments, to music, insofar as music gets dragged into this kind of imbroglio at all). The area within which I should like to tidy up can be indicated by these questions:

Is there anything in the nature of a moral obligation on the poet to convey opinions *in his work* about the sickness or health of the society he finds himself living in?

In the major poetry of our tradition, has social criticism been a preponderant theme or has it taken its place as one theme among many?

In responding to poetry which overtly sets out to make social judgments, ought we to apply any specialized criteria, or do we just approach it as poetry like any other?

And, most flatly of all, can poetry ever be straight propaganda? Or, if you prefer, can straight propaganda ever be poetry?

All of us who write are familiar with the person who comes up to us, on an average about once every three weeks in some shape and size, and asks, 'Why don't you use your writing to strive for a better world?' His (or her) tone will suggest, with a flavour of accusation, that the writer is heartlessly frivolous, or perhaps cynical, to leave so obvious a duty undone. A writer, with the power to attract people's attention, to engage their feelings, to channel their emotions in this and that direction — surely a

writer, of all people, ought to put on shining armour and slay his
dragon. The dragon, of course, always turns out to be the easily
identified villain of whatever mythology the questioner has em-
braced. Capitalism, imperialism, racism, fascism, discrimination
of all kinds — there is no shortage of dragons, wearing con-
spicuous labels. And, if one hesitates to dismantle one's art and
rebuild it as a missile-launcher, the hesitation does not neces-
sarily stem from any complacency about the world as it is. Per-
sonally, I am just as convinced as anyone that human society ought
to be changed; its cruelty and cynicism appal me; its greed and com-
petitiveness and prodigality leave me saddened; its ugliness
affronts me. And the misbehaviour of mankind is all the more horri-
ble in that it takes place on such a beautiful planet as the earth. We
are like a lot of delinquent children who break into a handsome
house, full of fine furniture assembled with love and good taste, and
proceed to relieve ourselves all over it. Yes, I agree that the world
should be changed! But are the imaginative arts the most suitable
instrument for bringing this change about? If you use a razor to
chop wood, don't you end up with very little wood and a spoilt
razor, no longer any use for its real purpose?

I am quite aware that the dedicated political activist will
answer at once: *So much the worse for art!* To such minds,
nothing matters except the struggle to change the world: indeed,
to let anything else matter, to give attention to personal
relationships or undirected art or the beauty of nature or
abstract intellectual questions, is merely immoral. It is easy to
feel small in the presence of such single-mindedness. On the
other hand, the single vision is usually a tunnel vision: it
achieves its clarity at the cost of a Draconian exclusiveness. To
see a single set of issues with such intense clarity is usually a
sign that there are other issues one is wilfully not seeing. And
here comes the fundamental split. The narrow, fiercely directed
vision of the revolutionary, or for that matter of the mystic or
the martyr, is entirely different from, entirely irreconcilable with,
the temperament that produces art. *So much the worse for art!*
again. But so much the better for it too, in view of the rich and
contradictory nature of human experience. 'Why don't you face

facts?' someone asked E. M. Forster. 'How can I', he replied,
'when they're all round me?'

Louis MacNeice, in his book on Yeats, had some wise words
to say about poetry and propaganda, writing at a time when the
claims of propaganda were being pressed as they are today.

> The propaganda poets claim to be realists – a claim which
> can only be correct if realism is identical with pragmatism.
> Truth, whether poetic or scientific, tends as often as not to
> be neither simple nor easily intelligible, whereas the
> propagandist is bound by his function to give his particular
> public something that they can easily swallow and digest.
> Realism, in the proper sense of the word, takes account of
> facts regardless of their propaganda value and records not
> only those facts which suit one particular public but also
> those facts which suit another public and even those facts
> which suit no one. The propagandist may have his 'truth'
> but it is not the truth of the scientist or of the realist; it is
> even further removed from these than poetic truth is. He is
> only interested in changing the world; any use of words
> therefore which will lead to that end – lies, distortions, or
> outrageous over-simplifications – will, from his point of
> view, be true. This again is a tenable position but it does
> not prove either that the poet will write better poetry by
> substituting propagandist truth for poetic truth or even
> that it is the poet's duty as a man to write propaganda
> poetry. Even if the poet believes in the *end* of the
> propagandist he can have legitimate doubts whether that
> end will be in the long run usefully served by a prostitution
> of poetry. Poetry is to some extent, like mathematics, an
> autotelic activity; if bad poetry or bad mathematics is
> going to further a good cause, let us leave this useful abuse
> of these arts to people who are not mathematicians or
> poets.

So coolly and so cogently argued, the case would seem to
carry itself. But there are very powerful magnets pulling in the
other direction. A good many writers, like a good many people of
every kind, have found themselves, at some stage of their lives,

participating in some activist movement or other. The hankering
for corporate action, for shared ideals, shared burdens, shared
discipline and danger, comes over most people at times. In the
particular case of the writer, there are some causes that make
him particularly vulnerable.

In the first place, a writer's life is lonely. If he gets on with his
work without the nuisance of other people, he is also deprived of
their comfort and support. After a number of years in the trade,
most people manage to come to terms with this loneliness, but it
is particularly hard to bear for young writers, who are in con-
sequence always forming groups, and issuing manifestoes, and
gathering in excited bunches. Often, this impulse takes a
political turn, and then the young writer has the delicious heady
sensation of being wanted. 'We need you. Our point of view
should be stated by someone like you with a gift for words.'

This kind of invitation is music in a young writer's ears, and
virtually the only way for him to hear it is to join a group who
are pushing towards some pre-defined objective. Otherwise, how-
ever well he writes, nobody will claim him, and young writers
want to be claimed. Such group-solidarity will, necessarily, lead
him often into solemn fatuity. All my life I seem to have been
opening magazines and books of poetry and finding solemn
fatuities based on political attitudes. In the 1940s, I promise you,
someone actually perpetrated the couplet:

> Bare, bitter with the truth, not posed, not slick
> Here's verse that's more than good, it's Bolshevik.

But the risk of fatuity is, to some, easier to take than the certain-
ty of loneliness. The subject-matter of art is, necessarily, as
generalized as the scope of human experience itself. Poetry is
about life, death, love, hate, heaven, hell, immortality, joy and
pain. But these things are everybody's concern; and what is
everybody's concern can often seem like nobody's concern.
Whereas, if he writes a poem arguing fiercely that the Palesti-
nian people must have their rights, or Basque militants be let out
of prison, or the British Army must get out of/stay in Northern

Ireland, he will find himself addressing a large, ready-made sec-
tor of the public who are looking for someone to say just *that*.
And he will be welcomed, and fêted. It is all an illusion, of
course; the welcome will turn to suspicion, the cordiality to
venom, as soon as he deserts the narrow path of that particular
subject-matter and goes back to his real work of writing about
unfenced-in human experience. But, till that moment comes, the
ride can be very exhilarating.

Then, again, there is the grudging tribute of envy that prac-
tical, demonstrable action always receives from those bound to
the desk or the easel. I always sympathize with the writer,
whoever it was (it was Augustine Birrell who told the story), who
attended a court sitting, and at the end of the morning's business
remarked ruefully, 'When that judge sentences some poor devil
to go to prison for five years, he goes. But when I publish a book
nothing happens!' In view of the sheer number of things that
have happened because books were published, this attitude
seems to me unrealistic; anything that involves people's
thoughts and feelings must surely accomplish more in the way of
results than the pronouncements of a bewigged and ermined
figure who is merely implementing the law that has been es-
tablished as much by the writing of books as by anything else;
but the attitude, understandably, persists, as witness Auden's
lines in the elegy on Yeats.

> For poetry makes nothing happen: it survives
> In the valley of its saying where executives
> Would never want to tamper; it flows south
> From ranches of isolation and busy griefs,
> Raw towns that we believe and die in; it survives,
> A way of happening, a mouth.

I find those lines memorable and somehow comforting, but
they contain a number of statements that seem to me untrue: to
begin with, executives (party bosses, for instance) very definitely
claim the right to 'tamper' with poetry if it seems likely to talk
back to them; and by that tampering they tacitly admit that 'the
valley of its saying' is a valley along which important rivers may

flow – perhaps that same 'peasant river' that was 'untempted by
the fashionable quays' earlier on in the same poem. And, if
poetry, and all art, survives mainly as 'a mouth', a mouth is
useful not only for making noises but for receiving nourishment.

Still, the point is that the writer, particularly the young writer,
doesn't *feel* as if anything has happened when he publishes his
thoughts; they don't seem anything like actions. Hence the
almost irresistible pull of activism to the literary temperament,
the kind of thing we read about in Renée Winegarten's
fascinating *Writers and Revolution*, aptly subtitled, 'The Fatal
Lure of Action'. One of Mrs Winegarten's prize exhibits is
Baudelaire: his view of the human condition, that its ills were
totally incurable, that the human animal was only at home in a
jungle full of cruelty and ferocity, and that the beauty of life was
to be found in the strange and lurid flowers that grew out of this
evil, and nowhere else – this view would surely inoculate anyone
against the temptation to participate in schemes for the radical
change of society; yet Baudelaire was seen by friends, during the
rising of 1848, among a crowd that had just looted a gunsmith's
shop, waving a gun and shouting slogans with the best of them.
I am equally fascinated by some examples that do not find their
way into Mrs Winegarten's muster. When the Spanish people
rose against Ferdinand VII and the Inquisition, well-wishers in
England raised a sum of money to help them, and two young
Cambridge men carried this money to a secret rendezvous in the
Pyrenees, to hand it over to the rebel leaders. The two young
Cambridge men were Alfred Tennyson and Arthur Hallam. The
future author of *Idylls of the King* and the 'Ode on the Death of
the Duke of Wellington', accompanied by the man whose death
was to inspire *In Memoriam*, bringing aid and comfort to
desperadoes in a mountain hideout!

Of course it is not only writers who are tempted by the cosy
togetherness of group action, and the short-term satisfaction of
doing something that has a demonstrable effect. But the
loneliness of a writer's life makes him, especially in youth,
vulnerable to the need for power. He wants to *matter* to
somebody, instead of being politely tolerated and half-heartedly

encouraged because literature is a Good Thing. And it is not lost
on him that the individual who is committed to a cause outside
himself, who is prepared, or appears to be prepared, to stake his
entire life on the chance of making his ideal come true, is a very
attractive figure: that he has, to use the word that we have con-
spired to burgle from the theologians, *charisma.* Even if the
writer did not know this from life, literature itself would instruct
him that it is so. Think of Turgenev's *On the Eve!* Think of
Elena, the intelligent, nervous, receptive Russian girl of good
family, who has the love of the decent young man of her own
class, Andrei Bersenyev, and could easily win that of the artist
Shubin; but it is neither of these she wants. The man who cap-
tivates her is Dmitri Nikanorovitch Insarov, the withdrawn,
austere Bulgarian exile, who takes no notice of her until she
begins to share his passion for the one shining ideal of his life,
the liberation of Bulgaria from Turkish rule.

Elena looked at him from the side.
'You love your country very dearly?' she articulated
timidly.
'That remains to be shown,' he answered. 'When one of
us dies for her, then one can say he loved his country.'
'So that, if you were cut off from all chance of return-
Bulgaria,' continued Elena, 'would you be very unhappy in
Russia?'
Insarov looked down.
'I think I could not bear that,' he said.
'Tell me,' Elena began, 'is it difficult to learn Bulgarian?'
'Not at all. It's a disgrace to a Russian not to know
Bulgarian. A Russian ought to know all the Slavonic
dialects. Would you like me to bring you some Bulgarian
books? You will see how easy it is. What ballads we have!
Equal to the Serbian. But stop a minute, I will translate to
you one of them. It is about. . . . But you know a little of
our history at least, don't you?'
'No, I know nothing of it,' answered Elena.
'Wait a little and I will bring you a book. You will learn
the principal facts at least from it. Listen to the ballad then.

. . . But I had better bring you a written translation, though. I am sure you will love us, you love all the oppressed. If you knew what a land of plenty ours is! And, meanwhile, it has been downtrodden, it has been ravaged,' he went on, with an involuntary movement of his arm, and his face darkened; 'we have been robbed of everything; everything, our churches, our laws, our lands; the unclean Turks drive us like cattle, butcher us—'

'Dmitri Nikanorovitch!' cried Elena.

He stopped.

'I beg your pardon. I can't speak of this coolly. But you asked me just now whether I love my country. What else can one love on earth? What is the one thing unchanging, what is above all doubts, what is it – next to God – one must believe in? And when that country needs. . . . Think; the poorest peasant, the poorest beggar in Bulgaria, and I have the same desire. All of us have one aim. You can understand what strength, what confidence that gives!'

Insarov was silent for an instant; then he began again to talk of Bulgaria. Elena listened to him with absorbed, profound, and mournful attention. When he had finished, she asked him once more:

'Then you would not stay in Russia for anything?'

Here, perfectly dramatized and with no intervening commentary from the author, is the moment of the girl's falling in love. And she loves the man not because he values *her* but because he values something capable of over-arching them both. The sombre consequences of this are the novel's theme: but the attraction, and its nature, are beautifully demonstrated.

To identify with a movement, to enjoy the admiration and loyalty of those who can see the beauty of a life given to the struggle for a tangible objective, must often seem to a writer the solution of his personal problems. But, then, if the writer can't face personal problems, and a lot of them, he shouldn't be a writer. And, having accepted the profession or, to speak more accurately, the vocation or, to speak more accurately still, the condition of authorship, one of the things he needs to learn is the extent to which the social and political situation, the general experience which impinges on him neither more nor less than on thousands of others, is a material that he can work into art: the extent, and the means.

The starting- and finishing-point, of course, is his experience as an individual. It will sometimes happen that a cluster of events describable as political will elicit a response from his entire being: it will affect him morally, imaginatively, emotionally, and the work he produces will unite all these.

Sometimes, when a large-scale political event erupts across the world, the reaction of poets is strange in the same way as the behaviour of the dog which attracted the attention of Sherlock Holmes.

 – Is there any point to which you would wish to draw my attention?
 – To the curious incident of the dog in the night-time.
 – The dog did nothing in the night-time.
 – That was the curious incident.

The most extraordinary occasion in our century when the dog did nothing in the night-time, I suppose, was the gradual disaffection of Western communists in the wake of Stalin's betrayal of the Left. When the Russian people rose and threw off their czars and their landlords, and proclaimed that power was now in the hands of the poor, young and generous people in every country in the world promptly fell in love with Russia. And when news began to leak out that the first, genuinely popular phase of the Revolution had been quickly succeeded by a cool power-grabbing operation by a group of dedicated and ruthless conspirators, when it began to be reported that the Russian people, having formerly been whipped with whips, were now being whipped with scorpions, of course these same generous-minded young rejected such reports as the expected backlash of counter-revolutionary propaganda, the sort of thing the bourgeois enemy would be bound to say. Time went by, the generous-minded young became less young and perhaps a shade less generous-minded, but they still believed in Russia and they associated this

belief with Stalin. Stalin was Russia and Russia was the Revolu-
tion, so how could he be wrong?

From this position they were dislodged, in a series of
sickening jolts. Some fell off with the Nazi–Soviet pact in 1939;
others with the refusal to permit free elections in the Soviet zone
of Germany immediately after the war, and the subsequent
bagging of an eastern European empire; the last and biggest
layer fell off after the bludgeoning of Hungary in 1956. A few, of
course, never fell off; there are still hard-shell Stalinists who take
the line that Stalin was right by definition, so if murder and
treachery were committed by Stalin, then murder and treachery
must be right. In this spirit, we must assume, did the poet Hugh
MacDiarmid rejoin the Communist Party in 1956, after being out
of it for some years, and declare that those who left were a bunch
of softies and the Party was 'well shot of them'.

The hard-shell survivors made their attitudes abundantly
clear; but what of those who fell off? What inward struggles,
torments, questionings, final resolutions did they undergo? And
why did the poets among them not bring this material into their
poems? No doubt there are many poems I have missed; but I
have read a great many poems written in the thirties, forties and
fifties, many of them by Socialists, and I do not remember a
single one that dealt with the agony of withdrawing one's loyalty
from Stalin, formerly the all-hallowed Leader.

The situation can be seen in all its singularity if we compare it
with the exactly parallel sequence of events that happened some
hundred and thirty years earlier. When the French people rose
and threw off their monarchy and aristocracy, and declared a
revolutionary democracy, young and generous people in every
country fell in love with France. And, when the revolutionary
society brought forth the Grande Armée with Napoleon at its
head, there were still people in every country who felt that
Napoleon must be right, because Napoleon was France and
France was the Revolution.

When Napoleon was finally broken at Waterloo, the occasion
was one of exultation for the bulk of the English people; at last
the suffering of the Napoleonic Wars was over, at last there had

been a great victory for British arms. But for 'progressives', who had never been able to slough off a certain awe of Napoleon, and had clung to a certain identification with France, the day was a sad one. Benjamin Robert Haydon's diary has a famous page about the effect first on himself, then by contrast on Leigh Hunt and William Hazlitt.

> ... I ran back again to Scott's. They were gone to bed, but I knocked them up and said, 'The Duke has beat Napoleon, taken one hundred and fifty pieces of cannon, and is marching to Paris.' Scott began to ask questions. I said, 'None of your questions; it's a fact,' and both of us said 'Huzza!'
>
> I went home and to bed; got up and to work. Sammons, my model and corporal of the 2nd Life Guards, came, and we tried to do our duty; but Sammons was in such a fidget about his regiment charging, and I myself was in such a heat, I was obliged to let him go. Away he went, and I never saw him till late next day, and then he came drunk with talking. I read the *Gazette* the last thing before going to bed. I dreamt of it and was fighting all night; I got up in a steam of feeling, and read the *Gazette* again, ordered a *Courier* for a month, called at the confectioner's and read all the papers till I was faint. . . . 'Have not the efforts of the nation,' I asked myself, 'been gigantic? To such glories, she only wants to add the glories of my noble art to make her the grandest nation in the world; and these she shall have if God spare my life.'
>
> June 25: — Read the *Gazette* again, till I know it actually by heart. Dined with Hunt. I give myself great credit for not worrying him to death at this news; he was quiet for some time, but knowing it must come by-and-by, and putting on an air of indifference, he said, 'Terrible battle this, Haydon.' 'A glorious one, Hunt.' 'Oh, yes, certainly,' and to it we went.
>
> Yet Hunt took a just and liberal view of the question. As for Hazlitt, it is not to be believed how the destruction of Napoleon affected him; he seemed prostrated in mind and body, he walked about unwashed, unshaved, hardly sober by day, and always intoxicated by night, literally, without

exaggeration, for weeks; until at length, wakening up as it were from his stupor, he at once left off all stimulating liquors, and never touched them after.

Hazlitt, who wrote a vast biography of Napoleon, simply could not adapt to the destruction of his idol. Not being an imaginative writer, he has left us no record of his inner struggles and sufferings. But his story is useful as a background to that of a great poet who endured all this and *has* left an account of it. The young Wordsworth toured France during the first heady, idealistic days of the Revolution, when every café and every town square was the forum for excited debate, when new ideas were springing up everywhere and 'human nature seeming born again'. And when revolutionary France became Napoleonic France, and entered on her expansionist phase, Wordsworth's agony was deep; a country boy, rooted in his environment and his neighbourhood, he could not make the effortless switch to supporting a foreign power against his own country, to cheering on soldiers who were killing his countrymen, that came so easily to the rootless Vietnam generation.

> ... I, who with the breeze
> Had play'd, a green leaf on the blessed tree
> Of my beloved country; nor had wish'd
> For happier fortune than to wither there,
> Now from my pleasant station was cut off,
> And toss'd about in whirlwinds. I rejoiced,
> Yea, afterwards, truth most painful to record!
> Exulted in the triumph of my soul
> When Englishmen by thousands were o'erthrown,
> Left without glory on the Field, or driven,
> Brave hearts, to shameful flight. It was a grief,
> Grief call it not, 'twas anything but that,
> A conflict of sensations without name,
> Of which he only who may love the sight
> Of a Village Steeple as I do can judge
> When in the Congregation, bending all
> To their great Father, prayers were offer'd up,

Or praises for our Country's Victories,
And 'mid the simple worshippers, perchance,
I only, like an uninvited Guest
Whom no one own'd sate silent, shall I add,
Fed on the day of vengeance yet to come?

There is the note of tragedy, too, in his description of France
under the Terror, when blood-lust attacked the nation like a
plague, and 'the crimes of few/Became the madness of the
many'. These passages remind us that there is nothing anti-
poetic, anti-imaginative, in public affairs as such. All that is
needful – but it is totally and at all times needful – is that the
situation should claim the poet entirely, going down to the roots
of his being and coming up as fresh foliage; there must be no
parading with boughs cut from Birnam Wood.

If a poem deals with the public situation, it must absorb that
situation into its metaphors, its rhythms and its entire verbal
fabric. Wordsworth in *The Prelude* succeeds in making his
experience of revolutionary politics as much a part of the poem,
as naturalized in its tone and pace, as his experience of moun-
tains or city solitudes. An example of the same kind of success
within a different area would be John Crowe Ransom's 'Captain
Carpenter'.

Here, if this were the spoken and not the written version of
this lecture, would come a reading aloud of the whole of 'Captain
Carpenter'. In print, that strikes me as unnecessary; it has been a
well-known poem since its publication in the twenties; Riding
and Graves quoted it entire in *A Survey of Modernist Poetry*, it
has appeared in several anthologies, notably the *Oxford Book of
American Verse*, and was published in the author's *Selected
Poems* on both sides of the Atlantic. Presumably anyone who
does not know it can easily look it up. But – as a reminder or a
preliminary sketch – Captain Carpenter is the Quixote-figure
who 'rose up in his prime,/Put on his pistols and went riding
out'. He is always riding out, and each time he meets an adver-
sary who defeats him with contemptuous ease. A 'pretty lady'
cuts off his nose with a sword; next comes a stranger rogue

That looked unchristian but be that as may
The Captain did not wait upon prologue

But drew upon him out of his great heart.

The stranger rogue cracks the Captain's shins; then the wife of
Satan bites off his arms; someone else cuts off his ears, then he
loses his eyes, and finally

I heard him asking in the grimmest tone
If any enemy yet there was to fight?

To any adversary it is fame
If he risk to be wounded by my tongue
Or burnt in two beneath my red heart's flame
Such are the perils he is cast among.

Finally, his most contemptible adversary cuts him open and
takes his heart; the 'neatest knave that ever was seen/Stepping
in perfume from his lady's bower'.
   The poem's conclusion is affecting; the poet utters a lament
over Captain Carpenter and a commination on his enemies. The
lines reverberate with tragic compassion.

I would not knock old fellows in the dust
But there lay Captain Carpenter on his back
His weapons were the old heart in his bust
And a blade shook between rotten teeth alack.

   But of course, just as strongly as compassion, the poem con-
veys a head-shaking irony. Captain Carpenter is gallant and
chivalrous, but he is also absurd. His knight-errant code governs
him as if he were a clockwork toy (the 'stranger rogue' might or
might not have been 'unchristian', but the Captain did not wait
to find out). He lives in a world that puzzles him; the other
characters do not stick to the script, any more than Don
Quixote's opponents. The wife of Satan 'should have made off
like a hind'; instead, 'the bitch bit off his arms at the elbows'.

'Hind' is interesting; she was supposed to run away as fast and timidly as a female deer, and also to be subservient like a menial ('hind' in the sense of 'farm servant'). She did neither. Nobody plays by the rules Captain Carpenter has been brought up to. And when we build in the information that John Crowe Ransom is a Southern poet, identified with agrarian ideas and with the Southern literary and social tradition generally, we see readily enough that this is a poem about the South; that it deals with the Civil War and its aftermath, and the humiliation of that society at the hands of enemies who did not comprehend, let alone share, its good qualities, but who had to win because the South was a natural loser, antiquated, unteachable and a bit comic.

This, by the way, is one of those cases where a little external information, coming in from outside the poem itself, is crucial. To a reader who had no idea of Ransom's associations, the theme of the South would not suggest itself — though the poem would still have the same basic diagram and the same emotional impact. But, after all, Ransom's Southern-ness is very much a fact within the public domain. He was associated with Allen Tate and Caroline Gordon and Robert Penn Warren in the Fugitive Group of Nashville, Tennessee; he contributed to a much-discussed volume of essays from a Southern agrarian point of view called *I'll Take My Stand*, etc., etc. To read Ransom with no awareness of his background would be as fruitless as trying to do the same for Auden or Yevtushenko.

I see no reason to doubt that the view of Southern history and Southern society that we find in 'Captain Carpenter' is Ransom's actual view. It is very much the view one would expect in a Southern American of his type. (It would probably not be the view of a black man.) And it is admirably conveyed not only by the poem's fable but by its physical nature too. The language is in a rather rusty fancy dress; it is 'tricked in antique ruff and bonnet', abounding in words like 'knave', 'rout' (for assembly), 'enow'. The punctuation consists of a single full stop after each stanza, thus conveying (as Riding and Graves pointed out) something of the atmosphere of a chapbook ballad. Linguistically, the poem is moth-eaten and sagging like a worn-out sofa, which is precisely what it is telling us that the South is like; but the sofa was originally made by good craftsmen to reflect the pride of some elegant house, the family are fond of it, and to chop it up for firewood is a melancholy task. Fable, metaphor, linguistic tone, rhythm – they all combine, with their Quixotry and faded elegance, to make a social and historical statement.

Of course the statement, like any statement, is made from a 'class' point of view; the moment we open our mouths to speak, let alone put pen to paper, we are of our social class, we reflect our upbringing and education – as I recognized glancingly, above, by the remark that Ransom's view of the South would not be that of a black man. Nor, for that matter, of a subsistence-level 'poor white'. The wave of populism that is washing over our society at the moment is an interesting phenomenon and deserves to be analysed calmly; one of its most striking features, when we come to any of the arts, is the deep-seated guilt about privilege. This has now reached the proportions of a mania. The other day I noticed someone airing his views in a correspondence column, maintaining that the Oxford Union, to whose usefulness as a training-ground several politicians had been testifying, was 'a private, privileged club' which should be abolished immediately. Setting aside the question of whether the Union is useful to an aspiring politician or merely misleading – I wouldn't know – it still seems worth pausing for a moment over this notion of privilege. The Society is open to anyone who becomes a member of Oxford University and is willing to pay a modest subscription; thousands of young people become eligible for membership every year and continue to be eligible as long as they live. If this is 'privilege', then so is everything that can't be joined by any casual passer-by in the street. Hasn't every school, every university, every regiment, every lodge, every trade union some organization that is restricted to its own membership – if only for mere manageability's sake? But we must breathe fire and slaughter over the Oxford Union Society because (I suppose) the word 'Oxford' has the same resonance as the word 'privilege' in its emotional field, and because Conservative (as well as Socialist) politicians acknowledge a debt to it.

Enough of this Aunt Sally game at three shies a penny. But the unimportant straw shows the direction of an important wind. It is this wind that makes young poets afraid to study their craft with any real professional devotion, lest their writing should appear to be losing that cherished note of the casual and the familiar, the four-letter and the street-corner, which is its party card. Back — or forward, or sideways — to a folk idiom! And the interest in folk art is in itself sympathetic, possibly even fruitful. Except that underneath it one scents a fallacy, a sentimental impulse to pretend. The fact is that the cult of folk art, in 'developed' countries, is exactly on a par with the cult of the steam traction-engine. It is nostalgic; it warms itself by keeping alive the memory of something kindly, and slow, and old-fashioned. (When the steam traction-engine erupts into literature in the pages of *Jude the Obscure* it does so as something alien, disruptive and terrifying; that was its heyday, when it was Progress.) The crowds at folk concerts, the crowds at cosy, slangy-poetry-readings, are indulging in nostalgia — which isn't, in itself, a sin; it only becomes hampering when it obscures a clear-sighted view of the situation. And the situation is that the folk idiom is dead. As soon as there is a popular press, let alone radio, film, television, then folk art lies with a dagger in its heart. And if we try to imitate a folk idiom, to put flesh and skin on those dead bones by an act of will, we are condemning ourselves to an art without roots.

The fact is that any poet who wants to work at the most effective level, to realize the power of his own imagination, and to communicate with the greatest number of people, will use the full resources of modern poetry as they have been developed, internationally, by experimentation and study. The 'difficult' modern poet, whose work is supposed to be unintelligible and is anathema to the populist, ends up being read by a much wider public than the *faux-naïf* or even the genuine *naïf*.

True, there is a perfectly reasonable counter-argument to this. The modern arts command a large public because they offer work in a bourgeois idiom and they address a bourgois audience. Since most of the people who expect to take any notice of art – to go to concerts, to buy books, to frequent art galleries – are middle-class, they naturally attend to the middle-class artist. And since these are the people who travel abroad, study foreign languages, attend international universities, and so forth, the bourgeois artist is addressing a large international public, able to dispose of large funds; sometimes privately, sometimes by influencing the channelling of public money. All this, we are assured, will be different when we have changed the structure of society and abolished the class system.

So be it. In an utterly changed society, there will be an utterly changed art, just as there will be utterly changed conceptions of justice, leisure and productivity. Perhaps even happiness and sadness will change their character, as they seem to have done already in the hippie jungles. But – to use an expression from the common tongue that was already well-worn when Jonathan Swift overheard it and transferred it to the printed page – let us not throw out our dirty water till we get clean. It would be a tragic mistake to abandon a tradition of art and literature that is still sound and fruitful, merely because it can be hastily stigmatized as 'bourgeois'. It is, doubtless, a thing to be regretted that the bourgeois person takes an interest in art and invests time and effort in appreciating it and the manual worker doesn't – but we shall not remedy that state of affairs just by ridiculing the bourgeois until he gives up and turns his time and efforts elsewhere. Thus leaving 'the field' clear – what field?

The bourgeoisie, as at present constituted, has one great redeeming feature as a public for art. It numbers many people who are not, or not totally and all the time, politicized. It contains many individuals who can look at a work of art simply as an utterance on behalf of general humanity, without asking whether it can be narrowed down to serve this or that Cause. Not that Causes aren't important, but their importance is not the same as that of art.

And why, in the end, does it matter so much? Why do we take so much trouble to protect art from the meaty hands of those whose wish is to grab it, package it, weigh and measure it, twist it into a shape convenient for their purposes and then another shape and another, till they tire of it at last and throw it out with the other broken toys? Why not let them have it?

We cannot let them have it because art, the free exercise of the imagination, is just about the only thing we have left, the only complete success our species can point to. Most of our techniques concern pure physical survival. But if we want to do more than survive, if we want to lift up our heads and assert that we, too, amount to something, what is there left but art? Everything else is a failure or a compromise. Men of science toil devotedly for years, breaking through time after time into fresh knowledge, and at the end of it their discoveries are absorbed into a technology that devises crueller and crueller weapons, that puts three men on the moon while three million starve for want of common bread. Politicians make power-structures which, at the most, give security and contentment to a bare majority. The most successful form of government is sixty per cent failure, if the object of government is to give people happiness and justice; and over most of the world's surface government is simply another name for bloody terror and exploitation. Turn to the inward life and the same picture is there. Mystics may be exalted but they cannot pass on their exaltation to their fellow-men; saints are imperfect and are tortured by their imperfection; every attempt at a life has failed. Others again base their ideal of fulfilment on personal relationships, and shrivel into dust at the first betrayal, which comes sooner or later as surely as the leaves fall off the trees. Only in the sphere of art is humanity able to rise totally above its failure and inadequacies. Contemplating a great painting, listening to a great symphony, watching a great play, reading a great novel or poem, only then are we in the presence of the human assertion without the human denial, the human achievement without the human failure, the human splendour without the human tarnish – if only because the denial, the failure, the tarnish are taken into that totality and orchestrated with it, and lifted up, so that we see our imperfections mirrored in our splendours, and we accept ourselves, at last, in peace and thankfulness. The glories of art are the only totally achieved glories we have left; and to the people who want always to cheapen them, to bring them down into the committee-room and the parade-ground, who want to use them as a means and muzzle them and discipline them and chop them into convenient lengths, our answer must be the same as it has been for hundreds of years, the only possible answer, the answer that is given in the closing words of *Love's Labour's Lost*: 'The words of Mercury are harsh after the songs of Apollo. You that way; we this way.'

*

According to my schedule of work, I ought to be getting on with a long, elaborate novel. And, indeed, I am interested in this novel, and have fallen in love again with the idea of the novel as a literary form: that form which Virginia Woolf described, in a marvellously pregnant aside, as 'so clumsy, verbose and un-dramatic, so rich, elastic, and alive'. The problem is that poems keep inserting themselves between me and the story and characters I am supposed to be maturing and elaborating. Well, they will just have to be matured and elaborated unconsciously for a while; for a novel, or any large-scale imaginative work, really does go forward, really does get itself together and take on clearer outlines, while one isn't 'thinking about' it at all. So during this spring and summer I let the poems come. There is nothing for it but to be led by the nose. And my nose seems to be pointed towards atavistic, ancestral root-thoughts. The death of my father, in May 1976, brings not only sadness but an emotional churning-up that is not unhappiness but a deep, fermenting excitement. I find myself writing a poem about Louis Wain, the successful light artist who charmed the Great British Public so totally and then went raving mad for twenty years. Was he a relative of mine? I cannot be sure, since like Samuel Johnson I can 'hardly tell who was my grandfather', but we must, I think, belong to the same clan; the name 'Wain' spelt in that way is very common in north Staffordshire, rare everywhere else, and Louis Wain's father came from Leek. I have a first cousin in Leek. Something, at any rate, tells me to write about Louis Wain, and why should it not be an ancestral voice?

Meanwhile I am involved not merely in practising my art as a poet but in trying to explain it. (Not 'defend' it. The time for defences of poetry is past.) The B.B.C. is putting on a series of talks by poets, called 'Finding a Voice', in which they try to explain the impulse that turned them towards verse in the first place, and the motives that keep them at it.

Shall I try? Is my 'craft or sullen art' one that will in any way yield to explanation, or seem more interesting when explained?

In the event, I try; it seems a legitimate effort, and the producer, Patricia Brent, is sympathetic and encouraging. She used to be a radio actress, and this in itself would be a passport to my good opinion, since radio drama has given me so many hundreds of hours of pleasure. So I tell the microphone what it was that made me into a poet.

As usual, the experience turns out to be tinged with farce. We get into the studio, I read my script and then Patricia comes through and says that we are running five minutes short. Can I improvise five minutes' worth of material? And what about quoting some of my own verse? I have none with me. I sit down for five minutes and reconstruct a short lyric from memory, then add a few notes which I hope to expand into sentences. (Five minutes is all the time we can have; the studio is booked by the next person.) So the talk, when it comes over, goes along smoothly and then suddenly hits a rough patch with improvised sentences and a verse quotation apparently inserted at random. Ah, well – we're all performers.

FINDING A VOICE

The people I knew in my formative years were hard-working, forthright, kindly and blessed with an earthy sense of humour. All these are excellent qualities, and I earnestly hope that some of them rubbed off on to me. It was a good society to grow up in: I am referring to the English Midlands in the 1930s and

1940s and specifically to the city of Stoke-on-Trent. On the other hand (there always is another hand), it was a society which had extraordinarily little place for the irrational. All those shadowy, unbiddable, immensely powerful forces which lie in the less accessible depths, and which are our deep sources of motivation and feeling, were neglected in a society devoted so wholeheartedly to the head and the sinews. Art was tolerated, even admitted, as long as it was representational; but the irrational and the numinous were handed over automatically to what was called 'religion'. There is nothing intrinsically wrong with this; a writer like D. H. Lawrence, who grew up in what was recognizably the same world as my own, though in a different sector, spent his life cultivating a religious vision based on 'the dark forces' which in his case he largely identified with the drives of sex. Probably any approach to the irrational has to be basically religious. The trouble was that in my boyhood religion meant the Church of England. Now, the Church of England has enough troubles without my joining in and knocking it, but the inescapable fact is that I, and everybody I knew, associated religion with going to church, and standing primly in rows singing hymns in a faint, droning voice that one hoped was not audible to the person standing next to one, and repeating prayers in which we said that there was no health in us, which was probably true but was rather lowering. As for the religion itself, all the theology had been filleted out of it, and it had become mainly a matter of being respectable, which in turn meant not doing things you would have liked to do.

When I look back on myself at the age of fourteen or fifteen, I see a being very deeply unfulfilled and frustrated at the spiritual level. Institutional Christianity was failing me – as, no doubt, I was failing it – and my *milieu* offered me nothing else. At this point, suddenly, I discovered the poets. The first poet who made an impact on me was Shakespeare – if only because we 'did' Shakespeare at school, and, though the classroom experience of literature is very much the worst way of approaching it, any approach is better than none and it did at least put the book in front of me. From Shakespeare, I discovered that certain lines of

verse seemed to jump off the page to me and flood my mind with
an extraordinary joy. It seemed entirely fortuitous; the lines that
worked on me so powerfully did not seem particularly related to
what I was interested in; the magical power of poetry seemed in-
dependent of the meaning that was being conveyed.

> In the most high and palmy state of Rome
> A little ere the mightiest Julius fell. . . .

I cared nothing for Rome or Julius; all that was just something
else we were dragged through at school. And yet those lines
moved me as unfalteringly as – say –

> Thou art not conquered; beauty's ensign yet
> Is crimson in thy lips and in thy cheeks
> And death's pale flag is not advanced there

– lines which, since they concern the death of a beautiful girl,
were more obviously in line with my adolescent broodings.

At fifteen, I could make myself drunk by repeating certain
lines of poetry. They put me into a state of exultation that was
almost trance-like. (We shall return to this point later.) It was
something like the experience of listening to music, or looking at
a painting; and it was something like the emotions that one
experienced in real life; but it came in a different package. And
poetry, however differently different people might define that
word, was the name of the package. In search of this milk
of paradise, I began to devour the English poets – from
Shakespeare I went to the Romantics, burrowed eagerly through
them, and came out via the Victorians to the moderns, then
swung like Tarzan back to the seventeenth century. At the same
time I began to try a little harder with school subjects like
French and Latin, because I wanted to see what their poets were
like. In other words, I had entered on that life of a man of letters
which I still lead today.

I realize of course that, though I have explained why I began
to read poetry, I haven't explained why I began to write it – and
for the good and sufficient reason that no explanation occurs to

me. It is simply a question of the difference between one man and another. Two people equally love music; one becomes a violinist, another a composer. Two people equally love the visual arts; one becomes a painter, the other becomes an art historian and never picks up a brush. I can offer no explanation of this, so there's no point in wasting time on the air discussing it.

In my youth, then, poetry came flooding in like a great healing tide in the desert of my personality. Because of course this excitation, this fascinated trance, was not an end in itself. It opened up deep sources of energy and illumination. But to explain what I mean here I must come at the subject another way.

Literature, to my mind, is primarily a useful art. Its utility to the human race is enormous. This utility is of two kinds. In the first place, literature helps us to understand our experience. In the continual closeknit series of events and perceptions that we call our life, we are always in danger of seeing the trees but not the wood. Things happen to us at bewildering speed but for the most part one at a time, and we always have some difficulty in arranging these discrete events into an over-all pattern. But when we read literature — that is to say, anything that offers us an imaginative interpretation of life — we are seeing our experience through the lens of another mind, offering us its perceptions and its ordering pattern. A form like the novel, which organizes large masses of information and sentiment, is an invaluable means of understanding both our individual lives and our lives in society. To read, say, Tolstoy, is to gain insight not only into what it was like to live then but what it is like to live *now*.

That is one usefulness of literature: a usefulness that I would expect to make an immediate appeal to the people I grew up among. (And, indeed, the one major writer to arise among them, Arnold Bennett, was a realistic novelist.) I respect this effort and try, from time to time, to make my own contribution to it. But there is another use of imaginative literature, which is not fully met by the realistic forms. This use is more like a divining-rod. It indicates sources of power and nourishment which are not im-

mediately apparent to the garnering intellect. We are powered
by deep instinctual and archetypal forces, but it would be a mis-
take to think of these forces as immediately available to our con-
scious minds at the touch of a button. They hide like great fish
in an opaque sea; they utter their messages in code, and they
never address themselves to the mind in its everyday, wide-
awake, rational guise. 'I know now', wrote W. B. Yeats, 'that in-
spiration comes from the self, but from the ancient memoried
self that shapes the intricate shell of the mollusc and the child in
the womb', and this ancient memoried self does not respond to
casual prodding. It needs a special state of mind, a state in which
the day-to-day considerations of life sink out of sight, and the
consciousness extends its range to pick up signals which are nor-
mally as far beyond it as the ultra-sonic bleep of bats or the
homing instinct of pigeons. These things are there, they exist in
the physical world, but we have no means of perceiving them
because our physical senses cannot get away from their limited
nature. The mind, however, can get away from its limited nature
if it rises on the wing-beats of art – which is why I regard art as
primarily a useful activity.

I have said that, as an adolescent, certain lines of poetry filled
my being with joy and put me into a trance-like state. They still
do, though not always the same lines. Now, this trance-like state
is not something that one cultivates merely for the sake of
pleasure. Indeed, I doubt whether in the ordinary sense it could
be described as pleasurable at all; the word is too flat, too take-
it-or-leave-it, to describe such a state of exaltation. What is im-
portant is that this unique blend of excitement and repose, of
intent self-forgetfulness combined with a confidence in the secure
fortress of the self, opens the way for an uttering of one's own
truth. For at such moments the imagination swims up and is
briefly seen and heard in the daylight of consciousness, and the
imagination cannot lie.

I do not wish to make extravagant claims for the imagination.
Perhaps we might say that great poets express great truths, and
minor poets express minor truths. What is certain is the wisdom
of the ancient tradition that every poet is to some extent a

visionary, a seer. 'The imagination', wrote Keats, 'may be com-
pared to Adam's dream – he awoke and found it truth.' Any
poet, at those times when a poem is beating its way out of him,
will be incapable of falsifying. Why this should be I do not know,
but that it is so I do know. And I think that this explains the im-
portance of the rhythmic element in poetry. To lay to sleep the
ordinary concerns of the mind, to put people individually or
collectively into a state of deeper receptivity, nothing works
better than a rhythm. For half a century and more, this truth has
been to some extent masked by the prevailing fad that poetry
ought to sound like conversation. At its worst, this imperative
has produced verse too flaccid to do its work on the nervous
system, for verse is to prose as dancing is to walking; a ballerina
in performance is not trying to make you think that this is her
normal way of walking down a street. She is moving in a con-
trolled, rhythmic, stylized way so as to transform the natural
movements of her body into an instrument of communication. In
the same way the poet uses the natural power of language, the
power that is latent in it and is to some extent used by everyone,
to form an instrument of total communication. This is the key to
the power of the poet and the difficulty of his task: he is using a
medium that is in the hands and mouths of all, but only he can
use it in such a way as to release its full range and depth, and
then only when the lightning strikes. I agree with Father Peter
Levi when he says, 'The nature of the power of poetry is nothing
but a natural fact; it is a law of the way in which language
works. But for poetry to be pure and strong without excluding
most reality, most of the language, and most people, in fact for it
not to become a game of devices like the Elizabethan lyric or the
nineteenth-century hymn, requires an individual power ap-
proaching to genius.'

The poem, like the dream, goes down into the depths of our
nature and brings up the hidden riches for inspection by the
waking mind. There has long been a flourishing industry in the
interpretation of dreams, and for that matter in the interpreta-
tion of poems. Just as we can have vivid dreams without being
able to interpret them, so a poet is not always the infallible guide

to the interpretation of his own poem. On the other hand, working close to the sources of dream, myth and archetype, he sometimes has an intuitive familiarity with them that makes his testimony valuable, so that criticism will never be able to get along entirely without the aid of the practitioner, though in our time it has strenuously tried to.

I'm well aware that this sounds like a general theory of poetry, without much reference to my particular case. And yet, why not? Why should I be so different from any other poet? When I began to write verse, I was writing to make sense of my experience of life, and also to surrender to those deep rhythmic and associative impulses that brought out my inner truth, the truth I couldn't drag out with the forceps of reason. That was why I wrote poetry when I was twenty, and why I write it today. Of course there are differences between myself now and myself as I was at twenty, both as a person and as a poet. In those days the immediate impulse that started my engine turning over was usually some other poet I'd been reading. I wrote very directly about what was happening to me, but the thing that incited me to write was usually literary – it was another poem. Both of those things have broadened out and diminished – it's very seldom another poem starts me turning over now – it's usually some general reflection about life or something I've found in a book of history or a biography, or fiction for that matter, but not necessarily the immediate rhythmic inspiration of another poem. And also I seem to be writing less personally, though I don't mean amorphously. I'm still writing as me, and yet I realize now that, even when I write of a very personal emotion, a lot of people have felt very similar ones before and a lot will again if the human race manages to survive. And somehow one feels able to be personal and at the same time to be general – to write in the name of all people who have had whatever experience it is.

About ten years ago, I published a poem called *Wildtrack* which is very much a bridge passage in my work. It's a poem on the theme of what unites people instead of what keeps them apart. I invented two little characters, the day-self and the night-self. The day-self is the self which copes with exterior reality,

which acquires skills and responsibilities, which learns languages
and procedures, and the day-self is balanced by the night-self
which is, of course, instinctual, primitive – in touch with the
archetypal realities. And, in order to write this poem, I had to
orchestrate an enormous amount of, as it were, non-poetic
material, things from social and political history and contem-
porary reality, and I had to do it with its mirror-image of symbol
and myth and dream. What I feel, looking back, is that I seemed
to develop an idiom there which I have tried to stick to. An
idiom which is personal, in that one is aware always of a speaker
and one is aware of an individuality, but it's not so personal that
one feels the writer has forgotten that anybody else exists in the
world. I'm thinking for instance of a lyric that's embedded in the
middle of it which describes a child in the womb and being born:

> Love held me soft and coiled,
> O but the mind, the mind!
> That tenderness was foiled.
>
> I fed on love alone,
> But in its tender rind
> My brain cried out for bone.
>
> I writhed in my own heat,
> I willed my heart to beat.

I feel that in a way that's personal – I think I'm speaking for
what it must have been like when I was a child in the womb, and
yet of course I'm trying to speak for humanity, if that's not too
pretentious a way of putting it. I think it's what Yeats meant
when he looked back over his early work and said, 'Players and
painted stage took all my love,/And not those things that they
are emblems of'; and I think perhaps I have managed to break
through into the things that they are emblems of. At least, this is
what I hope.

There is another difference between myself now and myself
when I was twenty, and that is that now I'm aware of the moral
aspect, the question of motivation. It's impossible to live

without a sense of purpose, though it might be possible barely to exist. My purpose in life is the same as that of any artist: to perceive such truth as I am able to perceive, and to pass it on to other people through the experience of the art I practise. This is my way of giving to people, as a doctor's way is to heal their illnesses or a scientist's to increase the stock of knowledge that is available to him.

It's difficult to speak of these matters without sounding like 'Thought for the Day' at a quarter to eight in the morning; and certainly it takes us beyond the bounds of the 'purely literary', whatever that may be. But, if I am to explain why I write poetry, I'd be falsifying if I didn't say that a major motive is to build bridges to other people, bridges without which I would be very lonely and frustrated. I like and admire many people, of many walks of life and many professions, but they have one thing in common; they are all contributing. Whether as performers, entertainers, artists, philosophers, scientists, historians, yes, even men of action and politicians, they are all givers, men and women who give prodigally, and because they give prodigally they can take prodigally, without the acid of selfishness eating into their souls.

I believe they get a reward. They have more chance, in the end, of finding out what life is really about than the non-givers have. And, if they are artists, it seems to happen that the constant building of bridges to other people, the continual challenge to produce something out of one's self that other people can enjoy, reveals to them in the end the basic diagram of the human being.

In one of S. T. Coleridge's notebooks occurs this jotting:

> If a man should pass through paradise in a dream, and have a flower given to him as a proof that his soul had really been there, and if he found that flower in his hand when he awoke — ah, and what then?!

The poem is the flower I find in my hand when I awake; and my readers are the people to whom I offer it.

●

A number of people wrote to ask me where they could look up that quotation from Coleridge. I did not answer their letters, for the good reason that I do not know. I read it somewhere years ago, it stuck in my mind, and now my memory retrieves it as the convenient summary of a point of view about imaginative creation. If any of my correspondents happens to read this, perhaps he or she will accept it as an apology for not replying.

Spring 1976 is a season of emigration. Wanderlust has taken over. As the mud dries, I accept invitations to go to Greece, and then to the south of France — working trips, both of them.

Athens in March was colder than Oxford. I flew from china-blue skies, strong sunlight and a boiling over of blossoms to cold grey streets and gritty winds. But my first sight of the Acropolis made me forget the weather.

Ideally, I should like to see Athens as Byron saw it, a lethargic village clustered on the hillside, with dogs scratching their fleas in the middle of the road and the slow, stately rhythms of Turkish mosque and Byzantine church washing through its arteries. Perhaps modern Athens is happier. At any rate, the country is nominally, and perhaps more than nominally, self-governing — though to say that is immediately to recall the appalling cruelties its people visited on one another during seven years of dictatorship.

Perhaps, when I wrote 'ideally', I meant 'visually' and nothing more. Early one morning, sitting on a rock below the Acropolis but above the city, I looked down at modern Athens, almost hidden by a thick industrial smog which was just beginning to yield to the pale rays of the sun, and longed to be able to clear it all away for just ten minutes and see the place as it looked — not to Pericles, because Classical antiquity is to me quite unimaginable, but as it looked to Goethe: the sheep and goats, the smoke rising gently from scattered houses, the morning silence pierced by a cock-crow and the clatter of pails. But then, of course, after the ten minutes of feeding my soul, I should want to be back in the twentieth century with anaesthetics and drains and electric light. It is the old, insoluble problem.

My hotel is next to a secondary school. Fiendish outbursts of yelling signal the intervals of leisure, but even when classes are being held the noise never quite stops. They seem to be perpetually having P.T. in the yard: the master's voice prods in through my window in a rhythmic series of commands that reach my ear as *Hyup . . . hoi . . . heu . . . yip*. The pupils march on the spot, arms swinging stiffly.

The school day is a long one, for they have a shift system that keeps the building (what our home-grown educational theorists would call 'the plant') occupied till seven in the evening. After that, silence, or what passes for silence in Athens, falls as abruptly as darkness.

On my first evening, I tried to spell out the headline of a newspaper, and succeeded inasmuch as the first word was ΒΟΜΜΕΣ and the last was φιασκο. I'm glad the bombs were a fiasco, whoever was trying to let them off: there are far too many bombs going off just now and they are not settling anything. All the same, it was not entirely a surprise. Not even happy countries, if there are any, can avoid outrages these days, and Greece is not a happy country. The government of Karamanlis is not that of Papadopoulos, the country is no longer under a dictatorship and a police terror, but the thaw is taking a long time and few Greeks are optimistic about the future.

Nikos Gatsos sits every afternoon at the same table in a high-ceilinged, old-fashioned respectable café, Floca, in the centre of Athens. The floors are marble, the wood is dark and polished, there are elaborate cakes and pastries arrayed on glass shelves, the waiters wear white aprons and walk with delicate, patient steps. In one section, it is also a restaurant, and a smart one. People give each other expensive lunches and pull off, or look as if they were pulling off, large business deals.

Gatsos is a big man, growing old gracefully, with a huge bald dome and dark, heavy-lidded eyes. He sits in the café like a wise old tortoise among the rocks.

This is the second time I have met him in two days. The first time, I was on my way somewhere else, and tired out, and we murmured a few platitudes. But this time we can talk. Eirian is with me for a few days; she will go back and I shall stay in Greece and give lectures, but this is her holiday. Peter Levi is here – he is our link with Gatsos and with so much else in this country of his near-adoption; and so is Sally Purcell, spending thirty-six hours in Greece as Eirian's guest. Gatsos looks round at three Oxford poets. He drinks cup after cup of coffee, and smokes cigarette after cigarette. The talk ranges.

One thing is clear at once: we are all equally aware that poetry, in our century, is under unprecedented difficulties. The whole tide of modern life is against it. The strength of poetry is the strength that is latent in all language. The poet does not put poetry into the language any more than the pianist puts music into the piano. He merely draws out what is there already, *in posse*. And this calls for a special art, even when the language is in normal health. But in our time language is sick, debilitated. It is used for the conveying of a torrent of information, used by a myriad human robots who have no love for it, and it has lost touch with its roots in soil and weather. All urbanized modern languages bear the same relation to their former selves as the wrapped sliced bread of the big English bakeries bears to real bread. We use the word 'bread' of both, but (whichever we choose) we know that they are different.

This problem of over-communication, of used-up, emptied-out language, has been with us since mass communications began with the popular press in the early twentieth century. But it accelerated violently in the 1920s, and has gone on accelerating ever since. Gatsos says sadly that the young Greek poets, the ones under thirty, seem to know nothing but this de-natured language, this sliced wrapped bread.

Professionally, he writes the lyrics for songs. This is not quite the comedown for a serious poet that it would be in England,

since a number of Greek composers, working close to the folk
tradition, collaborate with poets and even set to music, for a
popular audience, poems originally written with no thought of
being set, literary poems by literary poets.

Looked at externally, this is a hopeful sign, but Gatsos sees
the pitfall. When words and music compete, the music wins.
The convolutions and nuances of a poet's language do not sur-
vive the anvil of the composer's melody and rhythm; and when,
to complete the process, they are blasted out over loudspeakers
in crowded nightclubs the poet comes in a bad fourth behind
composer, singer and bouzouki-player.

Nevertheless, unsatisfactory as it is, this song-writing is vir-
tually all that Gatsos does nowadays. 'Amorgos', the poem that
established him as a major poet, was written during the war.
Thirty years of near-silence!

Yet, watching those hooded eyes so full of thought and
experience, hearing the deep melodious voice, one finds it pos-
sible to believe that, even yet, great poetry might be shaken out
of him.

Poets in Athens print their work at their own expense and
hand it out to friends. I get the impression that a poet's reputa-
tion flourishes best in, and probably does not go beyond, the
cultivated Athenian professional class. These are, for a small
capital city, numerous and impressive. Their interest in the arts
is evidently a mainspring of their life; they meet one another
regularly at the foreign institutes, hearing lectures, seeing films,
listening to music, looking at exhibitions of paintings; they are
informed and cosmopolitan far beyond their London counter-
parts. Moreover, they have money. A surprisingly large number
of them have substantial private means and can devote their
lives to appreciating the arts, if they want to. Perhaps, on reflec-
tion, this is not so surprising. Athens has grown since 1945 at
such a phenomenal rate that, if your father owned a plot of land
outside the city and had just room for two pigs and a goat, you
are now the ground landlord of an enormous block of flats.
Greece may be poor, but bourgeois Athens is very much private-
income country.

*

Olympia Karagiorga gives me her book of poems, across a red tablecloth. I stare in fascination at the beautiful paper, the elegant Greek print I shall never be able to read, the pen-and-wash drawing of the poet's face on the cover, the deep eyes both sad and joyful, the slightly hollow cheeks, the expression that manages at the same time to be fierce and vulnerable and contained, like a Maenad in repose.

She writes in my notebook a fragment in English:

The poet, yes, alone
always alone
after the falling of the rain
after the closing of the door
after the love forgotten.

The moment when someone walks out of your life and pulls the door shut: survive, or don't survive, I don't care.

I lecture on English poetry at the British Council. The clever, cosmopolitan audience listen politely. I see Peter Levi's face among them. He is one of the poets I must speak of. No account of contemporary English poetry would be adequate without some mention of his poems, their piercing individuality, their completely personal rhythm and imagery, totally of their time and yet not like any other poet's. He may be embarrassed at hearing me praise his poems and read one of them out; still, I cannot let that weigh against the impulse, and the duty, to speak of his work. I read, far less effectively than he would read it, a poem in which he meditates on timelessness.

The Break of Day and the Falling of Night

The break of day and the falling of night
birds fish moths in their generations
come without date: there is no infinite:
sea, rock and fossil are my creations.

Poetry without time is a sun-flame
flickering on the misty sea-surface
conversation has always been the same,
seen naked its body has strength and grace:

and I consider I have no future
but sea-blasted roses and foreshore grass,
the strongest languages are most impure,
· I wear love on my chest like a horse-brass.

O unwritten poem, secret mountain
peaks, bogmyrtle, bracken and idle men,
handfuls of birds in handfuls of rain,
repeat these words once and forget them then.

A few weeks later, I am in Provence, walking by the Rhône at
Avignon and contemplating the bridge. Memory, that uncon-
trolled roulette wheel, brings back the only previous time I was
in this spot. It was in 1939, and I was on a school tour of France.
I was clambering on the steep riverside, below the bridge, with a
boy named Fisher. He was a Sixth-Former, probably three years
my senior, and I never remember holding speech with him at
any other time, but he was a genial youth and was not standing
on his dignity. We were running down the bank when Fisher
caught his foot in something and fell heavily. When he got to his
feet, his trousers were torn, almost beyond repair, at one knee,
and through the huge rent I could see blood coming from the
torn skin.

My hosts at Avignon ask me if I have been there before. Yes, I
answer, in 1939. They were not born then, and they look in-
terested at the thought that I remember a vanished France, the
France of the 1930s.

I do; but of Avignon in 1939 I remember only Fisher and his
torn trousers. I can see him now, getting to his feet and inspec-
ting the damage. For thirty-five years, that is what the words 'le
pont d'Avignon' brought to my mind. No wonder the Greeks

made Mnemosyne the mother of the Muses. She is so unpredic-
table, withholding this and giving prodigally of that.

And where is Fisher? I never remember seeing him again.
Was he killed in the war that broke out a few months later, or is
he sitting in some office in Stoke-on-Trent today, a grave and
pursy citizen? Or has something quite unforeseeable happened?

As a matter of fact, my only other memory of Fisher was also
on this trip. In Paris, the Sixth-Formers, as part of their worldly
education, were taken to the Folies Bergères. I, fourteen years old
and not within this circle of privilege, was present when
someone asked Fisher if the show was as wicked and exciting as
it was supposed to be. 'Well,' he said judiciously, 'they seemed to
have their breasts bare most of the time, but, well ...' and
shrugged as if to say that it was all quite tame. Thereafter, I
looked at Fisher with the envy of a beggar for a millionaire. He
had seen girls with bared breasts!

Now it is time to settle back in Oxford and lecture on a living
poet. If Auden and Larkin were obviously right subjects for me
to talk about *con amore* and from long acquaintance, then by all
the same tokens I must obey my impulse to talk next about
William Empson, whose poetry has lived in my mind since I first
excitedly read it at the age of twenty-one, and always with fresh
accretions of strength and authority. This is a joyful task.

THE POETRY OF WILLIAM EMPSON

William Empson's first volume of poems came out in 1935, and the first poem in it is 'The Ants'.

> We tunnel through your noonday out to you.
> We carry our tube's narrow darkness there
> Where, nostrum-plastered, with prepared air,
> With old men running and trains whining through
>
> We ants may tap your aphides for your dew.
> You may not wish their sucking or our care;
> Our all-but freedom, too, your branch must bear,
> High as roots' depth in earth, all earth to view.
>
> No, by too much this station the air nears.
> How small a chink lets in how dire a foe.
> What though the garden in one glance appears?
>
> Winter will come and all her leaves will go.
> We do not know what skeleton endures.
> Carry at least her parasites below.

There seems to be some point in beginning, in a bull-at-a-gate way, with the first poem in the first book; a reader, perhaps one who bought the volume on the strength of the young Empson's already glittering reputation (he had been famous as a critic since *Seven Types of Ambiguity* in 1930), might reasonably have begun on the first page. First impressions are important. What are the impressions here?

First of all, a verbal and rhythmic tightness and trimness. The poem holds itself well, moves forward on springy feet. It is in

284

strict, though not particularly conventional, form – a sonnet, but with an unusual arrangement of rhymes in the sestet. And, even at a first reading, some of the lines have the quality, always important in poetry, of memorability; it is not likely that, having once heard the ring of

What though the garden in one glance appears?

or

Winter will come and all her leaves will go

one will soon forget them. Straightaway, then, we feel ourselves to be in the presence of a poet with authority. And when we settle down to work out the details of the poem, to investigate what it 'means', some of this authority seems to reside in the rapid, powerful, off-hand way the poet's mind throws up its ideas, links one to the next and tosses the whole heap across to us with a lack of ceremony that is casual but not unfriendly. The difficulty seems less a matter of conscious mystification than of the elliptical conversation of equals.

Empson's note is direct and helpful:

The Ants build mud galleries into trees to protect the green-fly they get sugar from, and keep them warm in the nest during the winter.

I knew, of course, about ants and aphides, but would have been baffled without that piece of information about the tree; since leaves and roots and branches are mentioned, there must be a tree in the poem somewhere, but it is helpful to have it on the line. The tree is addressed directly in the octet, as 'you'; in the sestet the angle changes, and the ants are talking among themselves, indicating the tree as 'her' and making their plans for survival.

The first line is mildly baffling; tunnelling out would normally be a matter of boring through darkness to get to the light, but these ants tunnel through noonday. They are going to tunnel into the tree, with their mud-lined tubes, but they start by

tunnelling out. I suppose *through* refers here to duration: 'all
through the long summer noon, we tunnel.' The entire first five
lines are devoted to a splendidly animated picture of ant activity.
Aphides are commonest during the soft warm days of high
summer, which is the tree's noonday (a time of day standing for
a time of year, as in Donne St. Lucy's Day is 'both the year's
and the day's deep midnight'). Bright and cheerful as the noon-
day is, the ants do not value it for these qualities; they carry
their tube's narrow darkness into the broad, leafy world of mid-
summer; the tree, which to us seems so beautiful, such a symbol
of the earth's generosity, is to them merely a source of greenfly,
as to the worshippers of Mammon all human impulses, needs,
likes and dislikes are simply a source of money. This is why the
sudden impressionistic glimpse of city life – black-coated clerks
scurrying about, some of them old men, and tube trains whining
along, everybody making money and keeping his head down – is
so apposite. The ants have a purposeful appearance of knowing
exactly what they are doing, a 'prepared air', though of course
the phrase refers primarily to the air within the mud-lined tube,
which is specially prepared to be at the right temperature for the
aphides. They are mindful of medicines and remedies, 'nostrum-
plastered', and this adds to the impression of fussiness, as of
Dickensian clerks, though it is primarily the tube that is meant;
it is plastered with mud as a nostrum, a medicine, against frost.
All this activity is irrelevant to the life of the tree, which may or
may not welcome it, but since the tree is rooted to the spot and
the ants are free to move about – well, all but free – the tree is
not consulted.

The height of the tree offers the ants a chance to see all over
the landscape, which they do not take. As the season goes on, the
high and exposed situation of the burrow, its 'station', seems to
them too bleak by comparison with their cosy underground nest;
the mouth of the tunnel, which offers a unique perspective of the
garden, lets in the dire foe of frosty air. The ants have a
foreboding of the approach of winter, not a precise vision. All
they know is that the tree will lose its leaves. Perhaps the
remaining skeleton will survive; that is not for them to say. The

only positive action they can take is to carry the parasites, at least, into shelter. The idea that the aphides are parasitic on the tree is strong throughout; 'We ants may tap your aphides for *your* dew', not '*their* dew'.

So much for the poem's surface (though doubtless there are things I have missed). But, if it were 'simply' a poem about ants and greenfly and a tree, it would be no more than mildly interesting. What involves our emotions is the reverberation of the poem, the sense that it is dealing by analogy with large and tragic realities. Small creatures, intent on their own limited concerns, inhabiting a large structure which they do not comprehend, either in its size or in its beauty, knowing only that they and it are to undergo an inevitable disaster which will be, whether they survive it or not, a time of severe testing: fussy, nostrum-contriving, tube-train-inhabiting, the ants begin to seem like the human race, and the aphides they guard so carefully, for whose sugary juice they crave, and which are acknowledged to be parasites, come to resemble those little rewards and compensations that human beings plan for themselves and give so much of their energy to pursuing. The tree may be killed by the winter frosts or brought down in a gale; we can take no responsibility for that, but we can look after the pitiful fragments of life that survive, though of course they will not survive long when their host has died. As it lingers in one's mind, a line like

Carry at least her parasites below

begins to take on a tragic, even lofty, resonance. We shall recognize that resonance more than once in Empson's poetry. Not that the analogy is in any way pointed up or overtly dramatized. The impression left by the poem is nothing so overt as 'We, the city populations of the nineteen thirties, aware of the approaching shadow of war, are busy with our little gratifications just like a lot of ants running about tending their aphides', though that parallel is certainly present; it is closer to 'Nature is full of examples of creatures who behave as we do; the world is like that.' Though gloomy, the poem has a steadying effect. The ants are ridiculous, and so are we, but this flavour of ridiculousness is something that runs all through creation, and it is calming to stand back and see ourselves and the ants in the same perspective. It may not do much for one's self-importance, but perhaps self-importance is a quality that city populations threatened by war are better without.

All this, of course, is my own construction on the basis of the poem. But, even if you have a different one, I feel we shall agree that the impulse to make a construction is quite irresistible. The poem presents us with its metaphor, and does so in such a vigorous way that, once the metaphor is in our minds, we cannot stop them from asking what it is a metaphor *of*, and then moving on to supply an answer. A great deal of poetry, of course, does this – most of it, perhaps. Empson's poetic method is not peculiar to himself, though his accent and his choice of metaphors is highly distinctive.

Turning back for a moment to 'The Ants', it may be that my reading the poem in terms of the threat of war is subjective, something I have imported. By 1935 it was obvious that a European war was likely and probably inevitable; Hitler was firmly in power, Mussolini had been in power for a long time, the Italians were fighting in Abyssinia, and the Japanese had already set about the Chinese in Manchuria, so it is not merely fanciful to see the anxieties of an approaching war in any imaginative work of that time (they are clearly marked in Auden's poems, for instance). On the other hand, though the volume came out in 1935 the individual poems might have been some years older; Empson had been publishing since the late twenties. And there is the evidence of that rough characterization he gave, during an interview with Christopher Ricks, of his two volumes of verse: 'The first book, you see, is about the young man feeling frightened, frightened of women, frightened of jobs, frightened of everything, not knowing what he could possibly do. The second book is all about politics, saying we're going to have this second world war and we mustn't get too frightened about it.' This, however, is so rough-and-ready that we need hardly feel bound to take it legalistically; clearly, several of the poems in *The*

Gathering Storm (1940) are not 'about politics'; there is an under-
current in the whole volume that relates to the public situa-
tion, but that I think can be traced in the first book too;
'frightened of everything' would cover it. Still, even if we reject
the suggestion that the oncoming winter, which will lay low the
greenness of the tree, is war, the situation could still be within
the same general framework; the poem might be voicing the nor-
mal fears of a young man who has to grow up and leave his
security. It is 'the garden' that appears in one glance from the
mouth of the tunnel, and a garden is a traditional symbol of
happy, protected comfort.

Having got this far in my exegesis, I took down the record
that Empson made in 1959 because I remembered dimly that he
had written sleeve-notes which were not just a reprint of the
notes in the books. Sure enough, there is a note on 'The Ants',
and it reads:

The Ants. It is a love-poem with the author afraid of the
woman.

Just that, and nothing more. My first reaction was to fall about
laughing. The coolness of it – to propose, in a take-it-or-leave-it
one sentence, an entirely unguessable interpretation of a poem
that had been, with its attendant authorial note, before the
public for twenty-nine years! But after I had finished laughing I
went back to the text, and it seemed to me that an important
Empsonian principle had come into focus. My interpretation of
the poem had seen it as basically an expression of fear, and of the
pathetic shifts of an endangered species, aware that they ought
to do something to save themselves but not at all clear about
their situation or about the nature of the disaster that is coming.
And I saw that the record-sleeve note did not in fact obliterate
this reading; it merely added a layer to it and suggested that the
new layer might be treated as the dominant one. Falling in love
always has an element of fear in it, since it matters so desperate-
ly what the loved person thinks of us; and there is a beautiful
aptness in the metaphor of the aphides – the ants do not drink

the tree's dew directly, but through the bodies of the parasites
who have been drinking it; thus the young man who is afraid to
approach the girl might derive joy and hope from touching her
life very timidly – ringing her up, making a date, treasuring
small souvenirs like pebbles or theatre-tickets. When disaster
comes and she gets rid of him, these small creatures are what re-
main. The poem is seen in a different focus, but it is still the
same poem, and the large reverberations remain in the mind
very much unaltered.

The whole question of 'difficult' poetry is one that seems to
merit a paragraph, certainly no more. Poems can be difficult
because the ideas and facts they incorporate, and the conventions
on which they are built, are unfamiliar to us, either because of
space (e.g., in modern Arabic poetry) or time (as in the poetry
of ancient Greece), so that effortful work has to go on before we
are in a position to appreciate the poem at all; a whole world has
to be built in our minds, the world the poem actually inhabits.
Of such poems we should more properly say that they are not
difficult in themselves but have been made so adventitiously, by
the passage of time or the distortions of perspective. The only
poetry that is difficult *per se* is that which a contemporary, living
in the same set of social and political conditions as the poet,
holding or doubting similar beliefs, would find hard to interpret.
This genuine, inherent difficulty results in most cases from the
poet's wish to make language behave in a new way, to rid it of
cliché and padding, to find metaphors that will come at the sub-
ject from a new angle, and rhythms that will act on the reader's
pulse. The thought to be expressed might be perfectly intelli-
gible, and capable of being expressed in words that were clear
but flat and unremarkable; in avoiding the flatness and un-
remarkability, the poet makes the thought more difficult to come
at, but more apt to be pondered and retained when it is found.
There is also a small category of poetry that is difficult because
the ideas it conveys are barely graspable in any case – usually
mental and emotional states bordering on the mystical – but the
difficulties here are not peculiar to the language of poetry, and do
not really need to be considered with it.

Empson's poetry is difficult because of his highly idiosyncratic idiom, an idiom that pays great dividends in flavour and memorability. Certainly one would not wish it away for the sake of making the poems easier. And, in a paradoxical way, it could be said that his poetry does communicate very directly. It conveys an attitude – a life-style, almost – immediately, by its rhythms, its imagery, and what in general I have called its reverberation. 'Poetry can communicate before it is understood,' remarked Eliot; that 'before' has always seemed to be a slight begging of the question, with its implication that all that is involved is a time-lag, whereas several of Eliot's own poems demonstrably made an impact on people, 'communicated' with them, who never at any stage fully understood them. My own experience as a reader of poetry has always been that, while a poet may baffle me in this poem or that, it is impossible to read thirty or forty pages of his verse without picking up a strong and on the whole very accurate picture of his subject-matter and attitudes; what *kind* of poet he is, what subjects attract him, and broadly how he approaches them; a mood, a colouring; as an actor can come on to an empty stage and walk across it, and without speaking a word can convey a great deal by his appearance and bearing, by whether he walks boldly and confidently or sidles or slinks, by whether he seems fresh or tired out. A poem conveys a great deal just by how it walks on to the stage, and it is possible to fall in love with a poem, as with an actress, just by seeing it move. (Feminists will kindly sort out those last sentences, redistributing the hims and hers and the -ors and -esses, to suit their preferences.)

There must be many people who were attracted to William Empson's poetry, as I was, long before they were ambitious enough to offer to construe it. What attracted us? How did these poems walk across the stage of our minds?

Wittily, of course; strongly; gracefully. The poems are flavoured with a lively, glancing wit that is as close to 'wit' in the modern sense, of making neat humorous epigrams, as to the serious seventeenth-century sense, metaphysical wit, multilayered alertness to meaning and implication, the power of 'continually forming new wholes'. Even where I don't see the joke, because it depends on some bit of mathematics or similar arcana, I can hear the crackle of it, as in

Two mirrors with infinity to dine
Drink him beneath the table when they please.

Then the movement of the poems is sinuous and athletic, the rhythms buoyant, the sound elegant. A line like

Heaven's but an attribute of her seven rainbows

is pleasant to speak, and any poet who turns out lines that are pleasant to speak is half-way towards claiming our attention. But it is no mere trifling hedonism, like eating chocolate creams, that this poetry offers. Quite apart from the bracing intellectual atmosphere, the agility with which ideas are thrown up and caught, there is something deeper: a bleak strength, a hint of tragic stoicism. Long before we have worked over the poems and decided on their meaning in detail, we have learnt to recognize the poet's idiom in lines like

Most wrecked and longest of all histories

or

The waste remains, the waste remains and kills

or, to come back to 'The Ants',

Carry at least her parasites below.

And even at this early stage, while we are still leafing through the poems, turning the pages idly, getting accustomed to the shape and feel of the verse, we can see already that this is a poet who attaches great importance to style in writing because he attaches the same importance to style in living. Ritual, convention, dressing up, the element of pretence and play in serious activities, are all part of the human game:

                        He who tries
Talk must always plot and then sustain,
Talk to himself until the star replies,

But in despair that it could speak again
Assume what answers other wits have found
In evening dress on rafts upon the main,
Not therefore uneventful or soon drowned.

The conquest a poet makes of us, not in person but simply on
the printed page, is not very different from any other kind of
conquest; there is something about style, outward appearances,
first impressions that we find (or don't find) immediately attrac-
tive. Deeper acquaintance follows — disillusion, perhaps — but
the conquest remains a fact. When as an adolescent I first read
Empson's 'Invocation to Juno' I was captivated by its ending:

Courage. Weren't strips of heart culture seen
Of late mating two periodicities?
Could not Professor Charles Darwin
Graft annual upon perennial trees?

I had only the foggiest idea then, or now, what it was all about;
but I liked the agile verse, the witty phrasing, the unmistakably
conveyed sense that ideas were amusing and interesting as well
as useful.

These may sound trivial considerations, but I believe they
guide our choice in important ways. There is, after all, a large
body of poetry which for one reason or another we find difficult;
some difficult poets attract us and encourage us to persevere,
others repel us. Some hold out the promise of valuable thoughts,
others give us on first acquaintance a depressing sense of confu-
sion, of the evading of meaning rather than the strenuous pursuit
and refinement of it. I believe the reasons why we form these ini-
tial impressions are real reasons, worth pondering; and certainly
the impressions are crucial for the poet concerned, for they win
or lose him a public. When the young Empson began to publish,
a great many poets were writing obscure verse. It was the

fashion. Eliot had laid it down in that famous essay of 1921, 'The Metaphysical Poets', that

> it appears likely that poets in our civilization, as it exists at present, must be *difficult*. Our civilization comprehends great variety and complexity, and this variety and complexity, playing upon a refined sensibility, must produce various and complex results. The poet must become more and more comprehensive, more allusive, more indirect, in order to force, to dislocate if necessary, language into his meaning.

Setting aside for the moment the question of whether or not that directive deserved to be followed, it is certainly the case that it *was* followed, enthusiastically, for something like forty years. The dog-like devotion of minor poets to the ideal of making themselves difficult to understand, to being 'comprehensive ... allusive ... indirect', resulted in a melting away of the readership for minor poetry. The major poets, of course, kept their audience, but (apart from the social-consciousness poets who yearned to be read by the working class and were in fact read, if at all, by people just like themselves) it is a fact that most poets in the twenties, thirties and forties, if they were of a 'modern' tendency, expected not to be read, and this is a factor to be taken into consideration when looking back at their work. In my youth, virtually every poet who claimed one's attention was 'difficult', yet one lingered over this poet and neglected that, eagerly read A and threw B aside. The poets who made an entry into one's consciousness were those who 'communicated before they were understood' – and into this category Empson fits very exactly.

Keeping these preliminary reflections in mind, we might go back to that first book, *Poems* (1935), and, ploughing straight ahead, considers poem no. 2, 'Value Is in Activity'.

> Celestial sphere, an acid green canvas hollow,
> His circus that exhibits him, the juggler
> Tosses, an apple that four others follow,
> Nor heeds, not eating it, the central smuggler.

Nor heeds if the core be brown with maggots' raven,
Dwarf seeds unnavelled a last frost has scolded,
Mites that their high narrow echoing cavern
Invites forward, or with close brown pips, green folded.

Some beetles (the tupped females can worm out)
Massed in their halls of knowingly chewed splinter
Eat faster than the treasured fungi sprout
And stave off suffocation until winter.

The syntax of the opening four lines is completely dislocated
from normal prose usage, and there is no point in trying to
straighten it out along ordinary lines. The juggler tosses up an
apple, soon to be followed by four others. He is standing on the
earth, which is a celestial sphere, and inside the Big Top. There
are certain points of correspondence between all three, here at
the outset and throughout the poem. The circus tent is the
colour of a cooking-apple; the planet dances in rotation with
other planets, like the juggler's apples. The last line of the four
introduces the next movement of the poem; 'smuggler' is there
for the rhyme and is not quite the *mot juste*; logically, the un-
identified passengers in the apple-core are stowaways, not
smugglers.

It makes no difference to the juggler whether the apples he
uses in his act are sound at the core or rotten; whether the seeds
are spoilt by frost or are healthy and fertile. As long as his skill
can keep them in equilibrium in the air, they will serve the pur-
pose. (The physical universe is morally neutral.)

The third stanza makes a jump from the juggler and his apples
to another theme from entomology, like the ants. Once again I
do not know exactly what kind of beetles are referred to, but
evidently the salient point about them is that once the fertilized
females have left the communal nest the males are left to survive
by a balancing act; the fungi that nourish them must be con-
sumed at exactly the right speed, so that they will not die out
and leave the insects to starve, nor proliferate till they cannot
breathe. When winter comes, presumably, the beetles die
anyway.

The thesis of the poem seems to me a strange one. Are we really like Wall of Death riders, who will crash if they slow down, and is this really the law of life? Still, one does not have to accept the doctrine of a poem before getting pleasure out of it; any cogent imaginative statement, of a proposition not actually lunatic, can hold one's attention and make a springboard for the poet's art, 'his circus that exhibits him'. And the writing here is magnificent, as usual; the images for decay and corruption within the core are so strong that they convey a deep sense of the tragedy of the endless warfare and suffering that underlie existence. And, then, the visual element in the poem is so strong and clear:

Mites that their high narrow echoing cavern
Invites forward. . . .

Perhaps the poem is a statement – an extravagant statement, in that metaphysical vein of serious joking – of a theme very much at the centre of Empson's thinking: equilibrium, the pull of balanced opposites. Everyone who has looked at this poetry carefully has seen this theme, and in the sparse notes he has provided Empson has drawn further attention to it. In the notes to 'Bacchus', a familiar *locus*, he says, 'life involves maintaining oneself between contradictions that can't be solved by analysis; e.g. those of philosophy, which apply to all creatures, and the religious one about man being both animal and divine'. A few lines further on: 'man cannot stand alone because he is dependent both on earth and heaven'. This thought was embodied very early on in a fine poem, one of Empson's best, and justly famous, though he says he has turned against it himself:

Arachne

Twixt devil and deep sea, man hacks his caves;
Birth, death; one, many; what is true, and seems;
Earth's vast hot iron, cold space's empty waves:

King spider, walks the velvet roof of streams:
Must bird and fish, must god and beast avoid:
Dance, like nine angels, on pin-point extremes.

His gleaming bubble between void and void,
Tribe-membrane, that by mutual tension stands,
Earth's surface film, is at a breath destroyed.

Bubbles gleam brightest with least depth of lands
But two is least can with full tension strain,
Two molecules; one, and the film disbands.

We two suffice. But oh beware, whose vain
Hydroptic soap my meagre water saves.
Male spiders must not be too early slain.

Without shredding out all the metaphors here, we can say that
the poem glides swiftly from one example to another of perilous-
ly achieved equilibrium, concluding with the most interesting
equilibrium of all, that of love. Empson's general alertness to
anthropology, his interest in the primitive, comes out in the
opening image; primitive man is supposed to have chosen cave-
dwellings that were just too far inland to be flooded by the tides,
without penetrating into the dangerous jungle; the heat at the
centre of the earth would kill him, and so would the cold of outer
space. Exactly what kind of arachnid is referred to by 'king
spider' I am not arachnologist enough to know, but clearly it is
one of those creatures whose life-area is not above the water, or
beside it, or within it, but actually on its thin tensile surface. Its
predators include fish, birds and man, so it is a parallel of the
human being who survives by an endless balancing act. The thin
skin on the surface of the water supports him; a soap-bubble is
constructed on the same principle, and this brings us to the
iridescent globe of love. Soap absorbs water and is thirsty for it
('hydroptic', eager to absorb fluid, carries an erotic suggestion);
the soap may be the more active element but the commonplace
water is necessary too, 'saves' it in fact. The hydroptic soap is
'vain' in the sense of 'conceited' (Empson's note says that

Arachne was a queen and 'disastrously proud'); the proud
beauty naturally has pride of place, like the female spider who
eats the male when he is no longer needed for procreation; but there
is no need to be in a hurry about it. (According to Ovid, Arachne
affronted Minerva by weaving a tapestry depicting the amorous es-
capades of her father Jupiter; was punished by the jealous goddess;
despaired, and hanged herself.) The poem ties all this up in a neat
parcel – a view of man's destiny, an avowal of love, a rebuke to
pride; like the best metaphysical poems of the seventeenth century,
it achieves a perfect balance of thought and emotion. The scientific
ingredients – water-spiders, molecules, etc. – are essential; so is
the anchoring in a personal situation and a personal emotion; but
the third leg of the tripod, the mythological allusion, is just as in-
dispensable as the other two. When Dylan Thomas wrote his clever
and affectionate parody of an Empson poem he called it 'Invocation
to Leda'. Empson uses mythology – generally the standard
Classical items that 'everybody knows' – throughout his poetry;
sometimes they furnish the titles ('Arachne', 'Invocation to Juno',
'Bacchus'), more often they crop up in the body of the poem. The
reason is clear enough. Myth is analogical. Whatever theory we
hold about the origin of myths – whether we believe with
Euhemerus that they come out of history, or with Frazer that they
come out of ritual, or whether our approach is via the Jungian sym-
bol – we all use them in the same way, as analogies. The persons of
mythology act out in their own scenario the events that happen in
the physical world and in the mind of man; they take a fact or an
experience that we recognize and repeat it in a different form. This
is the usual mode of operation of Empson's simpler (and often most
effective) poems, e.g., 'Note on Local Flora'.

> There is a tree native in Turkestan,
> Or further east towards the Tree of Heaven,
> Whose hard cold cones, not being wards to time,
> Will leave their mother only for good cause;
> Will ripen only in a forest fire;
> Wait, to be fathered as was Bacchus once,
> Through men's long lives, that image of time's end.

I knew the Phoenix was a vegetable.
So Semele desired her deity
As this in Kew thirsts for the Red Dawn.

Very large ideas are at work here. Semele, the human lover of
the god Jupiter, asked him to come to her in his true shape and
not in disguise. When he did, she was consumed and the child in
her womb, Bacchus, was with difficulty rescued from the flames
and allowed to finish his gestation in his father's thigh. Jupiter
would never have come to Semele with his fatal radiance had she
not so yearningly desired it, to allay the gnawing suspicion
planted in her mind by the jealous Juno. The girl's love led her to
desire her own death, and the tree is the same; it accepts
destruction as the price of regeneration, thereby enacting the
sacred drama of the phoenix.

These compressed, emotionally charged analogical state-
ments, conveyed to one's mind in powerful, rhetorical verse,
tend to leave powerful reverberations behind; it is virtually im-
possible to stop one's mind going on and on, piling up further
analogies beyond the initial one. It is heartening to know that
Empson himself regards this as a normal reaction to poetic
language. The reason why a poem contains this selection of facts
and not some other, he remarks in the *British Journal of
Aesthetics*, no. 2 (1962), is 'invented' by the individual reader;
'he will invent a variety of reasons and order them in his mind.
This, I think, is the essential fact about the poetical use of
language.' Thus, in an interesting article on '*New Signatures* in
Retrospect', it seems natural to Professor A. G. Stock to think of
'Note on Local Flora' as a poem which 'takes more direct notice
of Leftist standpoints'. Socialists at that time, given to pinning
their faith on revolution, naturally saw in the image of the forest
fire the symbol of the purifying destruction; in Professor Stock's
words, 'And are there seeds in man's nature that will never grow
till revolution has cleared the ground of those who nourished
them?' The poem in fact says nothing about 'Leftist stand-
points'; nor does it, except to the interested eye, say anything
about revolution; Empson's way is to state the analogy, strongly

and barely — but once stated it continues to echo through each individual mind, till in the end each of us has invented his own reasons and made his own poem, and all are legitimate.

Well, all except the lunatic ones — which is why Empson's work as a critic is so un-magisterial, so given to adopting the tone of rapid but reasonable argumentation (even, to use one of his own favourite words, 'argufying').

This, I think, is an essential orientation. Empson makes more use of scientific information than most poets, but this fact can easily bulk too large. Of course he went a certain distance with a scientific training, going up to Cambridge on it and taking the first part of the Tripos in Natural Science before switching to English Literature. The earlier poems, those published in the 1935 volume, could fairly be described as the result of taking a young scientifically nurtured mind and throwing it into the turbulent waters of seventeenth-century metaphysical verse; like everyone else at that time. Empson read Grierson's famous anthology, *Metaphysical Poems and Lyrics of the Seventeenth Century*, and there is a sense in which his own first volume might be described as an inspired criticism of that book, a demonstration of the fullest and most joyful response to what the metaphysical poets were doing. Nevertheless, the bent of Empson's mind was not and is not 'scientific'. It was and is analogical. It excels in forming new and powerful entities from materials not previously brought into focus; 'the most heterogeneous ideas are yoked by violence together', and the violence is the incandescent force of the creative mind.

In Empson's impartial hospitality to ideas and images from science, magic and religion we can see plainly the decisive influence of anthropology. In the Cambridge of his formative years, anthropology was, if not Queen of the Sciences, very much a member of the royal family; J. G. Frazer, who had been a Fellow of Trinity since 1874, was still a Fellow of Trinity. He had published *The Golden Bough* in 1890, and expanded it to three volumes in the second edition of 1900; and, though Empson undoubtedly read the work of many more up-to-date anthropologists (notably Emil Durkheim), he must have read

Frazer at a plastic stage in his own thinking. But perhaps 'thinking' is too narrow a word here; what Frazer obviously did for the first generation of his readers – yes, and the second generation, which was Empson's – was to give them a new way of seeing, of feeling, of reacting to phenomena, of relating insights to one another. We might as well add (since it involves all these things) a new way of writing poetry. 'Everyone' knows that *The Waste Land* would not exist, or would be a very different poem, without Jessie L. Weston's *From Ritual to Romance*, but it is equally true that Jessie L. Weston's book, and all that torrent of more or less popularizing books on human customs and beliefs, came into being because Frazer created a public that welcomed them. Was not Eliot's first book of criticism given a sub-Frazerian title, *The Sacred Wood*?

When we turn to *The Golden Bough*, and picture the young Empson reading it (as a sixth-former at Winchester, I dare say), certain passages stand out as likely to have been especially stimulating and formative. Frazer has laboured long, as he says, to point out that

> primitive man seeks to preserve the life of his human divinities by keeping them poised between earth and heaven, as the place where they are least likely to be assailed by the dangers that encompass the life of man on earth. [ch. LXVIII.]

Obviously that passage has a bearing on the recurrent Empsonian idea of survival by balance, of existence as a reconciling of opposites in themselves irreconcilable. But, quite apart from such direct clues, the whole texture and tone of Frazer's masterpiece could not have failed to make a profound impression on the imagination of any young poet. The old man has a vein of sombre rhetoric; he dates from the period when scholars who discussed important ideas did so in noble and stately prose; he offers nothing less than a view of human destiny. Take a passage like this:

> We must remember that at bottom the generalisations of science or, in common parlance, the laws of nature are

merely hypotheses devised to explain that ever-shifting phantasmagoria of thought which we dignify with the high-sounding names of the world and the universe. In the last analysis magic, religion and science are nothing but theories of thought; and as science has supplanted its predecessors, so it may hereafter be itself superseded by some more perfect hypothesis, perhaps by some totally different way of looking at the phenomena – of registering the shadows on the screen – of which we in this generation can form no idea.

Such a passage (it is in chapter LXIX) is a clarion-call to any young mind, especially to a mind like Empson's that was interested in theories of thought, ways of looking at phenomena, explaining the ever-shifting phantasmagoria of thought. A little later Frazer goes on, in grand and gloomy vein:

The dreams of magic may one day be the waking realities of science. But a dark shadow lies athwart the far end of this fair prospect. For however vast the increase of knowledge and of power which the future may have in store for man, he can scarcely hope to stay the sweep of those great forces which seem to be making silently but relentlessly for the destruction of all this starry universe in which our earth swims as a speck or mote. In the ages to come man may be able to predict, perhaps even to control, the wayward courses of the winds and clouds, but hardly will his puny hands have strength to speed afresh our slackening planet in its orbit or rekindle the dying fire of the sun.

And a little further on:

Without dipping so far into the future, we may illustrate the course which thought has hitherto run by likening it to a web woven of three different threads – the black thread of magic, the red thread of religion, and the white thread of science, if under science we may include those simple truths, drawn from observation of nature, of which men in all ages have possessed a store. Could we then survey the web of thought from the beginning, we should probably

perceive it to be at first a chequer of black and white, a
patchwork of true and false notions, hardly tinged as yet by
the red thread of religion. But carry your eye farther along
the fabric and you will remark that, while the black and
white chequer still runs through it, there rests on the
middle portion of the web, where religion has entered most
deeply into its texture, a dark crimson stain, which shades
off insensibly into a lighter tint as the white thread of
science is woven more and more into the tissue. To a web
thus chequered and stained, thus shot with threads of
diverse hues, but gradually changing colour the farther it is
unrolled, the state of modern thought, with all its divergent
aims and conflicting tendencies, may be compared. Will the
great movement which for centuries has been slowly
altering the complexion of thought be continued in the near
future? or will a reaction set in which may arrest progress
and even undo much that has been done? To keep up our
parable, what will be the colour of the web which the Fates
are now weaving on the humming loom of time? will it be
white or red?

We might add, from the viewpoint of our troubled decade,
that the black thread of magic, which Frazer seems to think
beneath mention as a serious challenger, is still very much part
of the pattern. (It would have been interesting to have the great
anthropologist's comments on a film like *The Exorcist*.) But,
since our immediate concern is with the poetry of William Emp-
son, what we need to note is that, despite the vast difference in
tone and approach, the same mental attitude is found in Empson
as in a father-figure like Frazer. Both take the view that the real-
ly illuminating sidelight, the key that opens some particularly
stubborn lock, might be found in science, or magic, or religion:
and they look at all three with the same eyes.

In 1935 Empson published his second book of criticism, *Some
Versions of Pastoral*. It is not my intention here to try to assess
his work as a critic, but this second book of linked essays, com-
ing in the same year as the publication of his first poems and five

years before that of his second, seems to me of all his prose books to do most to illuminate his poetry. For the casual reader, noting the highly wrought complexity of Empson's poetic language, the most obvious bridge has always been that between the poems and *Seven Types of Ambiguity* (1930); that first book, with its fascinating wealth of subtle analysis and exploration, the drawing-out of whole flocks of rabbits from the selected top hat, is certainly important, and some of its flights are justly famous and will probably never be equalled. But, just because it proceeds by means of the analysis of verbal texture, *Seven Types* left in many minds the impression of Empson as primarily a verbal analyst, and by extension they thought of his poetry as the spinning of complicated verbal webs. In fact, he has a much more complete approach to literature, both wide-ranging and fundamental. For those who read it attentively enough, *Seven Types* comes through in this way; the magnificent analysis of George Herbert's 'The Sacrifice', the last example in the book, takes the poem as a full-scale attempt, using all conceivable resources of language and thought, on 'the most complicated and deeply-rooted notion of the human mind', the god as scapegoat and tragic hero; and the terms in which he discusses the poem leave us in no doubt of the influence of anthropology. But *Some Versions of Pastoral* is more openly wide-ranging; it brings together every kind of consideration, social, political, philosophical; it is a fundamental inquiry into the question: Why is literature important?

Empson answers this question from many angles, but broadly speaking his position is that literature embodies the thoughts and feelings that are essential to the life of a society, that energize it and provide its motivations and resolve its conflicts. People live according to the rich, confused mixture of opinion and sentiment they carry about in their heads; as he puts it in a later book, *The Structure of Complex Words*, 'A man tends finally to make up his mind, in a practical question of human relations, much more in terms of these vague rich intimate words than in the clear words of his official language', and as he puts it in a poem ('Missing Dates'),

It is not your system or clear sight that mills
Down small to the consequence a life requires.

Empson is always on the look-out for the thoughts and feelings
that pack down into this day-to-day decision-making, into the
'consequence a life requires'. The logical, structured ideas, the
'system or clear sight', are all very well in theory, but Empson is
first and last a pragmatist; indeed, what is uniquely valuable
about his mind is that it is a mind able to comprehend abstract
ideas and take pleasure in them, without being tempted to make
the mistake of thinking that abstractions can be used to live by.

Some Versions begins with a chapter called 'Proletarian
Literature'. In the mid-thirties, when every alert young person
was looking for new ways of clearing up the sad social mess, and
Communism (not yet seen at close quarters) seemed an attrac-
tive solution, a title like 'Proletarian Literature' might have been
found in any one of a score of progressive magazines; it was an
'in' subject. Empson's treatment of it, though, could hardly have
satisfied any automatic expectations. He begins by finding the
term thin and unsatisfactory. 'One might define proletarian art
as the propaganda of a factory-working class which feels its
interests opposed to the factory owners'; this narrow sense is
perhaps what is usually meant but not very interesting.' Such
art, in any case, would disappear in a successful Socialist state,
and like everyone else in the mid-thirties the young Empson was
interested in what kind of art such a state would produce and
encourage. After worrying the notion of proletarian art for a few
pages, he decides to let it alone and move to the term 'pastoral',
which includes the same ideas but covers a wider and more
serious range. Pastoral, though a strange form, is permanent,
would not die out under any conceivable form of government,
does not depend on the exploitation of one class by another, and
crops up in widely separated areas.

> The essential trick of the old pastoral, which was felt to im-
> ply a beautiful relation between rich and poor, was to make
> simple people express strong feelings (felt as the most
> universal subject, something fundamentally true about

everybody) in learned and fashionable language (so that you wrote about the best subject in the best way). From seeing the two sorts of people combined like this you thought better of both; the best parts of both were used. The effect was in some degree to combine in the reader or author the merits of the two sorts; he was made to mirror in himself more completely the effective elements of the society he lived in. This was not a process that you could explain in the course of writing pastoral; it was already shown by the clash between style and theme, and to make the clash work in the right way (not become funny) the writer must keep up a firm pretence that he was unconscious of it. Indeed the usual process for putting further meanings into the pastoral situation was to insist that the shepherds were rulers of sheep, and so compare them to politicians or bishops or what not; this piled the heroic convention onto the pastoral one, since the hero was another symbol of his whole society. Such a pretence no doubt makes the characters unreal, but not the feelings expressed or even the situation described; the same pretence is often valuable in real life.

Since the whole book goes on at this cracking pace, we had better slow down just long enough to note that the pastoral figure, like the hero, is valuable to Empson because he is 'a symbol of his whole society'. Though he avoids the jargon and the easy assumptions of the officially leftist critics of his day, he is just as socially conscious as any of them; the importance of imaginative literature is the part it can play in 'the whole society'.

Not only literature, of course, but everything that sets out to communicate, can be seen as incorporating the driving sentiments of a society, and therefore would need to have its implications coaxed out of it:

It seems clear that the Worker, as used in proletarian propaganda, is a mythical cult-figure of the sort I have tried to describe. This is not peculiar to one party. As I write, the Government has just brought out a poster giving the numbers of men back at work, with a large photograph

of a skilled worker using a chisel. He is a stringy but tough,
vital but not over-strong, Cockney type, with a great deal
of the genuine but odd refinement of the English lower
middle class. This is very strong Tory propaganda; one
feels it is fair to take him as a type of the English skilled
worker, and it cuts out the communist feelings about
the worker merely to look at him. To accept the picture is
to feel that the skilled worker's interests are bound up with
his place in the class system and the success of British
foreign policy in finding markets. There is an unfortunate
lack of a word here. To call such a picture a 'symbol', like a
sign in mathematics, is to ignore the sources of its power;
to call it a 'myth' is to make an offensive suggestion that
the author is superior to common feelings. I do not mean to
say that such pictures are nonsense because they are
myths; the facts of the life of a nation, for instance the way
public opinion swings round, are very strange indeed, and
probably a half-magical idea is the quickest way to the
truth. People who consider that the Worker group of sen-
timents is misleading in contemporary politics tend to use
the word 'romantic' as a missile; unless they merely mean
'false' this is quite off the point; what they ought to do is to
produce a rival myth, like the poster. In calling anything
mythical I mean that complex feelings, involving all kinds
of distant matters, are put into it as a symbol, with an im-
plication 'this is the right worker to select and keep in mind
as the type', and that among them is an obscure magical
feeling 'while he is like this he is Natural and that will in-
duce Nature to make us prosperous'.

In seeing the Worker as a mythical cult-figure like something
out of *The Golden Bough*, Empson is acknowledging once more
that old and fundamental debt; but what particularly strikes one
here is his need to use both the terms 'myth' and 'symbol',
without being finally content with either. What matters is that
any potent suggestion-conveying image, like the worker on the
poster, whether we call it a symbol which carries over into myth,
or a myth that works symbolically, is recognizable by the fact
that 'complex feelings, involving all kinds of distant matters, are

put into it'; this has an obvious bearing on Empson's poetry, whose central metaphors (the forest fire, the king spider walking on the skin of the water, the plot of land whirling round and round in 'Legal Fiction', the earthquake in 'Aubade') all work in just this way.

The main thrust of *Some Versions* could almost be described as sociological; the author himself comes close to describing it so, back-handedly, when at the end of the first chapter he warns that it is 'not a solid piece of sociology'. In fact, like all Empson's writing, it is everything at once. He always follows where the argument leads him, and in the middle of discussing some technical point he will suddenly drop a remark of shattering import. Moral judgments are not shirked any more than any other kind of judgment. In a conversation about Empson's criticism recently, a friend remarked that many of his most basic statements about life are contained in parentheses that are simply left lying about. By contrast a critic like Lionel Trilling, who also goes wherever literature takes him, begins by stating his major position, putting it up on the mast-head, and then taking his illustrations from what he has been reading. My friend and I (it was Mr Andrew Harvey of All Souls) then searched our minds for a typically Empsonian fundamental judgment conveyed as a throw-off and both came up with the same one. It is from *Some Versions of Pastoral*, and from this first chapter I have been describing. Empson has been discussing Gray's 'Elegy' in terms of its social message; the poem tells us that, since the eighteenth century had no scholarship ladder, poor men could not get on in life however able they were, so that the rude forefathers of the hamlet may deserve the reverence due to great men whose qualities were never tested in action.

> By comparing the social arrangement to Nature he makes it seem inevitable, which it was not, and gives it a dignity which was undeserved. Furthermore, a gem does not mind being in a cave and a flower prefers not to be picked; we feel that the man is like the flower, as short-lived, natural, and valuable, and this tricks us into feeling that he is better off without opportunities. The sexual suggestion of *blush*

brings in the Christian idea that virginity is good in itself,
and so that any renunciation is good; this may trick us into
feeling it is lucky for the poor man that society keeps him
unspotted from the World.

Empson is inclined to disapprove of this as a kind of confidence
trick; but then, suddenly, he adds:

And yet what is said is one of the permanent truths; it is
only in degree that any improvement of society could
prevent wastage of human powers; the waste even in a
fortunate life, the isolation even of a life rich in intimacy,
cannot but be felt deeply, and is the central feeling of
tragedy. And anything of value must accept this because it
must not prostitute itself; its strength is to be prepared to
waste itself, if it does not get its opportunity.

The casual tone, the conversational prose, ought not to fool
us. Something important has been said: Empson as a poet will
explore that theme — 'the waste even in a fortunate life, the isola-
tion even of a life rich in intimacy' — with fortitude but also with
deep poignancy.

These thoughts provide us with a suitable approach to Emp-
son's second (and, as it turned out, final) volume of poetry, *The
Gathering Storm*. There is certainly a development from the
first volume to the second, but it seems to me that the differences
between the two collections have been habitually over-stressed.
The Gathering Storm is said to be more open in texture than
Poems, more accessible, less given to playing with ideas, coming
out of a wider life-experience, more concerned with current
problems. We may grant most of this as long as we keep in
mind: (1) that some of the best poems in the 1935 collection are
just as accessible as anything in *The Gathering Storm*: 'To an
Old Lady' or 'This Last Pain' or 'Note on Local Flora', for in-
stance; (2) that one of the most direct of the later poems,
'Aubade', was in fact written during the earlier period (Empson
tells us in the record-sleeve notes that it was written in Japan
probably in 1933; perhaps for personal reasons he did not in-
clude it in *Poems*, but it belongs there in time); and (3) both

volumes are haunted by the main Empsonian themes of fear and
equilibrium.

Empson's remark to Ricks during that interview, already
quoted, is of course the kind of thing that one says in conversa-
tion when seeking to establish areas of very broad agreement.
We must not build up any such neatly false picture as: first book
– English country-house background, Winchester, Cambridge,
books and ideas, youthful amours and hero-worshippings,
holidays in the Alps: second book – travel, exposure to reality,
maturing, threat of war. The threats are all there in the first
volume, even if they are not so specifically threats of war; a
foreboding echoes through many of the poems ('Winter will
come and all her leaves will go'), and it would be just as possible
to deduce from the first book as from the second, where the lines
actually occur, that this is a poet who believes

> No purpose, view,
> Or song but's weak if without the ballast of fear.

Empson taught English Literature in Japan 1931–4, and in
China 1937–9, so that whatever it is that happens to Europeans
in the Far East was happening to him pretty well all along. The
contact with a totally different culture would, of course, en-
courage and strengthen that tendency in his thinking which we
can loosely call anthropological and sociological. He has always
been interested in the underpinning ideas that keep a nation on
its pivot. By contrast with the extreme brevity of most of the
notes to his poems, the poem 'China' (which, unaided, I should
have found totally opaque) is explained, almost line by line, in
what is virtually a short essay, about five times as long as the
poem. Many of Empson's thoughts about China, and about
Eastern civilizations generally, find their way into this miniature
dissertation, which deserves to be looked up. But the passage in
it that caught my attention is in fact one that serves to illustrate
the continuity of Empson's poetry. He is commenting on the
stanza which ends the poem:

> A liver fluke of sheep agrees
>   Most rightly proud of her complacencies

With snail so well they make one piece
Most wrecked and longest of all histories.

The note says:

As to the liver fluke, who comes in the *Outline of Life* by
Wells, etc., its child does not kill the snail and cannot when
fully inside be distinguished anywhere from the body of the
snail; maybe it is not even cellular. It only puts red patches
containing its eggs on the horns of the snail so that these
are seen and eaten by birds. The horns grow again. There
is a third generation which gets from the bird to the sheep,
and the child of that has to leave the sheep and dissolve
itself in a snail. That the thing can play these tricks
without having any structure at all is what is so frighten-
ing; it is like demoniacal possession. However, to do the
Japanese justice, a normal Japanese is still rigidly Japanese
after twenty years of living among Chinese in China; no man
could be less like this eerie fluke. The idea that China unlike
other nations can keep its peculiar life going without a central
organisation was the excuse for bringing it in.

The liver fluke, maintaining its strange and to us repulsive
existence by means of total metamorphosis, perhaps without
even retaining a cellular structure, is exactly the kind of sym-
bolic–analogical idea that the earlier Empson built poems on; he
would have provided it with a mythological parallel and then
strung the poem between the two. In this instance, the parallel
comes not from mythology but from history; but when the note
remarks, 'it is like demoniacal possession', we realize that the
imaginative angle has not changed; we are still in the presence of
Frazer's three strands, red, black and white. The liver fluke is a
possessing demon in the same way as the phoenix is a vegetable.

At any rate, the themes handled in *The Gathering Storm* are
substantially the same as those in *Poems*. There is the tension-
of-opposites *motif*:

We could once carry anarchy, when we ran
Christ and the magnificent milord
As rival pets; the thing is, if we still can

Lacking either.

There is the concern with societies, with human aggregates, and what gives them their essential motivation:

It gives a million gambits for a mime
On which a social system can be based.

There is the central Empsonian concern with fear and the usefulness of fear. 'Courage Means Running', a rather pedestrian poem but a good repository of Empsonian ideas, starts out with two characters from *Pilgrim's Progress*, Fearing (here misnamed Fearful) and Muchafraid, both of whom exemplify the positive side of fear, which is not merely something to be overcome, like greed, but a useful instructor. One recalls how Empson, in one of those personal asides in *Milton's God*, confides in the reader that as a child he was haunted by the problem of whether, when it came to it, he would be able to show the courage that life evidently demanded of grown-ups. (He has.) To go back to *The Gathering Storm*, mythology is not quite so prominent as formerly (except in 'Bacchus', which is a hangover from the previous book, and a very bad poem it is too), but the analogical habit of mind is as strong as ever. There is the same stoical acceptance of tragedy, now and then expressed in an absolutely flat, unambiguous statement ('Verse likes despair'), the most famous being 'Missing Dates'. And there are love poems.

Empson as a love poet is first-rate, though usually at his most enigmatic. On this grand and mysterious subject, he gives full play to his sense of the richly baffling complexity of life. A great deal of love poetry (some of Shakespeare's sonnets, for example) turns on the unfathomable nature of the beloved, with the accompanying suggestion that this is appropriate even though it sometimes reduces the lover to despair; if she had a shallow nature that he could see right through, he would not love her so much. (One of Empson's early love poems begins with the striking line, 'Searching the cave gallery of your face'.) The whole package is contained in one of his most celebrated poems, 'Success'. The young man has arrived at the long-desired point; he has found the girl he loves, and she has accepted him; they are to marry (or whatever); he then finds — what, indeed, he suspected all along — that falling in love, even mutually, does not make life any simpler; its complexities remain; even in this happy state, there are discoveries to be made, new territories to map, not without effort; dangers and frustration, too, will have to be encountered. This marvellous poem gathers it all up; let us have it on the page.

> I have mislaid the torment and the fear.
> You should be praised for taking them away.
> Those that doubt drugs, let them doubt which was here.
> Well are they doubted for they turn out dear.
> I feed on flatness and am last to leave.
> Verse likes despair. Blame it upon the beer
> I have mislaid the torment and the fear.
>
> All losses haunt us. It was a reprieve
> Made Dostoevsky talk out queer and clear.
>
> Those stay most haunting that most soon deceive
>
> And turn out no loss of the various Zoo
> The public spirits or the private play.
> Praised once for having taken these away
> What is it else then such a thing can do?
>
> Lose is Find with great marsh lights like you.
> Those that doubt drugs, let them doubt which was here
> When this leaves the green afterlight of day.
> Nor they nor I know what we shall believe.
> You should be praised for taking them away.

The first three lines make a love poem on their own; also, whether in a sexual context or not, a wonderful sense of having arrived at serenity and the relief of pain. I remember a man telling me that he had been in a mental hospital with a very severe breakdown, had in fact been mad for some months, and that even during his worst patches he could find calm by murmuring those lines to himself. The poet is, among other things, a maker of runes, and these lines are one of Empson's.

'Those that doubt drugs, let them doubt which was here'
means both 'Those who are inclined to doubt whether drugs can
be efficacious, let them try doubting this one, which has so un-
mistakably worked', and also 'let them puzzle over exactly which
drug it was'. There is another and more pessimistic undertone,
which the poem proceeds to supply: drugs work powerfully but
they are not always good for us; this is introduced in the second
four lines, which bring in the note of disillusion; drugs as power-
ful as these emotions 'turn out dear', both expensive and dearly
valued. To lose one's torment and fear is a good thing but still a
loss. Dostoevsky was under sentence of death, had in fact dug
his own grave, when reprieve came; the shock was so unsettling
it turned him into a writer. The winning of love, which at the
beginning seems to stabilize everything, in fact leaves one's inner
life no less strange and complex than it always was ('the various
Zoo'). The last five lines of the poem are a beautiful and
memorable statement of acceptance. The onlookers, the people
who 'doubt drugs', are right to have reservations, but this is one
of those problem-clusters that are insoluble; we choose merely to
live with it, because there is no other way; the doubters, for all
their caution, are no nearer to a cut-and-dried answer than the
'I', for

  Nor they nor I know what we shall believe.

And so, with a kind of throwing up of the hands, we return to
the one thing we can be certain about, which is that

  You should be praised for taking them away.

You *should* be, and doubtless will be, but the simple 'I praise
you' is too direct to fit into this complex situation. Not that I
must make it sound as if the poem were cold, legalistic, hair-
splitting. The passion is there. Who that has ever been in love
has not sometimes wanted to say

  Lose is Find with great marsh lights like you

if he could only have found the words?

The love theme and the theme of history come together in the superb 'Aubade', one of the finest poems of our century. It is too long and too familiar to quote entire. Everything is there: the humour, the stoical acceptance, the impressionistic brilliance of the writing. The dramatic situation is clear and striking; whether or not the actual episode, of the two lovers in the house on a cliff being woken by an earthquake, 'really happened', the setting in a definite time and place gives the poem an anchor in the particular, as in Yeats's 'Among School Children'. Empson has explained that when he first went to Japan the old hands always warned the younger men not to marry a Japanese girl, because there would probably be a war, and then the family complications would be unmanageable. This meant that, if love did happen, it had to have that shorn-off feeling of impermanence; both sides knew it could not last. The earthquake that disturbs the lovers is thus one of Empson's fundamental symbols or analogies, like the forest fire that causes the tree to open its cones. The troubles and dangers of life are everywhere the same:

> Tell me again about Europe and her pains,
> Who's tortured by the drought, who by the rains.
> Glut me with floods where only the swine can row
> Who cuts his throat and let him count his gains.
> It seemed the best thing to be up and go.
>
> A bedshift flight to a Far Eastern sky.
> Only the same war on a stronger toe.
> The heart of standing is you cannot fly.
>
> Tell me more quickly what I lost by this,
> Or tell me with less drama what they miss
> Who call no die a god for a good throw,
> Who say after two aliens had one kiss
> It seemed the best thing to be up and go.

All this is clear enough; clear, and forceful, like something worked in hard stone. The third and fourth lines, there, incidentally, give us an amusing glimpse of Empson the countryman; he comes from a squirearchical Yorkshire

family (his birthplace is given as Something-or-other Hall) and
must, in childhood, have kept company with country people who
communicated to him traditional notions such as that a domestic
pig, when forced to swim, must never be hurried or its sharp little
front hoofs will lacerate its pendulous throat.

'The heart of standing is you cannot fly', one of Empson's
great reverberating lines (try *forgetting* it!), covers a wide range:
the whole point of turning to fight when cornered is that there is
nothing else to do; also, what gives brave men the heart, or
stomach, to fight is that running away will not save them and is
in any case contrary to their code. Here, as so often, there is a
link between the poetry and the criticism; in *Seven Types,*
chapter 7, his attention is caught by a line in Dryden's 'Song for
St Cecilia's Day',

> Charge, charge, 'tis too late to retreat.

> Evidently the thought that it is no good running away is
> an important ingredient of military enthusiasm; at any rate
> in the form of consciousness of unity with comrades, who
> ought to be encouraged not to retreat (even if they are not
> going to, they cannot have not thought of it, so that this
> encouragement is a sort of recognition of their merits), and
> of consciousness of the terror one should be exciting in the
> foe; so that all elements of the affair, including terror, must
> be part of the judgment of the most normally heroic mind,
> and that, since it is too late for *him* to retreat, the Lord has
> delivered him into your hands.

There is more, much more, to say about *The Gathering
Storm*, but one's space, and the patience of one's readers, is not
infinite. The main thing to say is that Empson's relatively small
body of verse, not added to for decades, has stayed wonderfully
solid; these poems do not go stale, or sink out of one's memory.
It so happens that I was the first person to think Empson's
poems worth writing a critical essay about; I wrote it before the
Collected Poems came out (though it was published a few

months later), at a time when Empson, back in China after a war-time spell in the B.B.C., was very much out of sight and out of mind. He was not, in those days, a big reputation, simply one poet among many, but his work stood out for me, and haunted my mind, and called for criticism if only to get my own ideas straight about it. I bring up the matter after a quarter of a century not, or not merely, to give a modest toot on my own trumpet, but to remark that it would have saddened me in those days to know that the poetry stopped there; that the two volumes I had in front of me were, substantially, all there was to be.

When Empson brought out his *Collected Poems* in 1949 (the American edition coming before the English, very much to the credit of American publishing) he added two poems not in either of his two volumes; one of them ('Let It Go') he has described as a poem about ceasing to write poetry; a few years later he wrote a beautiful and effective translation of a Chinese ballad and a somewhat more uneven 'Masque' for presentation at Sheffield University, and these were gathered up into the English *Collected Poems* of 1955. Apart from that, nothing. The blaze of poetic imagination which produced two such remarkable collections, only five years apart, threw out a few more sparks and then faded.

Empson has, of course, continued to write, and very interestingly; and he has worked away at the same themes that always attracted him, 'the most complicated and deeply-rooted notions of the human mind', the springs of action in societies and in men. No less in his later than in his earlier work, Empson's mind continually drives towards ultimates; the most routine piece of *explication de texte*, such as any Professor might harmlessly indulge in, will suddenly make a seven-league leap and land us in the most profound questions, not because Empson cannot keep his mind on his ordinary professional work but because the study of literature is based on concern for life. The most extraordinary, and yet in a way the most logical, fruit of this habit of thinking is *Milton's God* (1961, revised 1965). Milton has always attracted Empson – the loneliness, the arrogance, the superb artistry, the tremendous mental grasp that can co-exist with odd *lacunae*, they all challenge him. *Paradise Lost* seeks to justify the ways of God to men, but Empson happens to think that these ways, as viewed through the lens of the Christian religion, are not justifiable; so that the book opens out on to the wide and variegated hinterland of Empson's opinions about the nature of human society and the destiny of man. The basic thesis of the book is that the strains and contradictions in *Paradise Lost* come from its being a good poem, not a bad one, since the God it sets out to justify is wicked and not justifiable, so that the more acutely Milton's imagination works the more strange the poem seems to be. Always ready to follow up the implications of his judgments, Empson teases out all the strands until finally he reaches the point of having to say exactly why the God of Christianity seems to him unfit to be worshipped. The result is his remarkable chapter 7, 'Christianity', as fine an example as I know of Empson's mind working on a large general subject, with all its blend of acuteness and moral authority with a certain amateur casualness.

The gravamen of his charge against Christianity is that it is tainted with torture-worship and human sacrifice, and leads by devious routes towards a diseased indulgence in cruelty. His recoil from Christianity is so strong that he cannot bring himself to write temperately of it; understandably, since if you believe, as Empson does, that 'the Christian God the Father, the God of Tertullian, Augustine and Aquinas, is the wickedest thing yet invented by the black heart of man' (p. 251) there is no sense in being merely polite and equable about it.

Broadly, Empson's thesis is that human sacrifice may have been an emotional necessity in Neolithic societies, but that humanity managed to break away from that necessity, that feeling that the gods must be placated in the most extreme way, at about the time of the rise of the great religions. For primitive men, the cultivation of crops involves first an apparent waste of food and then a very anxious period of waiting, and this arouses a psychological need to implore the favour of the gods; when men move into towns, and live on the food sent in from the countryside, the ritual human sacrifice may accompany them but only because it is built into the pattern of their lives, and insisted on by the officials. Foreign conquest helped to break this down, when it became evident that a town could be occupied by people of different beliefs, who did not placate the gods in the same way or had different gods, and yet the food continued to arrive. 'To go on behaving sensibly after the loss of religious faith is an important capacity of the human mind' (p. 237).

Empson believes the human mind capable of progress, not the trivial progress of technical advance, but the deep progress of fundamental improvement in its attitudes; men can become more intelligent, more merciful, more tolerant, just as they can slip back and become less so. 'We do not easily realize how impressive it is to have the Second Isaiah and Pythagoras and the Buddha and Confucius all alive at the same time, because we think of that time, rightly enough, as the start of history; but the town civilizations had been going on for thousands of years.' During this miraculous phase, in the lifetime of these four representative sages, the race made the great advance of discarding its psychological reliance on human sacrifice. None of these great thinkers seems to have travelled much, and doubtless they were unaware of one another's existence, but the trade routes were opening up, and some ideas were 'portable' enough (Empson's word) to be carried from one centre to another and to spread light. 'What could cross the trade routes was a practical suspicion, very welcome to all decent persons, that the technique of obtaining benefits by human sacrifice was not really efficient' (p. 238). So that 'Thinkers began to talk about what is good or right or just for all men, instead of about the correct procedure for sacrifice to the local god or king.' Sweeping on, Empson throws out the fascinating aside that 'Greek tragedy is the reverberation after the fall of human sacrifice; no wonder its theology is adventurous and rather confused.' He then slows down long enough to hand out a few references (Sir Charles Eliot's *Hinduism and Buddhism*, H. G. Creel's *The Birth of China*, William Willetts's *Chinese Art*) to indicate the factual (or at any rate historiographical) sources of his notions here; the references, though cursory, are genuinely helpful, and

demonstrate his willingness to play fair with the reader. Then
we get this crucially important paragraph:

> Thus around 600–500 B.C. China, India and the
> Mediterranean basin behave like three great trees in a park
> in the springtime, doing the same things in parallel without
> apparent contact; and a mood of doubting the practical
> claims of murderous and expensive priests is about the only
> thing we can imagine them to catch from one another. The
> effect of giving up human sacrifice was that thinkers felt
> free to consider what was just and good for all men. The
> effect of this again, in various cases, was to make them
> conceive a God of all mankind, transcendent and meta-
> physically one with Goodness; though both India and
> China tended to conceive an Absolute rather than a Person.
> The belief in progress may sometimes be delusory, but this
> rapid simultaneous development is the most impressive
> case of progress on record; that is, of the kind of thing a
> theorist has in mind when he speaks of progress as if it
> could be expected to be quasi-automatic.

So much for the plus side. Now for the minus. This epoch of
religion-founding saw the start of one religion that has gone
drastically wrong; one set of believers started playing to the
wrong script:

> Among the various universal religions which were formed
> as a result of this change and still survive, Christianity is
> the only one which ratted on the progress, the only one
> which dragged back the Neolithic craving for human
> sacrifice into its basic structure. This is what is the matter
> with it; people recognized at once that the thrilling piece of
> religious engineering carried excessive strain at this crucial
> point.

For the next twenty-odd pages, before returning to *Paradise
Lost*, Empson delivers himself of an attack on Christianity that
is most impressive in its moral fervour. He really hates and fears
what he considers the basis of Christianity, its attempt 'to patch
the ancient Neolithic craving for human sacrifice on to the new

transcendental God of all mankind'. To him, the notion of a God
who tortures himself to death as an alternative to automatically
doing it to the entire human race, however sweetened by the
sugar-coating of the doctrine of the Trinity, is repugnant
because it ministers to these sick impulses in the human heart:
'Men always try to imitate their gods, so that to worship a
wicked one is sure to make them behave badly.' Naturally he
gets a good deal of mileage out of the barbarity of some of the
early Church doctrines, notably the idea, which he finds both in
Tertullian and Aquinas, that the redeemed soul, sitting in bliss
beside God the Father, is required to take pleasure in watching
the torments of the damned. It is true that this revolting doctrine
was not inculcated by Jesus, nor set forth anywhere in the Scrip-
tures, but the Fathers made it as a deduction from Holy Writ,
which would be enough to suggest that the study of Holy
Writ had made them worse instead of better, drawing them
away from mercy and towards vindictiveness.

Starting from that basis, Empson has no difficulty in
demonstrating that many kinds of neurotic foolishness and
wickedness are able to draw nourishment from Christian doc-
trine. For instance:

> A humanist, as I understand the term, says 'This world is
> good enough for me, if only I can be good enough for it'; an
> anti-humanist, however noble in personal character, at
> least appears to be committed to saying 'Nothing but
> Heaven is good enough for me; I ought to be there already'
> — nobody but God is aristocratic enough for him. The
> attitude is not always combined with interest in Hell, but
> that seems to fit on to it very easily, as one of the
> aristocratic pleasures of Heaven. A political-minded reader
> is inclined to reflect how easily this spiritual-minded author
> might instead have become a frustrated revolutionary,
> saying: 'If I had my rights, I'd be sitting in that police-
> station already, pulling out people's finger-nails.'

As polemic, all this is very enjoyable to read, and it certainly
fits in with part of what one feels about Christianity: that it is a
lofty and ennobling religion if you look at it selectively and see

only the lofty and ennobling parts. When Christianity is on the
defensive, as it has been for the last hundred years, its defenders
concentrate on those facets of it that are not likely to offend
ordinary decent people; when it is firmly in control and backed
by the secular power, the horrible sides of Christian doctrines are
apt to emerge and become paramount. At all periods when the
Christian Church has had effective power it has behaved con-
temptibly, though individuals within it have often been saintly;
it is, in fact, the usual human patchwork.

Having got this far, Empson has to make some sort of state-
ment of his own positives, which he does on page 259.
Christians assert that there can be no goodness without the under-
pinning of a religious belief; Empson believes that 'it would
be better to have principles'. His own principle is 'the theory of
Bentham which was in favour when I was a student at Cam-
bridge; that the satisfaction of any impulse is in itself an elemen-
tary good, and that the practical ethical question is merely how
to satisfy the greatest number'. This, obviously, is a piece of
Sunlight Soap that wouldn't convince a thirteen-year-old, since
some human impulses do not deserve to be satisfied, and the
process of sorting out the deserving from the undeserving among
our impulses must be based on something other than the mere
fact that impulses exist and drive towards satisfaction. A few
lines further on, Empson is admitting that 'unless some special
gadget can be fitted in, the satisfaction of an impulse to inflict
pain on another person must have its equal democratic right',
and this worries him; he toys with the idea that sadism can
perhaps be relied on to punish itself, but this won't wash either:
'No doubt, like other vices, it comes in the end to cripple the
normal satisfactions; but some people are clever at making
adjustments to their vices, and this one does not seem to punish
itself enough.' Finally he lets it all go with 'I recognize that my
own position about ethics is too indefinite.' He feels sure that
Christianity is wrong, but does not know what to offer in its
place; a perfectly honourable attitude, as one might warn people
to get out of a burning building without claiming to be able to
build them a new one.

In thus giving an explanation of his ideas about Christianity and how he arrived at them, Empson is not merely rounding out a fascinating piece of literary criticism (though he is doing that too); he is squarely in the tradition of English poets like Blake and Coleridge and Shelley, and for that matter Milton himself, who had speculative ideas, which to some extent they suppressed in their work but were in any case an important background to that work. The speculative ideas of poets have not always fared well at the hands of philosophers, but they have gone on being read and discussed, because of the attraction of the poetry and because of their own vitality. This will obviously happen to Empson's ideas, but I see no harm in combining a fondness for his poetry with a disinclination to take over his ideas wholesale; this, after all, is only to treat him as we treat Shelley or Milton. Empson's view of Christianity is interesting but not the only possible one. To begin with, it will seem irrelevant to many religious people of different faiths, because it treats all religions in a totally humanist way; the question of whether any religion is true, in the sense of offering a credible account of the universe, is one that does not even seem to him worth mentioning; they are simply systems by which men live, and the good ones are those that encourage them to live with kindliness and tolerance. This, of course, is an attitude that consistently underlies the poems:

All those large dreams by which men long live well
Are magic-lanterned on the smoke of hell,

and 'hell' means here, as the note tells us, 'only Sheol, chaos'. Belief, for Empson, is simply a function of the mind; doubtless he feels that ultimate truths are unknowable, and pragmatic truths can be verified or disproved empirically, which means that they do not involve belief in any deep sense — one simply takes them for granted. This is what I think myself, so that I feel sympathetic when Empson remarks of the doctrine of the Trinity, 'One can hardly discuss whether a man believes this doctrine, because it is merely a thing which his mind can be induced to do', but some people would not. To go back to Frazer for a moment, this is obviously the attitude which underlies the comparative method of *The Golden Bough*. It would not have been tactful for Frazer to spell it out, but nobody could ever have read his volumes without realizing that for Frazer, as for Empson after him,

Gods cool in turn, by the sun long outlasted.

Indeed, he comes very close to spelling it out in the highly emotional passage which concludes the whole work, that meditation on the Alban Hills in which the cult of the Virgin Mary at St Peter's is implicitly compared with the cult of Diana of the wood at Nemi, with its strong suggestion that such as the worshippers of Diana Nemorensis are, the worshippers of the Virgin Mary shall be.

Seeing religions as humanistic belief-systems, Empson naturally judges them according to their fruits, which in practice means judging them according to the behaviour of the people who believe in them. This of course is an extremely dangerous thing to do; I would not like to try to draw up a ledger of human wickedness and nastiness, and try to work out whether Christians, Muslims, Hindus, Buddhists or atheists have committed more of it.* Some dreadful things have been done in the name of all religions, or at any rate of all the active ones, the religions that tell their adherents to go out and do something. As for the religions of non-attachment, the sins of their followers are the sins of omission rather than commission, and I imagine the kind of Buddhistic doctrine preached in the Fire Sermon has never led anyone to become a Mother Teresa of Calcutta.

Mention of the Fire Sermon recalls a curious fact that seems apposite here. Empson's *Poems* of 1935 uses a page from the

---

* Empson's view of Christianity seems close to Macaulay's of Hinduism: 'The Brahminical mythology is so absurd that it necessarily debases every mind that receives it as truth; and with this absurd mythology is bound up an absurd system of physics, an absurd geography, an absurd astronomy. . . . All is hideous, and grotesque, and ignoble.' (Oration, 'The Gates of Somnauth', 1843.)

Fire Sermon, carefully put together from various translations to achieve the highest euphony and memorability, as epigraph, and this is carried over into the *Collected Poems* of 1955. To keep this flag at the mast-head across twenty years must surely indicate something; but, no, we find Empson a year later casually washing his hands of it. Mr Allan Rodway had written a review of the *Collected Poems* in *Essays in Criticism*, and very reasonably had taken the Fire Sermon into account when interpreting the various occurrences of 'fire' in the poems ('Not to have fire is to be a skin that shrills', etc.). Empson wrote a short reply (vol. VI, p. 481) in which he says:

> Like many others about thirty years ago, I looked up the Fire Sermon (recorded in Ceylon as one of the first sermons of the Buddha, given soon after he had decided that it was just possible to make himself understood) because of Mr Eliot's *Waste Land*. With all the repetitions it takes about ten minutes, and the experience is rather like having a steam-roller go over you. . . .
>
> . . . Of course I think Buddhism much better than Christianity, because it managed to get away from the neolithic craving to gloat over human sacrifice; but even so I feel that it should be applied cautiously, like the new wonder-drugs.
>
> The Fire Sermon itself is unlike most of Buddhism, and leaves Christianity far behind, in maintaining that all existence as such, even in the highest heaven, is inherently evil. Such is the great interest of it; but I think this all-embracing hatred commonly attracts only bad characters; and, to do Mr Eliot justice, I do not think that it is explicitly stated in his devotional verse.

Empson goes on to make an admiring reference to George Orwell's essay on Gandhi, in which Orwell makes the point that saintly renunciation is not a better version of ordinary human life but an alternative to it; the average person, who chooses to go on involving, loving, breeding, reacting to life on the level of day-to-day existence, is not just a failed saint, but one who has chosen to involve with life just as the saint has chosen not to;

e.g., 'love means nothing if it does not mean loving some people more than others'. This attitude evidently wins Empson's approval, yet it is, of course, the direct opposite of the doctrine of non-attachment that we find in the Fire Sermon. So why is the Fire Sermon up there? As Empson rightly recalls, T. S. Eliot had laid it firmly before his readers in the notes to *The Waste Land*, calling it the Buddhist equivalent of the Sermon on the Mount; but it does not seem characteristic of Empson to do something just because Eliot ordered it, and he goes on to offer some kind of explanation for sticking to the Buddha's words all that time. 'My verse', he says, 'sometimes tries to bring out these very sharp contrasts between one and another of our accepted moral beliefs', and goes on:

> though I probably never thought about the Fire Sermon when writing or revising, I had already decided that I thought its doctrine wrong, though fascinating and in a way intelligible. You might say that it is present as one extreme of the range of human thought, because the poetry often tries to take the position 'what I am saying is admitted to be true, though people look at it in so many different ways'; but even so it is pretty remote, and not appealed to.

So the Fire Sermon is important enough to Empson's poetry to be put up in front, and given a new lease there after twenty years, while being 'pretty remote, and not appealed to'. Is this, one wonders, a procedure Empson would expect from the poets about whom he writes such brilliant criticism? Would he expect Milton to come back from the shades and say that his Christianity was pretty remote, and not appealed to, in spite of being explicitly announced at the beginning of the epic? Obviously not; here, as in the matter of the explication of his poems, Empson is expecting other people to be more consistent than he is himself.

I labour this point about the Fire Sermon for a reason. The relationship between a poet's ideas and his poetry is usually a complex one. The text-books I read in my youth were based on the assumption that you could ascertain a poet's 'ideas' by going through his prose utterances, letters, recorded conversations, etc., and then turn to the poems and spot every line in which those ideas seemed to crop up; and when you had done that you had interpreted the poetry and everyone could go home. To be charitable, I think we can concede that this approach has its value as a first step, when dealing with a poet whose work is new and unfamiliar to us; I remember that when Wallace Stevens was first published in England, in the earlier fifties, and we had the job of coming to terms with his poetry and assimilating it into the tradition we were working from, most people adopted this simple approach to begin with; I certainly did myself. But as soon as the poems are familiar, and we begin to move towards a more sensitive and intimate approach, we have to realize that a poet may use his ideas in a number of ways, and directly versifying them is not the usual way or even a particularly common one. Empson might continue for years to draw some kind of strength from the Fire Sermon (even if he 'probably never thought about' it), by treating it as one of the stakes that supported a clothes-line (what was the other? Do the poems tell us or do we have to make it up?), and this explains why in spite of his detestation of the Christian God he can be a sensitive and sympathetic critic of Christian poetry. The cruder kind of anti-Christian – a party-line Marxist, say – is compelled to say of George Herbert or Hopkins that his poetry is based on a delusion fostered by capitalism, etc., etc., whereas Empson can always assume that the poet with a Christian subject-matter is using the theology in the way he himself is using the Fire Sermon. And this explains why the boiling indignation in that chapter of *Milton's God*, though it is more emphatic and narrowed-down than anything else in Empson's work, not excepting the poems, does not cloud the clear lens through which he looks at the work of other poets.

All in all, the mind of William Empson, scholar and critic and speculative thinker, seems to have remained very much the same over the last forty-five years, which makes it all the more strange that for the last thirty of those years William Empson, poet,

seems to have gone missing. Some writers, whether of prose or
poetry, simply burn out; they have no longer the vitality to offer
anything fresh, so they either repeat themselves or fall silent.
Empson's mind, as one knows it from his writings, from conver-
sation and from anecdotes (ah, yes, those anecdotes), has quite
clearly remained as athletic as ever; he thinks as incisively, and
his thinking is at the service of a broad, generous humanity that
one feels justified in calling wisdom. All he doesn't do is write
poetry.

Christopher Ricks has an interesting explanation of the poet
Empson's falling silent. Bearing in mind 'the enabling tension
. . . between the ordinary human wish to beget life and the equal-
ly ordinary sense that life is too dark and bleak a gift', Mr Ricks
notes that Empson more or less stopped writing poetry after his
marriage in 1941 and the subsequent birth of his two sons. This
tension is naturally 'more likely to precede than to follow
parenthood'; it has been a continuing preoccupation with Emp-
son, as witness the fact that 'Empson's criticism has always been
especially vivid, imaginative and central when it contemplates
parenthood, its responsibilities and the world's' (in speaking,
e.g., of *Hamlet, The Winter's Tale* or *Oedipus*). That particular
balance had to come down on one side or the other, and
becoming a father laid to rest a certain creative systole and
diastole in Empson's mind, with the result that he ceased to feel
the particular kind of pressure that forced poems out of him.
Certainly Empson has consistently held the view that the
writing of poetry is to some extent therapeutic, a means of
holding one's mental balance:

> Mr T. S. Eliot, some while ago (speaking as a publisher),
> remarked that poetry is a mug's game, and this is an im-
> portant fact about modern poets. When Tennyson retired
> to his study after breakfast to get on with the *Idylls* there
> had to be a hush in the house because every middle-class
> household would expect to buy his next publication. I
> believe that rather little good poetry has been written in re-
> cent years, and that, because it is no longer a profession in
> which ability can feel safe, the effort of writing a good bit

of verse has in almost every case been carried through
almost as a clinical thing; it was done only to save the
man's own sanity. Exceedingly good verse has been written
under these conditions in earlier centuries as well as our
own, but only to externalise the conflict of an individual. It
would not have been sensible to do such hard work unless
the man himself needed it.

Mr Ricks works out his theory very sensitively, with a wealth
of quotations from every area of Empson's work, which he
seems to know by heart in its entirety, and without the least
suggestion of intrusive biographical fingering. On the other
hand, I feel quite unable to comment on his theory one way or
another; I simply do not feel that I have the right, or for that
matter the impulse, to put forward any explanation of Empson's
silence. In the course of a long and arduous intellectual life, in
which his contribution to the general flow of ideas has been in-
calculable, he wrote poetry for rather less than twenty years —
wrote at heat and pressure, in fact, for just over ten, then
stopped. That is the fact, and beyond the fact I do not feel able
to penetrate.

If I have an impulse, it is not to find an explanation but to
offer a tribute. I happen to know, from personal sources, that
Empson thinks it a sound idea for a poet to do a certain amount
of writing for writing's sake. In that way, though he may go
through a period, or more than one, in which his work is not
very good, when he next has something important to say he will
have the habit of composition. Two distinguished poets of Emp-
son's own generation, Auden and MacNeice, carried out this
policy, and Empson believes that they were right and were
justified by the outcome. Only, it does not happen to be the way
he himself has chosen. When, for whatever reason, life no longer
exerted those particular pressures that forced poetry out of him,
when the particular urgencies gradually faded into the general,
he simply stopped. And it is a measure of our respect for him
that we feel, obscurely perhaps but unmistakably, that even this
is not entirely a failure but somehow a strength; that even the

silence of such a man has its dignity and its usefulness. To go
back to his own words, 'anything of value must accept this
because it must not prostitute itself; its strength must be to be
prepared to waste itself, if it does not get its opportunity'.

*

Dan Pagis is sitting in our garden, having lunch. He is in Oxford
to visit the Carmis; he and Carmi are close friends, poets who
sustain and incite each other. Now the two of them have
appeared in one paperback book in England, in the Penguin
Modern European Poets series. Are Hebrew poets 'European'?
It doesn't matter; both are classical modern poets, writing in
that idiom of 'pure', pared-down poetry that dispenses with dis-
course, and it is an idiom that was developed first in Europe and
then exported to the rest of the world.

   Their book is wonderful in its joint impact. Since they have
both been put into English by the same translator, Stephen
Mitchell, there is a surface similarity that probably doesn't exist
in the original. Even so, they come out as very different. Carmi
is rich, elusive, lyrical, glancing; Pagis is bone-hard and poignant.
What they share, apart from that vein of self-mocking Jewish
humour, is imaginative intensity. Both are poets whose work
seems to have no dead, explanatory passages. Every line is elec-
tric with imagination; every poem crackles and gives off sparks.
Their book could serve as an introduction to 'modern' poetry for
someone who has never read any, so completely does the life of
their poetry gather itself into image and metaphor.

   Dan Pagis has a long poem, 'Brain', which means a great deal
to me. As I read it and return to it again and again, it begins to
seem like an utterance of my own mind. He is speaking for, as
well as to, me. The theme of 'Brain' is the isolation and solitude
of the human identity. Reading it, living through it, I know that
the loneliness I often feel is shared and understood. Since its in-
gredients are by their nature incommunicable, they can be
flashed from one mind to another only by image and metaphor.

No one but a poet could do this work. As I read 'Brain' I feel an extraordinary release from suffering.

Dan Pagis is a physically frail man by comparison with the sturdy, shock-headed Carmi. He has a delicately boned face and large, wide-open eyes full of tranquillity, as if he had faced the worst of suffering and loneliness and found within himself the strength to get everything together again in an order that will endure and that he can live by. Like all people who have found this strength, he is easy to get on with; not solemn, full of humour and good talk, lively and affectionate.

This man is a survivor from a concentration camp.

Mulling over the entries for the Newdigate Prize, I find myself drawn to one in particular: the title is 'Hostages', and this writer has chosen to approach it *via* a painting by Berthe Morisot, *Le Berceau*, wherein a young woman (the mother, presumably) bends over a baby in its cradle. The poem is brooding, gentle, imaginatively penetrating. My two fellow-examiners are not sure at first whether they like this one best; one of them, by an oversight, has not been sent the postcard reproduction of the painting with which the entry was accompanied; but they read it again, and agree with me.

The entries are, of course, anonymous; but when the names are revealed, I am pleased to find that the winner is David Winzar. His name never entered my head. The poem showed so much sympathy with feminine thoughts and feelings that I had supposed it to be by a woman.

Another poet steps out!

Writing up my lecture and thinking of William Empson. Undoubtedly he is a great man. His work, in verse and prose, is one of the permanently valuable things in the English literature of my time. (Though, predictably, one looks in vain for the recognition, the *réclame*, the gongs and C.B.E.s and so forth.) It is first-rate, and it will live.

Everyone who knows Empson has anecdotes about him; I will

forbear to press mine on the reader. But his life-style is worth
pondering. It is, in fact, a tripod, and this is a great part of his
strength and solidity. His blunt directness is that of the
Yorkshire squire (though it was his elder brother, I believe, who
inherited the broad acres); his intellectual subtlety and depth are
Cambridge, and a wonderful example of what Cambridge at its
best can bring out; his London Bohemianism rests lightly on top
of all this like a cloak loosely thrown across the shoulders. He is
a natural inhabitant of three separate worlds, and his frequent
disconcertingness arises from his habit of jumping from one to
another without warning.

But, though Empson's personal character derives from the
tripartite nature of his experience, his professional *milieu* has
been the university. It was Cambridge that first made him a
poet; the work he published in *Cambridge Poetry 1929* became
famous far beyond the University; it was a Cambridge don,
F. R. Leavis, who wrote (however cursorily) the first criticism that
initiated discussion of his work. Then came the years of teaching
English literature in Japan and China. At one point, working in a
university that had to be evacuated in war-time, he was without
books and had to teach classical English poetry from memory,
writing the texts on a blackboard; this seems to align him with
the Oriental tradition of the sage who knows the sacred writing
by heart and teaches his disciples orally, and one cannot think of
anyone who would carry it off more gracefully. In later years it is
the English and American universities that have provided Emp-
son with his public, disseminated his work and discussed it,
employed and encouraged him.

This makes me think in turn of the fitness or otherwise of an
academic *milieu* for the writer whose work is primarily im-
aginative. Whatever its faults – and the most prominent of
these, obviously, is its too heavy involvement with teaching and
learning – it is at any rate free of the rank smell of competitive
publicity given off by the London literary world with its waves
of fashion, its skirmishes between ins and outs, and its reliance
on journalism to arbitrate and disseminate its values. If the
average don is slightly baffled in the presence of imaginative

writing, he is nevertheless far more tactful and unobtrusive than the publicity-conscious journalist who will be meddling.

But to criticize other people's attitudes is in all humility to take stock of one's own; and now, in the hot, vivid summer of 1976, I feel that I have reached a point of rest. My thoughts have been taking a personal, reminiscent turn; I am glad, allowing for the inevitable ups and downs, that things have turned out as they have, that my adolescence in Oxford is bearing some fruit in my maturity in Oxford. I write a poem 'To My Young Self'; it catches some of this mood. It is time to make a statement in public; after three years out of my five in the Chair, time to gather up what I have been thinking and saying, and make a parcel of it, interspersed with this commentary that has evolved, as I have gone on with it, into a kind of personal letter to the people who voted me into the Chair, and others who might think in the same way. I must bring out a book now, while I still have some time left in the Chair, so that when it comes out I shall still be here to answer criticisms, still carrying the can.

It is a mistake to try to wrench one's thoughts out of the course in which they have become set. Something deeper and less biddable than reason, some powerful tidal flow, is drawing them along, and the best policy is to go with them. Since the direction of my mind at the moment is towards reminiscence and biography, the sheer fascination of what happened, I decide to make my summer lecture biographical in vein. I want, that is, to produce not so much a spoken critical essay as a portrait, a biographical landscape with moving figures.

So I decide to tell the story of Edward Thomas, one of the poets I most admire, and the woman who loved him. Biography is not a substitute for criticism but, if I can bring those two deeply alive and deeply suffering people before the mind's eye, I shall perhaps have marked out an avenue to their writings, to his poetry and her prose.

I take pleasure in writing this lecture; and take pleasure, too, in the thought that this is the last I shall write. For the rest of

my term, I shall speak my thoughts into the air and let them fall
where they may, with no attempt to gather them up in print.
Giving a lecture is fun; giving a lecture and then writing it up for
publication is work. So this is the last of the work. When I finish
delivering it, and go across to the King's Arms, a long stint of
work will be over and I shall feel that I have gone some way
towards paying a debt.

EDWARD THOMAS AND HELEN THOMAS

They met in adolescence, in an ordinary little house in an ordinary street in a suburb on the edge of London. He was sixteen, a pupil at St Paul's School; she was seventeen and living at home.

Her father was a man of letters, not important but with genuine gifts and respectably established. He had published several books and was in regular work as a reviewer. Their home had been in Liverpool, but at the age of fifty James Ashcroft Noble moved with his wife and family to Wandsworth. Having made this move he settled down quickly again to his quiet, regular life. The household was a placid one, though the middle daughter, ambitiously named Helen Berenice, did not get on well with her mother.

James Noble was a kindly man, generous with his time and attention, well qualified and well disposed to help a beginner in the art of literature. One of his Wandsworth neighbours was Philip Henry Thomas, a stocky dark-haired man, hard-working, disciplined, ready of speech, assertive. Starting from a Welsh country background he had dragged himself up by severe effort into a responsible and secure, though by no means glittering, job in the Civil Service; he worked for the Board of Trade and had responsibility for tramcars and light railways. Mr Noble did not know Mr Thomas, but was informed by a local clergyman of the existence of Thomas's elder son Edward, who had literary talent and ought perhaps to be encouraged. He spoke of the matter at home; the girls giggled and dubbed this unknown schoolboy 'the Genius'. Mr Noble sent a message inviting Edward Thomas to call and talk with him.

He did so; they went into Mr Noble's study; after a time, Helen, out of curiosity to see 'the Genius', slipped into the room on some pretext, and they were introduced. The boy had been talking animatedly enough, but with the entry of the girl he fell silent, and soon took his leave, refusing an invitation to stay to tea. Helen has described his appearance at this time in *As It Was*, the memoir she wrote in the 1920s, in which she calls Edward 'David Townsend' and herself 'Jenny'.

> David was tall – just six feet – and slim, with a broad chest and shoulders, which he carried well – loose-limbed and athletic. He had a beautifully shaped head with a fine brow, and his thick fair hair, worn rather long, curled a little over his forehead and ears. His nose was long and straight, his mouth very sensitive, with the upper lip slightly overhanging the lower. The chin was strong. The eyes were grey and dreamy and meditative, but fearless and steady, and as if trying to pierce to truth itself. It was a most striking face, recalling a portrait of Shelley in its sensitive, melancholy beauty. His hands were large and powerful, and he could do anything with them from the roughest work to the most delicate: they symbolize for me his strength and his tenderness. It is his hands even more than his beautiful face that remain in my vision when I think of him; I shall never forget them.

And, more briefly and dismissively, her own:

> I was at the age plain, with a round healthy face and small nose; rather serious in expression, but not entirely unattractive. I had a lot of dark brown hair, which I wore parted in the middle with long plaits wound round my head – a simple style suiting my dress and my general seriousness. I was straight and tallish, and my own well-shaped and strong and – as I think now – really lovely body gave me intense delight. I loved being without clothes, and moving about naked, and I took a pride in my health and strength.

The only photograph of Helen Thomas that I have seen shows

her at the age of twenty-two: an attractive face, handsome
rather than pretty, with somewhat broad cheek-bones, a mouth
well shaped and strongly defined, and – her most striking feature
– eyes that look ahead intensely, as if welcoming life with eager
curiosity and acceptance. It is a girl's face, but already one sees
in it a woman capable of loving and being loved.

Helen Noble did not fall in love with Edward Thomas at that
first meeting, but he engaged her interest, and soon he was
taking her out for walks on Wandsworth Common, which in the
1890s was rural to an extent quite unimaginable today. Though
they both had the same urban or suburban background, he
already had a deep love of rural nature and a growing fund of in-
formation about birds, flowers, trees, fish, which he imparted to
her. Their love blossomed; one summer day, in some deep recess
of the Common, they became lovers in the physical sense.
Afterwards he gave her the signet-ring from his own finger,
which had belonged to his great-grandfather. They regarded
themselves as married.

In this attitude they were typical young people of their time.
It was the age of bold unconventionality in the face of the
narrow and rigid dictates of Victorian respectability. This revolt
did not take the form of an insistence on the right to
promiscuity; it involved a code of behaviour not much less strict
than the official code, but claiming a freedom from convention
and social rite. In his own autobiographical fragment, Edward
Thomas has described how his deep dislike of the official world,
the world of rules and regulations and assemblies and outward
appearances, was rooted in him by enforced Sunday attendance
at a Unitarian chapel.

Chapel and Sunday-school were to me cruel ceremonious
punishments for the freedom of Monday to Saturday. I
have still a profound quiet detestation of Sunday in
whatever part of England or Wales it overtakes me, but
most of all in London. I think I began learning to hate
crowds and societies, and grown-up people, and black
clothes, and silk hats and neatly folded umbrellas and

shining walking-sticks, and everything that seemed a circling part of that deathly solemnity as I was not.

So matters stood. Their lives were no different from the lives of thousands of young people at that time: a narrow round of simple pleasures and inexorable duties, watched over by parents who would be outraged at any deviation from the solemn respectability of Victoria's last days, but aware already of the stirring of a new spirit. Like finds out like, and Helen had a knack of striking up acquaintance with 'advanced', even 'Bohemian' families, of making herself welcome in households frequented by writers and painters. Edward, for his part, was intensely solitary, feeling at ease only with simple people who lived close to the earth and knew its ways. In childhood holidays at Swindon he had met an old man called David Uzzell, a character of the hedgerows and canal banks, an ex-poacher who knew the name and nature of everything that grew out of the ground or moved on it. He had kept in touch with Gaffer Uzzell, and now took Helen down to the tiny cottage where the old man and his wife lived. They delighted her by treating her as a bride, spoiling the young couple, showing a genuine love for Edward. Perhaps these two or three days were the happiest of her life.

This little honeymoon was to buttress them against a separation, for Edward Thomas had persuaded his reluctant father to let him read for a scholarship to Oxford. He won it, and entered the University first as a non-collegiate student and then as a member of Lincoln College. Here, he blossomed into the typical rather precious young aesthete of the time, reading and writing chiefly for fine phrases and adopting a generally willowy stance. It was a slightly tiresome phase (and particularly so to energetic duty-ridden Thomas *père*), but we need not be harsh about it; no one becomes wise overnight, and no writer becomes a mature artist without some uncertain period of development. Helen went off contentedly enough to take the first of several jobs as a governess. She loved children and her dearest wish was one day to bear some for Edward.

That wish was granted prematurely. Helen became pregnant

during Edward's second year at Oxford. Their first action was to get married, taking the view (one that persisted until very recently) that, while mating did not require official sanction, parenthood decidedly did. Then they broke the news to their parents. Mrs Noble, whose relations with Helen had never been good, at once broke them off for ever. Edward's father groaned, complained, but continued his allowance for another year, to enable him to take his degree.

He did so, getting a decent Second, and then at once left Oxford and plunged into the brackish water of literary journalism and hack book-making. After their child, a boy, was born in 1900, he and Helen settled in a London slum, a real slum, with drunkenness and ill-health and despair on every side, while he trod the stairs of literary editors and publishers and she struggled to keep a cheerful and decent home. Work came in slowly, and was wretchedly paid; they moved, again to a slum, and finally decided that come what may they must get out into the countryside. Edward went house-hunting in Kent; the only affordable place he could find was a hideous little house on a knob of raw earth, and Helen's heart sank when she saw it, but at least they were out of the city, never to return, and in closeness to the natural rhythms of the earth they felt more themselves.

For the next dozen years their life was no more than normally eventful. They moved from house to house and from village to village, but always in the countryside. Edward Thomas wrote reviews and articles and books as publishers and editors wanted them; uncongenial work wasted his time, frustrated his energies and soured his temper, but there was rent to pay and mouths to feed. His one deep abiding solace was the countryside, the contact with simple people and the beauty of the earth; and, since he was known principally as a writer on rural themes, many of his commissions were for books that involved him in long solitary journeys of exploration. He covered hundreds of miles on foot, sleeping at inns and cottages, and always, however deep his melancholy, responding with quiet joy to trees, flowers, stones, birds and animals. Mostly he preferred to be alone

among these sights and sounds, but in sunnier moods he would
take Helen along, with or without the children, and then her joy
and content were boundless, loving him, as she did, utterly. With
no gush, no sentimentality, but with her usual simple truthful-
ness, she has conveyed the nature of the happiness she found in their
country pleasures.

> All this work I loved, as I did the housework, the gardening
> or any work which gave my strong body exercise, and
> which satisfied my spirit with its human necessity. David
> too was glad for me to do these things, and I tried my hand
> at brewing, wine-making, hop-picking and even reaping. Of
> course hay-making on the lovely slope of Blooming
> meadow was a festival for us all at the farm, and we learnt
> how the ricks that rose like a town in the rick-yard were
> shaped so symmetrically, and thatched as carefully as a
> house. It is this full life of homely doings that I remember
> chiefly at the farm – the early morning expeditions with
> David to a large pond about three miles away to fish for
> perch and roach and even pike; the walks to Penshurst and
> Leigh and Ightham Moat; the pickings and storing of
> apples; the making of quince jam; the finding of an owl's or
> a nightingale's nest; the woodpecker which cut the air in
> scallops as it flew from oak to oak; the white owl which
> brought its young to the roof ridge to be fed; the beautiful
> plough-horses with their shining brass ornaments; the
> cows going into their stalls like people going into their
> pews in church; the building and thatching of the ricks; the
> hedging and ditching; the wood-cutting and faggot-binding
> by men whose fathers had done the same work and whose
> fathers' fathers too; the work of the farm, leisured as the
> coming and going of the seasons; the lovely cycle of
> ploughing, sowing and reaping; the slow experienced
> labourers, whose knowledge had come to them as the
> acorns come to the oaks, whose skill had come as the
> swallows' skill, who are satisfied in their hard life as are the
> oaks and the swallows in theirs.

These are not progressive sentiments. If Helen had been an
up-to-date young woman of her time – if, for instance, she had

been a Fabian Socialist – she would have said that the rural labourers were not happy or, if they were, they were fools, tamely putting up with low wages and long hours and primitive accommodation, and that they ought to unite and do something about it. But, with the clear sight of her simplicity, she saw what was in front of her: country people, exploited as they were no less than the town population, were often happy in the beauty of their surroundings and the skill of their work. The rural population of England have never been materially prosperous, and now they never will be, since with the mechanization of agriculture and the disappearance of its work-force the rural poor as a class are no longer with us. And yet during their long history of privation, in such glimpses as we catch of them through their songs and stories and dances and feasts and festivals, they seem to be happy quite as often as miserable, and if they were happy then it must have been for the reasons that Helen Thomas gives, for certainly there were no others.

When there was happiness about, Helen reflected it like a mirror, and always she was a faithful moon to the sun of her husband's moods. Often these would be black and bitter. When the toil of hack-work caused a normal fatigue and depression she could understand and bear it, but sometimes this fatigue and depression linked up with a deeper, innate melancholy that would, they both realized, have worked in him whatever the circumstances of his life. Then he went through hell and she followed him, and at times her hell was deeper than his because she had to suffer guilt (her body had brought forth the children who had to be fed, she ran the home that had to be paid for) and the even worse pain of knowing that her love could not help him. During her second pregnancy, while Edward grimly parcelled up some of his beloved books to be sold against the extra expenses, Helen wrote despairingly to a friend, 'He cannot love, Janet, he cannot respond to my love. How can he when all is so dark, and I, I have deprived him of it all, the joys of life and love and success. If he would only begin life again without me my heart would rejoice. I should be very happy, for his happiness is all I care for.'

And in *World Without End*, the continuation of *As It Was* (the two are nowadays always printed together), she has described one of the bad times in agonized detail.

In spite of the lifting of financial cares the attacks of gloom and wretchedness had become of late more frequent and more lasting, and there were terrible days when I did not know where he was; or, if he was at home, days of silence and brooding despair. Often during this period while I was doing my housework or playing with the children or working in the garden I was straining to hear his coo-ee from the hillside, or his foot on the steps up to the gate. And often when he came I was terrified by the haggard greyness of his face, and the weary droop of his body, as he flung himself into his study chair, not speaking or looking at me. Once in one of these fits, after being needlessly angry with one of the children who cried and ran away from him, he rummaged in a drawer where he kept all sorts of things like fishing tackle and tools, and where I knew there was also a revolver. This he put into his pocket, and with dull eyes and ashen cheeks strode out of the house up the bare hill. I watched him go until he was lost among the trees at the top. I thought 'perhaps I shall never see him again', but I knew he would not leave me like this; it would not be like this that he would save himself. Nevertheless my limbs went weak and slack, my tongue was dry in my mouth, the questions and chatter of the children were an agony to me. I wanted to be alone and listen. But I could not. I took the children down to the stream in the hollow where they could paddle and sail their boats without wanting me to join in their play. There I sat with my hands in my lap unable to sew or read or think, and while the children played I listened. I prayed too that he might be released from his agony and I from mine. When the sun set and the children got tired of their game I took them home and put them to bed. I changed my dress, made up the study fire, drew the curtains, and got the tea things ready on a little table. I was in the kitchen, ironing, when he came in.

'Hello,' I called, though the word came out like a croak.

He was safe. When I could control my voice and face I
went to the study. He was taking off his shoes by the fire,
and I saw they were coated with mud and leaves. He did
not look up.

'Shall I make the tea?' I said.

'Please,' he answered, and in his voice I was aware of all
he had suffered and overcome, and all that he asked of me.

Though they faced honestly their frequent unhappiness, and
each insisted on taking the blame for the other's sufferings, there
was never any question of a separation. Edward Thomas,
though he could often be harsh and cruel to Helen when the
despairing mood was on him, would tell her at other times that
she was the essential underpinning of his life. 'If you turned to
anyone else,' he told her in a letter, 'I should come to an end
immediately.'

Even when another woman brought him at least intermittent-
ly a happiness strong enough to lift his melancholy, Helen never
felt her marriage threatened. The young and gifted Eleanor
Farjeon came into Edward Thomas's life in 1912 and has drawn
a sympathetic and sensitive portrait of him in *Edward Thomas:
the Last Four Years*. He enjoyed her company, responding both
to her intelligence and her femininity, but their involvement was
not physical and Helen seems to have viewed Eleanor as an ally
in the struggle against Edward's melancholy. Her account in
World Without End of a visit Eleanor paid to them shows the
two women united in the effort to help the man.

Exactly why Edward Thomas was so melancholy and reserved
can, of course, never be known. It would be simpler to dismiss
the question, to say 'he was melancholy and reserved' and leave
it at that. Yet it is also tempting to speculate on how his par-
ticular mental composition got itself together. His photographs
show a thin, sensitive face marked by deep lines of strain, with
large, emotional eyes, and obviously such people suffer in the
rough arena of human life. But one feels that the special cir-
cumstances of his own life were also to blame. If Philip Henry
Thomas had not left his Welsh background, he would have been
a poor man but his children would have known a richer tapestry

of relationships and stories and customs, a more nourishing soil
than the bleak examination-passing existence among suburban
chimney-pots. Edward Thomas reacted against his parental
background and escaped back into the countryside, but he did so
as a solitary being, an escaped animal doomed to isolation from
others of his kind. This drove him further into inhibition and
aloofness. The warmth of Helen's love for him might well have
melted this frost, but unfortunately he never loved her as deeply
as she loved him; the rays of her being did not penetrate into the
recesses of his; and, after their idyllic beginning, he came all too
soon to identify her love for him with domesticity and financial
pressure.

Oxford, though he enjoyed it, seems to have done little for
him, except in the narrow sense that an Oxford degree may have
made it slightly easier for him to get a toe in the door when he
came to look for literary work. (But he had already started his
career as a *feuilletoniste*, had published articles and even a book,
before he went there.) It has been wisely said that the university
is the place where you go to have the nonsense put back that was
knocked out of you at school; where a young man can delight in
colour and individuality and variety after the harshness and
narrowness of school life. Edward Thomas certainly took Oxford
in this spirit, rather than seeing it, as his father wanted him to,
simply as a means of 'getting on'. But the effect was not lasting.
He relapsed into his shy, solitary melancholy. Though it was his
fate to tramp round looking for literary piecework, he so
abhorred any taint of salesmanship that his interviews with
editors and publishers would have been comical if the situation
had not been so dismal. The kindly H. W. Nevinson, whose
befriending of the Thomases was crucial, remembered their first
meeting and Edward Thomas's characteristic style in offering
his services:

He was tall, absurdly thin, and a face of attractive distinc-
tion and ultra-refinement was sicklied over with nervous
melancholy and the ill condition of bad food or hunger.
Almost too shy to speak, he sat down proudly and asked if

I could give him work. I enquired what work he could do,
and he said 'None'. . . . I asked whether he would like some
reviewing on any subject, and was quite sure he could not
write, but certainly he did want work of some sort. . . .

As in professional life, so in personal, it was extremely difficult
for him to build a bridge to another human being; he was one of
those to whom, as he put it in a letter to Gordon Bottomley,
'social intercourse' was 'only an intenser form of solitude'.

This isolation was so intense that the family life of which, as a
father, he was necessarily at the centre seems to have impinged
on him mainly as a remote play of shadows. Not that he failed to
do his best as a provider and organizer. The Thomases were in-
clined to worry about the schooling of their eldest child, Merfyn,
and at some point in his boyhood they heard of the existence of
Bedales, one of the then new 'progressive' schools: no repressive
atmosphere, no school uniform or regimentation or conformism.
To Bedales, then, Merfyn should go, and the family moved to be
in that neighbourhood, taking a cottage in Ashford, near
Petersfield, in 1907.

During their years here, Edward and Helen each behaved in
an entirely characteristic way. He continued to live a life as
solitary as a badger's; she threw herself warmly and eagerly into
contact with people, which meant partly the villagers but mainly
the personnel of Bedales School. The relationship, though she
persevered at it, was anything but a success. High-minded
theoretical libertarians, seeking simplicity in conscious recoil
from the complexities of modern living, engaging in the un-
complicated life according to a rational plan, confronted a couple
who, whatever their temperamental differences from one
another, were at least united in living the simple life for no
theoretical reason but because it was the only one they knew.
With the breed of reasonable, hygienic, self-approving reformists
represented by Bedales, Edward and Helen Thomas had no
more in common than an unkempt hedge full of wild roses has
with the lawns of the Trianon. On the surface, they might have
some beliefs in common; but as soon as that surface was dis-

turbed, as it inevitably was in a few minutes' conversation, the fundamental non-recognition showed itself. Helen Thomas assiduously attended discussion meetings for parents and teachers, and at some of them she even found herself speaking, but these speeches were never a success. She agreed with the Bedales clan, on the surface, about Women's Rights, but when she stood up before an audience to defend the feminist position somehow the wrong words came out: instead of taking the required anti-masculine line, she spoke frankly as a woman who enjoyed her work in the home, delighted in looking after her children and husband, found fulfilment in cooking and keeping a house. Helen tried; Edward did not try; but, in any event, no lasting friendships were formed.

One man, though even he did not form a real, living link with the Thomases, was an honourable exception. Geoffrey Lupton was a simple-lifer like the others, devoted to William Morris and the dignity of craftsmanship, but, like Morris himself, he had the skill and the devotion and the patience to do real work of value. He had money and was able to please himself, and his idea of pleasing himself was to make fine things with his hands, using stone he had seen quarried, and timber he had seen felled and then seasoned in his own workshop. This man now offered to build a house for Edward and Helen. He used perfect stone and seasoned oak, he built the house up from the ground with his own hands, perching it dramatically on a high platform of rock from which the ground fell away steeply on every side, and when it was finished it was the perfect home for a poet and his wife and children to be happy in. That was the blueprint. But the Thomases, though grateful to Lupton, were not happy there. It was too new, like a suit of clothes that has not had time to become comfortable; and, more than that, it was too planned, too intentional. They could love oak beams and stone walls in some centuries-old cottage that seemed like a natural thing grown out of the earth, fed by sun and rain and the generations of history, but this house seemed like an extension of Bedales.

We were not there long enough [wrote Helen] to conciliate

the spirits which for ever moved and complained about the house. Human birth and sweat and tears of joy or grief had not had their way with that house. The stone threshold was still unworn. Doors had not opened to welcome a bride, nor shut on hushed and darkened rooms. The great oak planks of the floor were unmarked by human usage; no swallows had found the eaves nor lichen the roof. These changes would come, but not in our time.

Edward Thomas's answer to it all was either to be out on long solitary walks or to escape to his study, a small room he had succeeded in humanizing and where he could work contentedly enough. But these were thin, sour years, and the relationship with his family seems to have done little towards releasing the central current of his energies. He seems to have drudged on very much in the spirit of some eighteenth-century Grub Street hack, despising most of what he had to do, making book after book just to be working and earning money, and never earning enough to put any aside and buy himself some time for peace and concentration.

It is an appalling life to contemplate, the more so knowing, as we do, what was building up inside him. Edward Thomas was a poet long before he began writing poetry in December 1914. His sensibility was forming itself, the physical materials of his poetry were being taken on board and stacked away, his imaginative compass-bearings were being worked out, and all without his knowing it. When Eleanor Farjeon asked him why with his knowledge of poetry and acknowledged authority as a judge of it he did not try his hand as a poet, he replied dismissively, 'I couldn't write a poem to save my life.'

Obviously the inhibiting factor, the thin but impenetrable membrane that stood between Thomas's consciousness mind and his deep creativity, must have been related to that self-consciousness, that inability to build bridges to other people, which he recognized as an illness. In 1911, when he seemed at breaking-point, Helen took the desperate step of appealing for outside help; she wrote to a friend of theirs, E. S. P. Haynes,

civil servant and man of letters, who promptly gave them money
and advice. Haynes suggested that Edward should see a 'nerve-
specialist', as psychiatrists were called in those days. Edward
jibbed at this, but apparently did seek medical help at various
times in the next few years. I have no idea what kind of treat-
ment was tried on him, but it had no effect. Poets, in any case,
are immune to psycho-analysis; being too subtle and intuitive,
they elude the analyst at every turn, and any analyst who takes
on a poet is himself courting a breakdown. When deliverance
came, it came from within, abetted by a curious combination of
circumstances. Three things came together. Thomas met Robert
Frost and they became friends; the war began; and Thomas
started to write poetry. The three are inter-related beyond un-
picking. Frost undoubtedly gave Thomas the nudge that set his
machinery in motion. But that machinery was already fully
formed, waiting to begin its work. It was not merely that
Thomas found stimulus and encouragement in friendship with a
practitioner. He already knew many poets, notably Gordon
Bottomley who was a fellow-protégé of Mr Noble's, and he was
recognized as a perceptive critic of poetry. When Harold Monro
opened the Poetry Bookshop with a party in 1913, Edward
Thomas was invited, and accepted on condition that he should
not be introduced to any of the poets. As a reviewer of verse, he
felt it would be embarrassing and hampering to meet the writers
on whose work he had been, or would one day be, passing judg-
ment. (George Orwell, at a similar stage of his life, had similar
feelings.) Frost was at that party, but they did not meet until
Ralph Hodgson introduced them later in the same year.

There is no need to make an elaborate search for the reasons
why Frost was so important as a catalyst to Thomas. Both poets
were in pursuit of the same ends, and in reviewing *North of
Boston* in 1914 Thomas stated his own poetic in a description of
his friend's.

Mr Frost has, in fact, gone back, as Whitman and as
Wordsworth went back, through the paraphernalia of
poetry into poetry again. With a confidence like genius, he

has trusted his conviction that a man will not easily write
better than he speaks when some matter has touched him
deeply, and he has turned it over until he has no doubt
what it means to him, when he has no purpose to serve
beyond expressing it, when he has no audience to be bullied
or flattered, when he is free, and speech takes on form and
no other. Whatever discipline further was necessary, he has
got from the use of the good old English medium of blank
verse. . . .

The effect of each poem is one and indivisible. You can
hardly pick out a single line more than a single word. There
are no show words or lines. The concentration has been
upon the whole, not the parts. Decoration has been
forgotten, perhaps for lack of the right kind of vanity
and obsession. . . . Naturally, then, when his writing
crystallizes, it is often in a terse, plain phrase, such as the
proverb, 'Good fences make good neighbours', or . . .
'Pressed into service means pressed out of shape'. But even
this kind of characteristic detail is very much less impor-
tant than the main result, which is a richly homely thing
beyond the grasp of any power except poetry. It is a
beautiful achievement, and I think a unique one, as perfect-
ly Mr Frost's own as his vocabulary, the ordinary English
speech of a man accustomed to poetry and philosophy,
more colloquial and idiomatic than the ordinary man dares
to use even in a letter, almost entirely lacking the emphatic
hackneyed forms of journalists and other rhetoricians, and
possessing a kind of healthy, natural delicacy like
Wordsworth's, or at least Shelley's, rather than that of
Keats.*

Without doubt it was Frost's handling of language that at-
tracted Thomas. Of course, what draws one poet to another is
always, in a broad sense, 'technical'; words, rhythms, rela-
tionship to the singing or speaking voice. Frost's New England
rhythms fell on Thomas's ear like the sound of his own voice
coming back to him. The point is not without interest at a

---

* Cited in William Cooke, *Edward Thomas: a critical biography* (1970),
p. 71. The excisions are Mr Cooke's.

time like the present, when in some English circles there is a critical orthodoxy that sweeps aside the native tradition and preaches a subservience to American poetry at the point where it is most different from English. To exhort a young English poet to imitate, say, William Carlos Williams is to urge him to abandon his own language altogether in favour of one that he must learn as a foreign tongue. Between Frost and Thomas no such gulf existed. In those months between their meeting and Thomas's beginning as a poet, he listened with rapt attention and complete sympathy to the rhymes and cadences of such poems as 'The Death of the Hired Man' and 'The Wood-Pile'. 'You really should start doing a book on speech and literature', he wrote to Frost, 'or you will find me mistaking your ideas for mine and doing it myself.' In that same letter he mentions for the first time his own impulse to poetry. 'I wonder if you can imagine me taking to verse.' That was in May 1914. On 3 December of that year, Thomas wrote his first poem – the first, that is, since the inevitable adolescent verse of twenty years earlier. It was 'Up in the Wind'. The barrier was down, the membrane of diffidence and self-doubt was broken, and now poem followed poem at an unbelievable pace; five poems in the first five days, and from then on several every week. Or, rather, the pace would be un-believable if we did not know that this was the opening of a long-buried treasure-chest. In the central core of his being, Thomas had been making his poems for years. Like Hopkins, he had worked out his idiom unconsciously, in silence; and, again as in the case of Hopkins, the releasing impulse came from what seemed accident.

How shall we briefly characterize Edward Thomas's poetry? There is a good deal of the man in it; while never aiming at 'self-expression', whatever that is, he reveals his own nature and his own situation with that unvarnished directness that he and Helen have in common. He presents himself simply and honest-ly, as a sad man; one who finds no particular welcome in the society of human beings and the system of life; who is so far from being well adjusted and happy that he hardly envisages the possibility. He is rather like a visitor from some other world, accidentally landed here and unable to go back home, who contemplates without resentment an order of things in which he has no meaningful part, but which he does not seek to change. A poem like 'The Long Small Room', for instance, presents him as an uncomprehending spectator of the revolving machinery of life.

The long small room that showed willows in the west
Narrowed up to the end the fireplace filled,
Although not wide. I liked it. No one guessed
What need or accident made them so build.

Only the moon, the mouse and the sparrow peeped
In from the ivy round the casement thick.
Of all they saw and heard there they shall keep
The tale for the old ivy and older brick.

When I look back I am like moon, sparrow, and mouse
That witnessed what they could never understand
Or alter or prevent in the dark house.
One thing remains the same – this my right hand

Crawling crab-like over the clean white page,
Resting awhile each morning on the pillow,
Then once more starting to crawl on towards age.
The hundred last leaves stream upon the willow.

The sadness there, the resignation, never degenerate into self-pity; the originality and distinction of the writing would ensure that, if nothing else did; the satisfying trajectory of the poem, the way the willows, seen through the small window in the first line, reappear in the last, now singular and an unmistakable personal emblem.

Thomas accepted his fate, and part of that fate was an intense loneliness and sense of exclusion, beautifully distilled in 'Gone, Gone Again':

Gone, gone again,
May, June, July,
And August gone,
Again gone by,

Not memorable
Save that I saw them go,
As past the empty quays
The rivers flow.

And now again,
In the harvest rain,
The Blenheim oranges
Fall grubby from the trees

As when I was young —
And when the lost one was here —
And when the war began
To turn young men to dung.

Look at the old house,
Outmoded, dignified,
Dark and untenanted,
With grass growing instead

Of the footsteps of life,
The friendliness, the strife;
In its beds have lain
Youth, love, age, and pain:

I am something like that;
Only I am not dead,
Still breathing and interested
In the house that is not dark: —

I am something like that:
Not one pane to reflect the sun,
For the schoolboys to throw at —
They have broken every one.

What saves this sadness from any taint of mawkishness is that
it is accepted so calmly and that the poet is not primarily
engaged in probing his own feelings; he is looking outward,
'breathing and interested'.

This introspection or, more precisely, self-contemplation is also the clue to one of the most important features of Edward Thomas's poetry, its modernity. He is perhaps the first, as he is certainly one of the best, of the English modern poets. By 'modern' I mean not chic, avant-garde, having the external trappings of international modernism; I mean reflecting accurately those characteristics of the present-day world which mark it off from the world before. Chief of these qualities is isolation. Belief in a coherent system underlying the universe gives the human a sense of kinship both with other human beings and with 'nature', insofar as he thinks of himself as standing outside the merely 'natural'. When these beliefs go, the loneliness that results is far more intense than the loneliness that arises from the mere absence of other human beings.

The unformed, chaotic nature of 'modern' art also has affinities with this isolation of unbelief. If we think of ourselves as part of a meaningful structure, we take more naturally to the discipline of building meaningful structures in our work, and the public whom we address enjoys them more. It is impossible to imagine, say, the music of Mozart coming out of an age that accepted as its dominant metaphor emptiness, isolation, the black metaphysical void of a merely accidental universe. This metaphor is what modern people, at any rate in their characteristic majority, do accept, and modern art is one of the results, as modern politics is another.

If we come to Thomas after reading any of the English nineteenth-century poets, this isolation is one of the first things we notice. The religious poet could look at a beautiful landscape and say, 'This is beautiful, therefore the Creator is good.' If he happened to be of an anti-God turn of mind, he could look at an animal dying of gangrene in a trap, and say, 'This is hideous, therefore the Creator is evil.' Either attitude is equally religious; Hardy is just as much a religious poet as Hopkins. But when we pass to Thomas we become aware of the working of the modern mind in poetry. Thomas does not build bridges. If he looks at a landscape, he does not connect with it, feel it to be part of a system that includes him. He looks at it,

writes down what he sees, and . . . what else? What further step
is possible? Only one, obviously; he can look at himself looking
at it, study his own mind in the process of contemplation. This
self-consciousness is the one hallmark that all modern art has in
common. Now that the human mind feels itself to be alone in a
universe of fragments, the only relationship it can form is with
itself. Hence the typical modern poem is a poem about writing
poetry. This is the process that Yeats saw at its beginning, and
unhesitatingly faced and described, for instance in 'Ego
Dominus Tuus':

> *Ille.* By the help of an image
> I call to my own opposite, summon all
> That I have handled least, least looked upon.
>
> *Hic.* And I would find myself and not an image.
>
> *Ille.* That is our modern hope, and by its light
> We have lit upon the gentle, sensitive mind
> And lost the old nonchalance of the hand;
> Whether we have chosen chisel, pen or brush,
> We are but critics, or but half create,
> Timid, entangled, empty and abashed,
> Lacking the countenance of our friends.

Thomas is that gentle, sensitive mind. Even when he paints a
water-colour for its own sake, his thoughts are always partly
directed towards the act of perception. Take his delightful
vignette, 'Thaw':

> Over the land freckled with snow half-thawed
> The speculating rooks at their nest cawed
> And saw from elm-tops, delicate as flower of grass,
> What we below could not see, Winter pass.

This, of course, conveys perfectly the physical quality of a
mild February day after snow; but its real subject is perception,
the awareness of the man at ground-level that the birds at
treetop-level are attuned to a change in season that has not yet

reached him. And as with physical, so with mental and emotional perceptions. What attracts him is the thing half-remembered, the truth that is only to be seen out of the eye's corner. All the miraculously close-knit observation of natural shapes and colours is in the service of this evanescent perception. 'The Glory' begins with a short, intense hymn to natural beauty, 'The cuckoo crying over the untouched dew', and all the other unsmirched loveliness, and quickly passes to an effort to pin down 'the happiness I fancy fit to dwell/In beauty's presence'; the poem works away at this problem with no conclusive result, ending in a gesture of relinquishment:

And shall I ask at the day's end once more
What beauty is, and what I can have meant
By happiness? And shall I let all go,
Glad, weary, or both? Or shall I perhaps know
That I was happy oft and oft before,
Awhile forgetting how I am fast pent,
How dreary-swift, with naught to travel to,
Is Time? I cannot bite the day to the core.

In 'Old Man', the particular scent of a herb, the crumbling of it between his fingers, leads back to some unattainable memory, and it is this memory or, rather, the lack of it, the fruitless rummaging for it, that makes the poem's subject.

I have mislaid the key. I sniff the spray
And think of nothing; I see and I hear nothing;
Yet seem, too, to be listening, lying in wait
For what I should, yet never can, remember:
No garden appears, no path, no hoar-green bush
Of Lad's-love, or Old Man, no child beside,
Neither father nor mother, nor any playmate;
Only an avenue, dark, nameless, without end.

Thomas does not build bridges; he perceives states. And the more subtle they are, the further they lie outside the hard circle of light that we experience as normal consciousness, the more he

reaches out towards them with all the direction-finding power of
his imagination. As in 'The New House':

> Now first, as I shut the door,
>   I was alone
> In the new house; and the wind
>   Began to moan.
>
> Old at once was the house,
>   And I was old;
> My ears were teased with the dread
>   Of what was foretold,
>
> Nights of storm, days of mist, without end;
>   Sad days when the sun
> Shone in vain: old griefs and griefs
>   Not yet begun.
>
> All was foretold me; naught
>   Could I foresee;
> But I learned how the wind would sound
>   After these things should be.

One of the marks of a good poet is his ability to make his
poem capacious without turning it into a mere rag-bag. Simple
poems, of course, have their place ('My love is like a red, red rose'
could not be improved, in its own terms), but an important poet
– Burns himself, to stick to that example – can organize his
poetry along sufficiently complex lines to include most of what
he really cares and thinks about. It is this capacity that marks off
Edward Thomas from the ruck of 'Georgian' poetry, sub-
sequently so disapproved of that the name of their movement
had, by 1935 or so, become a synonym for bad poetry, weak,
false and artificial. Edward Thomas was in most things a
Georgian poet; in terms of a literary programme, in respect of
things like diction and versification and choice of subject-matter,
his aims were their aims. Since he was a good poet and it has
been an axiom of criticism for forty years that Georgian poetry
means bad poetry, this created a difficulty from which the usual

way out has been to deny that he was a Georgian poet at all. In fact, he was that critical non-person, a good Georgian poet: a poet who used the Georgian idiom and made out of it a poetry that could be the vehicle of major statements. 'Roads', for instance, is a subject on which the run-of-the-mill Georgian poet could easily spread himself or herself: one of the ancestors of the Georgian style, A. E. Housman, had used the beautiful image of

> Where under branching elms the highway
> Would mount the hills and shine

in a way that opened it up for a use mainly picturesque. Edward Thomas's way is different, subtler and more comprehensive:

> I love roads:
> The goddesses that dwell
> Far along invisible
> Are my favourite gods.
>
> Roads go on
> While we forget, and are
> Forgotten like a star
> That shoots and is gone.
>
> On this earth 'tis sure
> We men have not made
> Anything that doth fade
> So soon, so long endure:
>
> The hill road wet with rain
> In the sun would not gleam
> Like a winding stream
> If we trod it not again.
>
> They are lonely
> While we sleep, lonelier
> For lack of the traveller
> Who is now a dream only.

From dawn's twilight
And all the clouds like sheep
On the mountains of sleep
They wind into the night.

The next turn may reveal
Heaven: upon the crest
The close pine clump, at rest
And black, may Hell conceal.

Often footsore, never
Yet of the road I weary,
Though long and steep and dreary,
As it winds on for ever.

Helen of the roads,
The mountain ways of Wales
And the Mabinogion tales
Is one of the true gods,

Abiding in the trees,
The threes and fours so wise,
The larger companies,
That by the roadside be,

And beneath the rafter
Else uninhabited
Excepting by the dead;
And it is her laughter

At morn and night I hear
When the thrush cock sings
Bright irrelevant things,
And when the chanticleer

Calls back to their own night
Troops that make loneliness
With their light footsteps' press,
As Helen's own are light.

Now all roads lead to France
And heavy is the tread
Of the living; but the dead
Returning lightly dance:

Whatever the road bring
To me or take from me,
They keep me company
With their pattering,

Crowding the solitude
Of the loops over the downs,
Hushing the roar of towns
And their brief multitude.

The poem uses four separate ingredients, which it sets out
to blend into a unity: the discriptive, the personal, the
mythological, and a fourth that I think we can best call the
historical, in that it points to the stage at which the history of
European man has arrived *now*. (Perhaps some people would
prefer the word 'topical', but I would not.) The four ingredients
are not, of course, laid mechanically end to end; the opening
stanza brings in the mythological element and, though in the
next six stanzas the descriptive prevails, it is very much a
description of mood and atmosphere, with the most serious
issues everywhere implied ('Heaven' and 'Hell' are not empty,
descriptive terms).

In stanza 8, the 'I' of the poem makes an appearance, and
forms the necessary hinge between the purely contemplative – a
poetic essay on the theme of the permanent and the evanescent –
and the more dense central argument of the poem. Quickly, we
pass to the tale of Elen in the Mabinogion, which Thomas
himself retells in the first chapter of his book on the Icknield
Way. (The Roman Emperor Maxen, in a dream, saw a castle
with a girl sitting therein, so beautiful that he saw her again
whenever he slept, and could think of nothing else when waking.
He sent his emissaries across the whole Empire to find a place
that corresponded to his description, and they found the castle

and girl at Caernarvon. She became his Empress, he built her three castles, and she caused roads to be built between them, connecting up three areas of the kingdom of Britain. As Thomas himself mentions, Elen of the Roads has become fruitfully confused in the popular mind with Helen the mother of Constantine.) The spirit of Elen, part ghost and part symbol, walks beside the poet as he strides the roads, and with her, naturally, come other ghostly presences, all those unknown multitudes who have traversed these roads and left no trace except the numinous air of their passing. 'Troops that make loneliness/with their light footsteps' press' conveys this perfectly, but because it introduces the word 'troops' it reminds us that this, like all Thomas's theory, was written between the declaration of war and his own arrival on the battlefield. Thomas is a war poet in the sense that a poem about a brick wall, in war-time, is a war poem; anything as all-pervading as war is bound to make its presence felt on the pulse of a sensitive man. And so the poem enters its last phase, when the ghosts who throng the roads are at last identified with the young men who, passing in an endless stream towards the slaughter, return in another endless stream as their dead selves.

To remark on the fineness of this, the delicacy and accuracy with which the emotions are gathered into the poem, would be superfluous.

When the war was less than a year old, Edward Thomas enlisted as a soldier, though he was well past normal military age. As a shy, proud man, he feared ineptitude and failure at the menial tasks of soldiering more than he feared the enemy, and before joining his unit he got a friend to take him to a quiet stretch of Hyde Park and show him the rudiments of drill so that at least he would not have to endure the sarcasm of a sergeant-major. He worked conscientiously to turn himself into a good soldier, and did well enough to be accepted as a cadet at the Royal Artillery School in Handel Street, London – a place vividly described in C. M. Bowra's *Memories* – and to be commissioned.

His enlistment came just about half-way through his life as a poet. The flow of poetry went on as fast as ever, allowing for the inevitable disruptions of military life. Whether as a soldier or a civilian, the war-time Edward Thomas was a much freer man than his peace-time equivalent had been. With the end of the long Edwardian peace, as normal habits and normal expectations were uprooted and no one could be certain of the future, he seems to have slipped his collar of grinding financial responsibility. Regular literary piece-work, though it might still exist, could not be counted on, and in any case no one could seriously think of sitting at a desk and turning out a string of books with titles like *Feminine Influence on the Poets* or *A Literary Pilgrim in England* as Europe slithered into red ruin. After August 1914, though Thomas's material prospects were no better, were indeed sharply worse, he seems to have stopped worrying about them. As John Moore sensibly put it in his *Life and Letters of Edward Thomas* (1939):

> ... while the War had not really solved any of his problems − in fact it had increased the difficulty of making a living − it had at any rate relieved him of the necessity for worrying about them. It had not lessened his responsibility; but it had lessened his sense of responsibility.

How often one comes across it, when reading about the lives of writers − that liberation through débâcle, that moment when the situation becomes so bad that it is good!

Of course enlistment must always have been in his thoughts, and with it the knowledge that Helen and the children would have the routine financial support which, pittance though it was, kept alive thousands of families and put households up and down the land on an equal footing. He hesitated for a few months, as was natural for an older man, with no military training, in a situation where many were still predicting a short war; but his world was changed overnight, war-time England was not the same as peace-time England, and the war makes itself unobtrusively felt as a theme in his work from the beginning. Edward Thomas is not a 'war poet' in the ordinary sense in which that term is applied to the civilian generation who found themselves in the trenches in those years: he does not

write about the horrors of the battlefield, and his poetry was all
written before he saw action; but it is war poetry in the truer
and deeper sense, that the world it describes, and the sensibility
out of which it comes, are moulded by being within a context of
war. 'The Owl', 'As the Team's Head-Brass', and other familiar
poems refer to the over-arching reality of conflict and death,
refer to it in an unemphatic, unstrained fashion; Thomas is
accepting the world, as he always did, taking for granted that it
was not arranged to suit his purposes, finding it too remote from
his ways to try to alter it by protest.

On Helen, meanwhile, a blow had fallen that hurt her in the
recesses of her being. Lupton was at the front; his wife inhabited
the house he had built for the Thomases, while they crowded
into a poky, but cheap, dwelling down below in the village of
Steep. Lupton had made Edward Thomas a gift, for a nominal
rent, of the study he had grown used to, and his books awaited
him there. Now Mrs Lupton began to find this arrangement in-
convenient. She needed the room for a woman who was moving
in as her companion; she sent Helen Thomas a letter asking her
to clear it of her husband's possessions; she ignored a long letter
in which Helen made a passionate plea for Edward to be spared
this final uprooting, this loss of a refuge where his books and
papers could quietly await his visits on leave. Mrs Lupton was
immovable; she would have the room, and Helen must take
away everything that was Edward's. Helen fumed and raged.
After years of trusting optimism and adaptability, after all that
long effort to like and agree with people of that well-washed and
well-planned unconventionality, she suddenly saw the deep
fissure that ran between them. People of the Bedales stamp,
cushioned in well-being and self-justification, comfortably disap-
proving of the war, comfortably patronizing about men like
Edward who were so misguided as to go off and fight, suddenly
seemed to her the worst enemies she had ever known.

The rumour of their dispute spread. A young Bedales master
paid a well-meaning social call on Helen, asking if he could in
any way minister to a better understanding. Helen turned on
him like a fishwife, the submissiveness of years boiling over in

corrosive resentment. He must have been glad to get away. Afterwards Helen, equipped only with a donkey-cart driven by an ancient villager, took Edward's books away, load after laborious load, under Mrs Lupton's stony eye. The old man could not help her handle the books; he had just strength enough to drive the cart.

On his next leave, which was his last visit to Steep, Edward Thomas picked out the few books he wanted to keep and burnt the rest. Review copies, books he had read for no better reason than to earn a guinea, all the detritus of his long servitude, books he had kept because his library was his only asset and because, after all, books were books, he tossed in among the flames, burning his past, triumphing over his years of drudgery, till the flames mounted so high that he was seriously afraid his neighbours would think he was signalling to Zeppelins. Edward Thomas, hack writer, died in that fire; his discarded books made a better showing against the night sky than they would have done on well-planned shelves in Mrs Lupton's house.

What angered Helen about the episode of the study was, of course, that it was an attack on Edward. Her entire life was given to thoughts of him. Seeing their situation as she did with complete clarity, she found from somewhere the courage to face the knowledge that her love for him was not returned in anything like its full radiance. He was not a man to wrap anything up in evasions, and she always knew the state of his feelings, but when he wrote his poetry he set down his feelings about Helen for the rest of us also to read. On four successive days in April 1916 he wrote four poems to his family — the elder daughter, the younger daughter, the son, and Helen. W. B. Yeats liked the first poem in the sequence, 'If I were ever by chance to own', so much that it is the only specimen of Edward Thomas's work in the *Oxford Book of Modern Verse*, which Yeats edited in 1936. One sees why, because it is jaunty and skipping and fits in better than Thomas's more characteristic work with Yeats's odd notion that 'the Muses' loved 'gay and warty lads'. But the best poem of the four, the one with the deepest flow of felt life, is certainly 'And You, Helen'. It is not in the ordinary sense a love poem, and yet there is love in it; he looks at her and sees her as a real woman, whom he knows in her depths and who shares his life. And in that concluding gesture, half love and half helplessness, when he tells her that he would give her

      myself, too, if I could find
Where it lay hidden and it proved kind,

we have distilled into a line and a half the essence both of their sharing and their suffering. Even in its withdrawn way it comes closer to an expression of love than the equally beautiful but much bleaker poem he had written to her in the previous month. 'No one so much as you' is a bare, honest, despondent poem, beautiful and lonely in its refusal to take comfort. Iris Murdoch says somewhere that most of the things that cheer us up are illusions; Edward Thomas made his poem out of the refusal to be, or to permit Helen to be, cheered up by any false rainbow-colours in their steel-grey landscape.

No one so much as you
Loves this my clay,
Or would lament as you
Its dying day.

You know me through and through
Though I have not told,
And though with what you know
You are not bold.

None ever was so fair
As I thought you:
Not a word can I bear
Spoken against you.

All that I ever did
For you seemed coarse
Compared with what I hid
Nor put in force.

My eyes scarce dare meet you
Lest they should prove
I but respond to you
And do not love.

We look and understand,
We cannot speak
Except in trifles and
Words the most weak.

For I at most accept
Your love, regretting
That is all: I have kept
Only a fretting

That I could not return
All that you gave
And could not ever burn
With the love you have,

Till sometimes it did seem
Better it were
Never to see you more
Than linger here

With only gratitude
Instead of love —
A pine in solitude
Cradling a dove.

This is not a poem of rejection: the pine is 'cradling' her, and she
is not a woodpecker but a dove. The extent of his feeling for her
is very accurately conveyed. Nevertheless, it must have taken all
Helen's courage to assimilate that poem when it finally reached
her. Just once, many years later, that courage momentarily
failed. In a radio interview in April 1967, she gave it as her opi-
nion that 'No one so much as you' had been written to Edward's
mother. Her own strength was failing by this time and, if ever a
lapse into human weakness could be perfectly understood and

forgiven, this one can.

The war ground on, events took their relentless way, and in January 1917 Edward Thomas was given his last home leave before going overseas. Helen's description of their last night together cannot be quoted. It must be left in its natural setting, tightly folded in the petals of the flower she grew for Edward out of her memories and her suffering. Dragged out, it would be too much like a bleeding torn-off limb. It is personal, but universal; universal because personal – the agony of one woman, repeated in thousands of women whenever nations go to war.

So their last night was over; he was ready to go; he must go. The children were to go with him to the station, and she was to stay behind in the house. The last words of *World Without End* say it all.

> A thick mist hung everywhere, and there was no sound except, far away in the valley, a train shunting. I stood at the gate watching him go; he turned back to wave until the mist and the hill hid him. I heard his old call coming up to me: 'Coo-ee!' he called, 'Coo-ee!' I answered, keeping my voice strong to call again. Again through the muffled air came his 'Coo-ee'. And again went my answer like an echo. 'Coo-ee' came fainter next time with the hill between us, but my 'Coo-ee' went out of my lungs strong to pierce to him as he strode away from me. 'Coo-ee!' So faint now, it might be only my own call flung back from the thick air and muffling snow. I put my hands up to my mouth to make a trumpet, but no sound came. Panic seized me, and I ran through the mist and the snow to the top of the hill, and stood there a moment dumbly, with straining eyes and ears. There was nothing but the mist and the snow and the silence of death.
>
> Then with leaden feet which stumbled in a sudden darkness that overwhelmed me I groped my way back to the empty house.

She never saw him again. He was killed at the battle of Arras on 9 April, Easter Monday, 1917; and she lived on without him for fifty years.

Appendix I

'Children, children'
(See page 217)

Music L.

KITTY'S SONG

369

2.

Appendix II

Poems 1973–6

Furry Bundles

Homage and Pity for Louis Wain, 1860–1939

Note: Louis Wain, born in London of north Staffordshire stock (his father came from Leek), was one of the most successful light artists of the Edwardian era. His sentimental and whimsical pictures of cats were as well known as Tom and Jerry to the present generation. In about 1920 he went mad and spent the rest of his life as a patient in a mental hospital. In his madness he continued to paint cats, but now in strange and compelling schizophrenic shapes. His paintings can be seen in the Guttman Maclay Collection in the Maudsley Hospital.

Cats filled his mind. Why cats? Of course it was easy
    to sell them;
charm too straightforward to miss, a beauty in no
    way demanding,
every Aunt Tabitha needed a picture as well as a live
    one.
Sweet Pussy who sits by the fire, blinking and licking
    her paws clean,
then like a nesting bird settles down, or with pads
    neat and noiseless
moves on her own little errands: a self-centred life but
    a calm one.
So, in the ordered world that preceded the bangs and
    the blood-rain,
he painted cats for the public, and these hexameters
    praise him.
He was a household name in the street of a thousand
    households.

Oh, Louis Wain had a skill
he painted cats dressed up to kill

Louis Wain, Louis Wain, he was clever:
people looked at his cats and said *Well I never,*

we must have pretty Pussy on our parlour wall.
To Louis Wain it was no trouble at all

he painted lovable fluffy pussies with eyes
of green or yellow larger than realistic size.

Oh, Louis Wain had a trade
he was well off, he needed no aid

Louis Wain had a wonderful gift
not for him the scraping and thrift

of the poor hill farmers of Leek
he lived on his marvellous technique

and did so well at his one chosen thing
that people said *Louis Wain, Louis Wain for king.*

The fluffy pussies got him in the end.

I love little pussy, her coat is so warm,
And if I don't hurt her she'll do me no harm.
So I'll pet her, and stroke her, and feed her with food,
And Pussy will love me because I am good.

Oh Louis Wain, Louis Wain,
he painted furry bundles again and again,

and of course spending so much time with the
    creatures
he must have been well acquainted with their natures

he must have known those things about them that are
    not cosy
however he chose to keep his own spectacles rosy.

Louis, the artist has a duty to teach as well as amuse
qui miscuit utile dulci and all that, but you did not
choose

to tell us what cat-nature is really like
no no you dressed them up and painted them like Van
    Dyck

and if you did not make them fluffy you made then
    funny
which made people laugh and then they gave you
    money

and all the time Louis you must have known
there are some things about cats that make one weep
    and groan

they let mice run away and then leap and catch them
    again
just to give them a little longer to suffer fear and pain

when they kill a bird they seem to savour its fright
their copulation is a horrible sexual fight

'I have myself found, as the result of many years of inquiry and
study, that all people who keep cats, and are in the habit of nurs-
ing them do not suffer from those petty little complaints that all
flesh is heir to, viz., nervous complaints of a minor sort. Hysteria
and rheumatism, too, are unknown, and all lovers of "pussy" are
of the sweetest temperament.'
Interview, 'Canine and Sublime, a chat with Mr Louis Wain',
                                          The Idler, January 1896

Louis, Louis, the artist has a duty
to see things as they are, not just skim off beauty

or comicality because they have a ready market
he must look for the gunpowder of truth and spark it

otherwise Louis it will ultimately get up his nose
and one by one the apertures of his mind will close.

It seemed a cheerful fire no rain could dowse.
He never knew half-truths are worse than lies.
His streets were cosy and his pastures green.

And then one day he felt his silent house
Patrolled by cats with murder in their eyes.
His mind split wide. He was a schizophrene.

No tail, no whiskers. Yet he is a mouse.
Why is there not a hole of the right size?
Where can he scamper, crouch, and not be seen?

He sweats, he groans, he envies flea and louse.
The tomcats mew in mockery of his cries.
Their teeth are honed. Their claws are white and
    clean.

I fear little pussy, her eyes open wide,
they smoulder and show me the furnace inside,
so I'll shun her, and flee her, and hide in my bed,
or Pussy will hunt me until I am dead.

'Wain picked out the important features of the English cat,
raised its forepaws off the ground, made it smile, enlarged its
eyes, dressed it sometimes in a feathered bonnet or in a cap and
Norfolk suit, and made it ready for human company, between
the years 1890 and 1920.'
Brian Reade, *Louis Wain*, Victoria and Albert Museum, 1972

I fear the big tom-cat, his cry is so shrill,
I know what he's saying, 'Let's kill him, let's kill!'
and all my past kindness has turned out in vain,
for the toms they are marching to get Louis Wain.

And then, the long stillness.

The fame and money gone, the story over.
Outside the window, urban seasons: dead enamel
   winter,
spring with corrosive light, the asphalt summer:
cars going by on the long featureless roads
and inside, the artist.

A quiet clean old man in a mental ward.

A kind of peace, a kind of resolution:
but the eyes were looking.

Those unforgiving jewels,
hard with a light that came from his shocked mind
a beauty he had never seen before
flashing a new language of fire and ice.

The people were very kind, they brought him
everything he needed:
a proper little studio he had!
'Mr Wain is an artist, he used to be quite well known,
it will do him good to paint some pictures, even
if they are a bit strange.'

It did him good.
He painted his fear and his penitence
and the joy that flickered from a coal of terror
and the new beauty that was revealed.

Louis, Louis, I see that life of yours
in the fumed-out quiet at the end, when
too much of life had been lived to go back now:

when the lonely mind turns to self-accusation
and even the good memories condemn
and only the beauty is left to rejoice in,
seen purely at last by the unshelled spirit
unhoused, hunted from refuge, forced to admire
the unassuaged glitter that pierces all evasions:

the topaz, the chrysolite, the ice, the pinnacle.

With these, finally, you were paid: at last, in peace.

Performers

Tensed, flexing, they make the leap.
Notion to enactment. Flesh gathered to a purpose
outside its own needs, yet fuelled by them.
Bruised, always ready to be bruised again:
and cherished, suckled, dreaming within a dream
of another dream, never-ending, lit from within,
a dream small enough to swallow like a pill,
big enough to wander in hand in hand
with everyone you ever loved, where the present
moment never comes to an end. This is
surely what they are searching for. Look at their eyes.
The dream within the dream: it has to be that.

Their trance-state must be catching: normally I
feel my mind realistic, ballasted. Now
among them, I feel less sure. Outlines flicker.
Flat shorelines become thickets of dark-green weed.
A mountain fades into cold white smoke, then
    becomes
a cloud that hardens into snow. Then thaws.
Let's pretend. And now we've finished pretending,
let's pretend that what we're doing now is real.
And if it isn't real, let's still pretend.
Ought I to resist? They confuse me, but gladly
I embrace confusion. Their petulant moments,
even, are a sharp game I relish. Why?
What spell do they put on me? It must be
the deep assent they give to transformation.
Their openness is beyond morality.
To take so readily might just as well be to give:
take, give: take, give: the words change places

till one tires of watching: do a swallow's wings
take from the wind, or offer themselves to it?
Their egotism is a sacrifice
of self. I breathe the pyre's sky-climbing plume.
So the cardboard turns out to be rock, the paints
are really the true colours of nature.
That girl's feigned tears fall for all slow griefs.
To simulate passion is to remember it,
to remember passion is to invite more:
watching them pretend, I become more real:
their rehearsed movements unlock my limbs to
    freedom.

So ritual makes hard truth into a dream
that could come true. And as Imagination,
the red-nosed clown, squirts from his button-hole,
true laughter rises up, true tears run down.

To My Young Self

I remember you so well, lank-haired restless one.
Shall we attempt a dialogue at last?

If I could roll up three decades like a worn carpet,
and walk with you among these trees,

or in this lane by the old blackened wall,
where your starveling footstep often came,

among these scenes that keep the same outline,
it might calm both of us.

After all, we came through it together,
you changing slowly into me.

Came through what? Ah, *diablotin*,
we both know how jagged was the path

and how our joint footfall altered its nature:
becoming heavier, more poised, less free.

You wandered in a hailstorm of choices,
each choice numbered and coloured like snooker.

Decisions, choices, possibilities,
rolling on the green cloth of your life.

One by one they disappeared into pockets:
now only a few are left to invite collision.

I chalk my cue for the shots that will decide the game.
I need skill, where you needed only appetite.

Cadaverous joker, the feelings that shook your bones
and broke your health, were in fact your best friends.

Your voice echoed among Easter Island heads:
mine shouts along a valley littered with broken
    waxworks.

You had to break iron bars to get out:
I have to unpick silken ropes to stay out.

Nothing could help you but the stubbornness to live:
Nothing can help me but the stubbornness to live.

The word led you upward into a mountain landscape:
The word leads me downward to the banks of a
    strong river.

You were in danger of falling and being broken.
I am in danger of sinking and being engulfed.

But after all, we are the same person, gallowglass,
both the same timorous but untrainable animal:

more easy under the cold sky than in a kennel,
rooting for bitter grubs, not waiting to be fed mince.

You with the wild laughter and the apprehensive eyes,
wondering where the next smash on the nose would
    come from:

I, knowing by this time just where it will come from:
no longer laughing like a madman, my eyes calmer.

Well, I have enjoyed our talk together,
though I admit I did most of the talking

and found it rather difficult to draw you out:
but then I am fifty-one, and you are what? twenty?

twenty-one, twenty-five? in any case, bambino,
though I do not suppose you trust me, I will trust
    you,

having not much else to trust, and no patrimony
save the few battered belongings that used to be
    yours.

At Jowett's Grave

Majestic he sailed,
flagship of a navy
sails puffed with every wind
that pride could summon.

They were going to *rule*:
to command, to direct, to prescribe,
to categorize, to set in order:

and always with his eye on them.
And damn it, they *did* all those things,
and always with his eye on them.
Never apologise, never explain!
And they never did.

So majestic he sailed
until at last he docked by these flat stones,
got out of his high painted ship, and lay down.

Lay down in sour earth
with nettles, docks and mares' tails
amid the cut-price comforts of small lives
in a graveyard no bigger than a tennis court.

And it is all there today,
for the small lives persist like the mares' tails
(common and beautiful as the veined wings of flies)
and will have their cut-price
comforts and conveniences,
the dock-leaves to assuage their endless nettles:
small pubs, small shops, a factory where they work,
off-licence, fish and chips, a laundromat.

While a few streets away, in the same rooms
where he lived out his life, the port goes round,
the talk goes on, the truths are shredded out
and the points scored, with stroke and counter-stroke
('That was damned bad sherry you gave us, Master,
if it comes to that,' and it still does come to that):
and he lies in unsunned earth, almost near enough
to catch what they are saying, and join in,
but for the little accident of death.

There is no memorial: I stumbled
on his grave by chance one day,
waiting for my wife to have a baby
in the hospital down the road.
(You were the baby, Toby, and I want
you to accept this poem, if you will —
not that I want you to grow up like Jowett.)

And yet a man could do worse,
worse I mean than grow up like Jowett:
and much, much worse than lie like him in death.

Shaded by the factory wall he lies,
among the docks and nettles and mares' tails:
his navy sunk, his ship burnt long ago:

a candidate for elegy, but not pity.
He is still there, strong in six feet of earth:

secure in the overhead flight of swans
that make the air hiss through their heavy pinions:
in the embrace of earth, the nearness of water,
the cheerful stubbornness of the springing weeds —

still not apologising, never explaining.

The Launching of Two Iron Narrow-Boats
on the Oxford Canal in 1863

There would be different willows then.
A plank of water laid across the fields.
Cows cluster at bridges: may-flies hatch.
Fish glide or nibble in the reeds.

O dark, still mirror of the changing sky!

Arrived in town, it swims out placidly
into a round basin. People stand about.
Something is happening. Children are held
by the hand. Dogs wait.

A speech
seems to be being made. With slow stamping,
horses have drawn a wagon to the slipway.
The two hulls slide, and splash. It has happened,
the different marriage, the new dance of molecules.

Metal knows a new way of kissing water.

The idlers smoke and stare. A scholar, thinking,
sees the crowd, chooses another path.

Two narwhals lie on the uncomplaining sheen.

And now, disperse the idlers, send the children home:
the horses lean to their sweat-softened collars,
stamp a few times, blow through dilated nostrils,
and are ready to pull the narwhals.

Muscle pulls metal: this will not last,
it is a brief kingdom. Oats, sweet musty urine,
warm hair, the ring of metal on cobbles,
and the narwhals patiently gliding behind.

No, it cannot last:
these are the landing-craft of an army
that will destroy the horses and the men.

The willows rustle the silver of their leaves
in the old way, the may-flies do not notice,
the fish as alway keep their counsel.
But
the water feels the change.
When winter comes,
through the stiff reeds the wind will breathe differently:
having, I think, a taste of iron.

Evening over the Place of Cadfan

Over again, these gifts: the high bareness:
the spear-grass, the sheep carved in stone
watching me pass, the darkening granite
still dabbed with lyric green. And at my back
the levelled-off tips dead quiet, these man-made cliffs
too surgical for grass, human work to the end,
but work of departed giants, all that determination

signed off for ever, the hubbub of silenced voices:
after such purpose, nothing but loneliness, wildness:
and out at sea,
the day's sun in his lead coffin.

In the Beginning

Now, in our perfect hour,
while the green stem supports the weightless flower,
before the rains, before the blurring mist
disturb the globe of silence where we kissed,
let us be calm and tranquil in its power.

There may be love
as daily and enduring as a glove:
this may be granted when perfection fades,
but never the silken magic that pervades
this first fine tapestry our fingers wove.

Your beauty lifts my heart
to a dimension where time has no part.
It must come down, I know: we take our places
among the normal names and normal faces:
but not in these first hours, not from the start.

This equilibrium,
most rare and perilous balance, leaves me dumb
to say it all, to name the gems and metals
(flame of a butterfly before it settles)
before the troubles and the questionings come.

Before our ship is tested,
before we sail where seas are cold and crested,
for this one hour let lust be pure as laughter:
let your love breathe without before and after,
soft as the hollow where a bird has rested.

Juliet and Her Nurse

Under the hot slanting Italian sun,
two woman-shapes.

This one casting a lean upright shadow:
that one casting a soft rounded shadow.

Here, all quickness, insistence:
there, a habit of circling.

And why should she not circle?
She ranges for nourishment far distant.

Her landscape lies spread beneath the crags
where she sits memoried, brooding: she sails out
on broad dusty wings now and then,
to look it over.

And why should she not be insistent?
(She, she: haec, illa: our tongue does not say it.)
Needs newly awakened are needles.
One night in his arms is a down payment:
the rest is to come soon, it must come, it must.

They are like water:
this one leaping from the rock, unwarmed, unstained,
exclaiming in diamond spray, avid for contact,
contact with stone, wood, air, clay, skin,
with the throats of animals and men:

that one broadened out, standing,   .
in places very deep, calm on the surface,
in places shaded by old trees.

The young woman is hungry.
She wants love, which is to say she wants suffering,
joy, fury, repletion and forgiveness.
She wants to throw herself over the steep rocks.

The old woman is satisfied:
her body moves slowly and needs little,
stored with the rich protein of her memories.

Memories of dawn when she, too,
cast a lean upright shadow:
when she threw herself over the steep rocks
and he was standing below, eager, and caught her.

The young woman will not be caught.
Down the rock-face dashes the clear water
unwarmed, unstained, wasted:
no old trees will shade her,
there will be no quiet depths.
We know the story.

Song of the Far Places

Before I saw any of the postcard places
I lived among Staffordshire names and faces

before I knew where the warm Gulf Stream went
I staged twig-races on the sickly infant Trent

I read of Mississippi bayou, fjord, calanque
and I watched the wind-stirred water from the canal
   bank

dreaming of wildebeeste and voortrekker
I went voyaging on a Potteries double-decker

reckoning up sheikdom and emirate
I cycled to Woore, Black Brook and Pipe Gate.

They told me tales of antarctic and equator
and the broad snout of the questing alligator

afloat on jungle rivers, Orinoko and Amazon
and I watched the canal water grow dark as damson

and the turquoise dragon-flies hover and disappear:
the black tips fumed but nature was always near.

The pylons marched overhead but the long grass
    waved
nothing in nature was tidy or well-behaved:

I had not seen the Alps in spring blue with gentians
but I watched hedgerow lovers with their warm
    intentions

and though the males were hot-blooded in Brindisi
among ferns in Trentham Park they had it just as
    easy

and if girls were submissive in Japan and Korea
in nettle-green alleys between Longton and the Meir

they showed no more sign of prudish alarm
than their stark-naked sisters in Dar-es-Salaam.

Before I saw any of the postcard sights
I heard the loud cold wind on winter nights

throwing tiles off roofs and slashing at the trees
roaring in Penkhull as it roared in the Hebrides

and in the long summer when the baked soil hardens
the winged seeds came floating over the back gardens

teaching me what the earth is like in the burnt south
where spring water is sweeter than kisses to the
    mouth

for Hanley Deep Pit seemed ready to throw up lava
Trent Vale and Hanford were tropical as Java.

Yes, before I saw any of the postcard views
I knew the richness of land and water was mine to
    choose

which parts excited or lulled or frighteningly chilled
    me
and pierced my marrow with beauty or in dreams
    fulfilled me.

The hymnody of the earth is the same for you and for
    me,
which means childhood is the same wherever you
    happen to be,
except in a high-rise apartment with a colour TV.

Index